WHO DO YOU SAY THAT I AM?

28

WHO DO YOU SAY THAT I AM?

CHRISTOLOGY AND IDENTITY
IN THE UNITED CHURCH OF CHRIST

EDITED BY

SCOTT R. PAETH

UNITED
CHURCH
PRESS®

Cleveland

United Church Press
700 Prospect Avenue
Cleveland, Ohio 44115-1100
unitedchurchpress.com

Printed in the United States of America on acid-free paper

11   10   09   08   07   06   5   4   3   2   1

Library of Congress Cataloging-in-Publication Data

Who do you say that I am? : christology and identity in the United Church of
    Christ / edited by Scott R. Paeth.
        p. cm.
    Includes bibliographical references.
    ISBN-13: 978-0-8298-1702-7 (alk. paper)
    1. Jesus Christ—Person and offices. 2. United Church of Christ—Doctrines.
I. Paeth, Scott.
BT203.W476 2006
232.088'285834—dc22
                                                        2006023750

ISBN-13: 978-0-8298-1702-7
ISBN-10: 0-8298-1702-6

CONTENTS

ACKNOWLEDGMENTS

A project of this nature requires the hard work, time, and patience of many people. I have been grateful for the confidence and faith of Timothy Staveteig and the entire staff of The Pilgrim Press, who saw this project as a necessary and fruitful investment of their time and resources. That this book exists at all is wholly to their credit.

Elizabeth Nordbeck of Andover Newton Theological School deserves special mention. It was she who invited me to a meeting with Timothy Staveteig in which this project first began to take shape, and who encouraged me to push the project forward to completion.

Mark Burrows of Andover Newton also deserves much credit for his encouragement and support in the early stages of this project, as I sought contributors and ideas for organization.

Of course, the contributors to this volume deserve particular thanks, and I consider myself deeply in their debt. Each of them took time from enormously busy schedules to write their contributions. In some cases, the contributors had never even heard of me, yet they were willing to lend their support to this project. I attribute this entirely to the importance of the Christological question to the existence and the future of the United Church of Christ. Each of them could have written on another topic or for another editor, and I am grateful that they trusted me with their hard work. I hope that I have proven a worthy steward of that trust.

I should mention the particular inspiration of those of my teachers who were also contributors to this volume: Gabriel Fackre and Max Stackhouse. Both during my time at Andover Newton and at Princeton Theological Seminary, I was fortunate to be mentored by two great scholars of the church, each of whom understood that it is only by conscientious and faithful reflection on the person and work of Jesus Christ that Christian faith, life, and practice can be rightly understood and ordered. To the degree that this project embodies such faithful reflection, it is wholly due to their inspiration and instruction. Needless to say, however, any deficiencies in this project are attributable solely to myself.

Last, but certainly not least, I would like to thank my family for their patience as I worked to bring this project to completion. Of all of the gracious souls who were patient with me throughout the production process, they were by far the most patient, if only because it was they who had to live with me daily as this project moved, often slowly, forward. To my wife, Amy, and my daughters I offer my special thanks and gratitude.

Solo Dei Gloria!

Contributors

Lee Barrett
  Mary B. and Henry P. Stager Chair in Theology,
  Professor of Systematic Theology
  Lancaster Theological Seminary

Mary Schaller Blaufuss
  Executive for Volunteer Ministries
  United Church of Christ

Gabriel Fackre
  Abbot Professor of Christian Theology, Emeritus
  Andover Newton Theological School

Deirdre King Hainsworth
  Assistant Professor of Christian Ethics and
  Director of the Center for Business, Religion and Public Life
  Pittsburgh Theological Seminary

Scott R. Paeth
  Assistant Professor of Religious Studies
  DePaul University

Stephen G. Ray, Jr.
  Associate Professor of African American Studies
  Lutheran Theological Seminary at Philadelphia

Max L. Stackhouse
  Stephen Colwell Professor of Christian Ethics
  Princeton Theological Seminary

John H. Thomas
  General Minister and President
  United Church of Christ

Theodore Louis Trost
  Assistant Professor of Religious Studies
  The University of Alabama, Tuscaloosa

Lydia Veliko
  Minister for Ecumenical Relations
  United Church of Christ

INTRODUCTION
WHO DO WE SAY THAT HE IS?
SCOTT R. PAETH

Talking about Christology in the United Church of Christ is akin to wrestling an octopus. The complexity of the issue, when understood in light of the history and values that have been central to the UCC's mission and identity for a half-century, is rooted in our simultaneous commitment to diversity on the one hand and Christian unity on the other. The problem of holding these two commitments in tension with one another is only further complicated by the question of what roles the history of the Reformed theological tradition, the sensibilities of our ecumenical partners, and the interpretation of scripture play in defining just what we mean when we refer to the *United* Church of Christ.

Perhaps this is why, as a denomination, we are so reluctant to address the subject of Christology.

This volume represents an attempt to overcome that reluctance. The articles here represent a variety of attempts to understand the significance and identity of Jesus Christ in the common body known as the United Church of Christ. That we claim to be a church united *in Christ* is at the heart of the need to struggle with who Christ is and how we understand his relationship to us. Was Christ a wise teacher—a good man—but no more (or less!) than that? Was he the incarnate Son of God, the second Person of the Trinity? Was he the eternal *Logos* of God made flesh and a continuing Presence within the church, or is it sufficient to say that he lives on through his example of a life lived fully transparently to God? And, perhaps most significantly for the life of the church, what does the identity of Christ mean for the identities of those who follow him? What does it mean for the idea of discipleship, for our commitments to justice and peace, for our openness to "new light" breaking forth in the world? Each of these questions has the potential to create enormous controversy within the UCC, yet all of them warrant precisely the kind of intensive theological reflection that is only possible when we turn our whole attention to them. Our hope is that this volume will contribute to creating precisely this kind of sustained attention.

The dual commitment to diversity and unity that has characterized the spirit of the UCC since its inception is evident in these essays. Implicit in the variety of approaches represented here are answers to the question of how we can remain a *united* church, given our many understandings of the significance of *Christ*. Each of these essays honors that diversity of perspective while also making the case that there is a deeper unity that underlies who we are and what we stand for as a church.

The Mystery of Christ's Identity

The mystery of Christ's identity lies at the heart of the Gospel of Mark. From the beginning of his ministry in Galilee, Christ goes out of his way to hide the truth of his identity. In the first chapter of the Gospel, almost immediately after his baptism and temptation, we find the following curious exchange:

> That evening, at sundown, they brought to him all who were sick or possessed with demons. And the whole city was gathered around the door. And he cured many who were sick with various diseases, and cast out many demons; and *he would not permit the demons to speak, because they knew him.* (Mark 1:32–34, emphasis added)

A short while later, in the same chapter, we find the well-known encounter between Jesus and a leper:

> A leper came to him begging him, and kneeling he said to him, "If you choose, you can make me clean." Moved with pity, Jesus stretched out his hand and touched him, and said to him, "I do choose. Be made clean!" Immediately the leprosy left him, and he was made clean. After sternly warning him he sent him away at once, saying to him, "*See that you say nothing to anyone*; but go,

show yourself to the priest, and offer for your cleansing what Moses commanded, as a testimony to them. (Mark 1:40–44, emphasis added)

Jesus' seeming reluctance to reveal the true nature of his person or his mission is strangely at odds with the very public nature of his preaching and his healing, yet throughout Mark's Gospel, Jesus' identity remains elusive.

Even among his followers, Christ's identity is mysterious. His followers habitually misunderstand Jesus' intentions and misinterpret his statements. Even in the pivotal moment when Peter proclaims his faith that Jesus is the Messiah, he immediately botches it by trying to force Christ into the customary messianic role of a political and revolutionary leader:

> Jesus went on with his disciples to the villages of Caesarea Philippi and on the way he asked his disciples, "Who do people say that I am?"
> And they answered him, "John the Baptist; and others, Elijah; and still others, one of the prophets."
> He asked them, "But who do you say that I am?"
> Peter answered him, "You are the Messiah."
> And he sternly ordered them not to tell anyone about him.
> Then he began to teach them that the Son of Man must undergo great suffering, and be rejected by the elders, the chief priests, and the scribes, and be killed, and after three days rise again. He said all this quite openly. And Peter took him aside and began to rebuke him. But turning and looking at his disciples, he rebuked Peter and said, "Get behind me, Satan! For you are setting your mind not on divine things but on human things." (Mark 8:27–33)

Once again, Jesus insists—"sternly" in fact—that the disciples not reveal the nature of his identity. But the disciples themselves, even after Jesus explains clearly what that identity entails, refuse to believe him. Peter goes so far as to rebuke Jesus, only to be rebuked in return: "For you are setting your mind not on divine things but on human things." Whatever insight Peter seems to have had about Christ is obscured by his complete failure to understand its significance. Even at the very hour of his resurrection, the disciples have to be *told* what it means, incapable as they are of figuring it out for themselves:

> But he said to them, "Do not be alarmed; you are looking for Jesus of Nazareth, who was crucified. He has been raised; he is not here. Look, there is the place they laid him. But go, tell his disciples and Peter that he is going ahead of you to Galilee; there you will see him, just as he told you." (Mark 16:6–7)

Is it any surprise then that the identity of Jesus remains elusive even today, even among those who claim to be his followers? We seem to be possessed of no better wisdom than Peter had in coming to terms with Jesus. Yet, like Peter, we find ourselves in the position of needing to speak about Christ in order to follow Christ. But speaking of Christ means entering into the mystery of his identity.

The United Church of Christ has attempted to enter into this mystery through its Statement of Faith, which seeks to understand Christ in terms of the "Deeds of God" in relation to creation. Jesus is thus described as "the man of Nazareth" and "our crucified and risen Savior." These brief words carry the weight of two thousand years of theological reflection behind them, but bring us no closer to penetrating the mystery. In reflecting on the doxological version of the Statement of Faith, Roger Shinn comments on the shear power of what is implied in these two statements: "In this person Jesus, a genuine human being, you, the true God, have entered into our midst. You have not simply sent a messenger, a representative, but you ('very God of very God') have entered into the life of this person and through him the life of human kind."[1] Simple explanations of how this could be so, either by collapsing Christ's divinity into his humanity or by absorbing his humanity into his divinity, fail to take with full seriousness the paradoxical nature of Christ's identity. Yet the mystery of Christ's identity continues to confound our attempts to corral it into an easily comprehensible formula.

It is in the nature of mysteries that they can neither be escaped from nor resolved. This is particularly true of the mystery of Jesus Christ. The further one delves into the meaning of his life and work, the deeper the mystery becomes. At its most profound, the meaning of Christ's identity leads us beyond that which can be expressed in theological categories and into the act of worship. In the United Church of Christ, the sacramental theology of the Mercersburg movement represents an insistence that worship, and particularly Communion, is a place where we come into direct contact with the mystery of Christ's identity, and indeed enter into that mystery in partaking of the bread and wine. It is in coming together in worship and in praying together as a community of faith that we move from the act of *explaining* the meaning of Christ's identity, to encountering Christ in direct relationship.

However, Christ's identity cannot simply be reduced to an impenetrable mystery. The evidence of encounter is confirmed in a transformed life. In the UCC, following the path blazed by the Abolitionist, Social Gospel, and Civil Rights movements, that transformation is understood, at least partially, in terms of the relevance of the Gospel to the tribulations of contemporary society. This prophetic dimension of Christ's identity, and the determination to understand that prophecy in light of today's concerns for peace, justice, and social responsibility, lead us to ask what it means to speak of Christ's identity right here and now.

WHO IS JESUS CHRIST FOR US TODAY?

The question of Christ's identity is not about determining a truth that lies in the past, but is rather a deeply urgent and pressing question. Dietrich Bonhoeffer's much quoted question—"who is Jesus Christ for us today?"—cuts to the heart of the church's theological self-understanding.[2] It is actually three separate questions, each of which draws us back in its own distinct way to the question of Christ's identity. Who *is* Jesus Christ? Who is Jesus Christ *for us*? Who is Jesus Christ for us *today*? Each iteration of the question intensifies the significance of the previous one. It is not enough to seek to understand Jesus in an abstract and ahistorical way. Nor is it enough to understand him only in light of his own time and place. Rather, Christ's identity must be tied to the present reality of Christ in the context of modern society.

The UCC has taken this mandate to heart. Since the 1957 merger of the Evangelical and Reformed and Congregational Christian Churches, the UCC has been active in movements for social change, including the civil rights and anti-Vietnam war movements. From the beginning, the UCC has understood its vocation as a church to be rooted in the struggle to create a better, more humane, and more just world.[3] How that vocation is related to the person and work of Jesus Christ is a more complicated question, subject as it is to the myriad interpretations of Christ that are represented in the UCC, where Christ is understood variously as Moral Teacher, Power and Presence of God, triumphant resurrected King, and Friend of the poor, oppressed, and downtrodden. One need not choose one from among these understandings, for each of them is true simultaneously with the others.

As a church, the UCC has never insisted on "tests of faith" but rather "testimonies" of the community of faith to God's spirit of love and grace in action.[4] This freedom has allowed the UCC and its predecessor denominations to be at the forefront of movements for justice, including civil rights, women's ordination, and the full participation of gay and lesbian persons in the life of the church. Some of these decisions have raised, and continue to raise, controversy both within the UCC and in society as a whole. Yet, for better and for worse, the UCC has been committed to understanding what it means to follow Christ, and to interpret his significance for us today in terms of social and moral action on behalf of those who are pushed to the margins of society.

To ask who Jesus Christ is for us today is not, however, only to ask how we can understand him in light of the most recent social struggle or political problem. It also raises difficult theological questions: Are we bound to understand Christ today in light of how he has been understood in the past? What debt do we owe to the theological heritage from which we are descended? Can we continue to speak of Christ as the Son of God, the second Person of the Trinity? Do these titles continue to have meaning in a world of war, oppression, poverty, and genocide?

No single answer to these questions predominates in the UCC (nor, given our polity, can it be imposed). What we are left with is simply the question, in all of its open-ended immensity, with all of its significance: Who is Jesus Christ? For us? Today? What is more, given the huge diversity of different ways this question is answered within the UCC, a further question is raised: If we are a *united* church, what in fact is it that unites us, if not a common understanding of the identity of Jesus Christ?

UNITED IN CHRIST?

"The United Church of Christ acknowledges as its sole Head, Jesus Christ, Son of God and Savior," according to paragraph 2 of the Preamble of the Constitution of the United Church of Christ. In this sentence we can find three affirmations about Jesus Christ: he is the sole Head of the UCC, the Son of God, and Savior. But affirmation is not explanation, and it is precisely by refusing to insist on an extensive set of theological requirements that the UCC has been able to allow for such a wide diversity of Christological opinions to flourish under its auspices. But this is also what makes it so difficult to determine what it means to be a church united in Christ. Gabriel Fackre has argued that Jesus Christ is the "norm" of theological authority for Christians.[5] But what does it mean to accept Christ as our norm? In what way does he unite us? Are we united by his moral example? His spiritual teachings? His mystical presence? Is it all of these together, or something else entirely? In what sense is Christ the "Head" of the church? In what sense, in other words, is the UCC a United Church of Christ?

This may be the most trenchant problem that the UCC faces in coming to terms with its identity as a Christian denomination. Is what distinguishes the United Church of Christ from other Protestant churches—beyond issues of polity, history, and worship—finally, simply, its inability to decide what it means to *be* a Christian church? Yet, even in the midst of the plurality of theological possibilities that has allowed the UCC to engage creatively and faithfully with the world in which it finds itself, is it not possible that there is a deeper unity, a unity found in Jesus Christ, even though we cannot agree on who Christ is and what it means to be *in* him?

It is impossible, in raising these questions, to begin to formulate an authoritative answer, since the issue of authority is precisely at the heart of much dispute within the UCC! As a denomination, we do not recognize the national office as having binding authority over conferences, associations, or churches. Nor do we recognize the declarations of the General Synod to be binding and authoritative. From the perspective of church polity, only the local church has definitive authority over doctrinal matters, and yet even the principle of local church autonomy is in some sense tied to an understanding of what it means to vest *final* authority in Christ. Thus, every local church decides for itself the significance of Jesus Christ.

What then ties us together? Perhaps nothing but the desire to remain together faithfully as followers of Jesus Christ, "the man of Nazareth," with the great wealth of understandings of what that means. As a community of faith, we may be *unified* without being *uniform* if we can leave adequate room for generous and loving difference among us. The mystery of Christ's identity creates the room for that multiplicity to exist within a community dedicated to living together in love. At the same time, as followers of Christ, we have all recognized in Jesus Christ a teacher, a prophet, a unique connection to God. To be united in Christ means to hold on to that recognition in the face of mystery, in the face of disagreement, and in the face of doubt.

Yet, it must be said that as a community of those who are called to follow Jesus Christ, our differences should not become an excuse to avoid speaking of Christ altogether. On the contrary, it is because of our differences that talking about the meaning of Christ is our most important theological task. It is through an understanding and appreciation of the various ways that Christ is understood and spoken of in the UCC that we may better understand our own beliefs about the identity and significance of Jesus Christ, and thereby become more faithful, more generous, and more dedicated disciples.

Overview

The aim of this volume is to make a contribution to the task of interpreting Jesus Christ in the United Church of Christ. Our goal is not to interpret for the church, but simply to offer a set of perspectives out of the multitude available within the UCC. Our desire is to foster a conversation on the centrality of Jesus to our denomination, not to insist that there is only one proper perspective. Whether one defines the identity of Christ in terms of his status as Resurrected Lord, or his moral teachings, or the breaking of the bread, or in the Great Commission, one will find material for discussion and reflection in this book. Since limited space makes it is impossible to address every possible angle, we make no claim to an exhaustive survey of positions, but rather hope to provide a "sampler" of some of the available options.

At the same time, some common themes emerge. For many of the authors, the Mercersburg theology of John Williamson Nevin and Philip Schaff is a significant and relevant contribution to a contemporary conversation about the meaning of Jesus Christ. The sacramentology of the Mercersburg movement offered a way of connecting the individual believer directly to Christ through the experience of Communion. By taking seriously the dual nature of Christ as both truly divine and truly human, Nevin and Schaff attempted to offer an understanding of Christ that was neither reductionistic nor fundamentalist, but stood in the tension between the ancient and the modern. They were strongly *Christocentric*, but not *Christomonistic*.

Rather, they sought a way of speaking of Jesus Christ that was simultaneously present and transcendent, contemporary and eternal. In many ways the seriousness with which the Mercersburg theology took the question of Christology is a direct inspiration for this volume.

Another common theme running through these essays is the seriousness with which the authors take the texts and history of the United Church of Christ. Far from embracing the cliché of the UCC as being anchorless and ungrounded, the authors have sought for grounding in those documents through which the UCC has defined itself and its character: its constitution and bylaws, the resolutions of synods, and the theologies of those who have been recognized as leaders in the church. Beyond that, the authors have sought to situate the UCC within the broad tradition of Reformed theology, the inheritance of its predecessor denominations, and the perennial touchstones of Christian faith. At the very center of this reflection is an attempt to understand Christ as he is portrayed through the words of the Bible, for this is the first and final source for almost all we know of Jesus of Nazareth. If these stories of his life, his teaching, his death and resurrection are at all meaningful, or even revelatory, then the Bible must be the keystone of any interpretation of Christology within the UCC.

Yet another theme that emerges is the relationship between theology and Christian life. Though the *idea* of Christology can often seem abstract, and perhaps less than totally relevant, the *practice* of living as a follower of Christ is not. The ethical imperative that has always motivated the United Church of Christ can be seen throughout this volume. How we understand the meaning of discipleship is wholly dependent on how we conceive of who Christ is. It is thus the form of life that we adopt for ourselves as individuals, and more importantly as a church, that defines in a practical sense just what our Christology *really* is. By seeking to interpret the meaning of Christology within the UCC, the authors of these essays also, implicitly and explicitly, make the case for the kind of life that is appropriate to his followers.

Closely connected to this is the recognition that our understanding of Christ cannot only be backward-looking, but must also be "of the moment." Each of these essays addresses, in its own way, Bonhoeffer's question: Each author seeks to understand the meaning of Jesus Christ for today. If our faith is related to our response to the pressing concerns of the world in which we live, then how we conceive of Christ will govern our answer to those who are beset by the evils of injustice, poverty, disease, and death. The hope of the Christian faith is that, in Christ, these evils will not have the last word, but will be overcome, to "let justice roll down like waters, and righteousness like an ever-flowing stream" (Amos 5:24).

Other themes will no doubt become apparent to readers as they consider the conversation among the contributors to this volume, and engage in that conversation themselves through their reading. The reflection that we hope to engender does not end when one arrives at a particular answer. The truth of Jesus Christ cannot be reduced, as the saying goes, to a "laundry list of propositions," but opens up to an ever deeper understanding the more it is pursued. Our hope is that these essays may provoke such a pursuit in our readers.

In this vein, the volume begins with a consideration of the theological heritage of the United Church of Christ. For Max Stackhouse, the relationship of Christians to the world is a central Christological issue. In his essay he considers how the threefold office of Christ can serve to provide groundwork for thinking about Christian social responsibility. The offices of Christ present a way for Christians to understand the offices that they occupy in their own lives. In recognizing Christ's authority over these public roles of Prophet, Priest, and King, Christians relativize the claims made on those roles by earthly prophets, priests, and kings. In the increasingly global world in which we live, the recognition that Christ is sovereign over all spheres of human existence empowers Christians to act as deputies of Christ in society.

In the second essay, Lee Barrett frames the diversity of Christological perspective in the UCC in terms of a "kaleidoscope" of viewpoints, each of which contributes to the unity of the whole. Barrett begins by considering some of the various "plot lines" that describe how Jesus can be spoken of. He then turns to the classical theological categories of the "person" and "work" of Jesus Christ. The meaning of Christ's person revolves around our understanding of his dual nature as both true God and true human being, while his work is best understood through the traditional *munus triplex*—the threefold office of Christ as Prophet, Priest, and King. Given the amazing array of possible interpretations that these ideas elicit, the question becomes whether the UCC can or even should seek to embrace them all.

Gabriel Fackre's article draws our attention to the way Jesus Christ has been understood in the foundational texts of the United

Church of Christ. In going "back to the sources," as it were, Fackre examines some of the Christological affirmations that were central to the creation of the UCC. These documents represented a formational body of theological reflection that helped to ground its sense of ecclesial identity. These texts should be understood within the "narrative framework," as Fackre calls it, of the Great Story of God's work in history, the culmination of which is the incarnation and ministry of Jesus Christ. At the same time, these texts are "ministerial" not "magisterial" in the UCC. That is to say, documents such as the UCC Statement of Faith do not have binding authority within the UCC, but do serve to orient us theologically toward the key affirmations of the church.

The second part of the volume deals with the ecumenical connections that have been so essential in the life and history of the United Church of Christ. Considering the question of Jesus Christ in light of the issue of religious pluralism, Lydia Veliko examines the tension between unity and diversity in the life of the UCC. The identity of Christ, the theology of the Reformed tradition, and the question of the meaning of salvation offer resources through which we may understand the nature of the church as both "united" and "uniting," and opens up possibilities for the role of the church in interfaith dialogue.

John Thomas's essay explores these issues with his gaze firmly fixed on how the meaning of Jesus Christ factors into the UCC's role in ecumenical discussions. Beginning with the idea of "visitations" in the Gospel of Luke, Thomas examines the way that Christ's messianic identity is recognized by those with whom he comes into contact. Thomas connects these passages to the idea of sacramental "presence" in the theology of the Mercersburg movement. He then turns to consider how this theology has contributed to the UCC's participation in the Lutheran-Reformed dialogue that eventually produced the 1997 "A Formula of Agreement." The question of Christ's presence in the Eucharist is connected to the presence of Christ in the work of the church in the world.

Part three of this volume moves to questions of the role of Christology in light of the issues and challenges facing the UCC today. Mary Schaller Blaufuss considers how our understanding of Jesus Christ affects how the UCC goes about missionary work in a pluralistic world. Framing her essay around the encounter between Jesus and Martha in John, chapter 11, Blaufuss explores what it means to transcend social limitations in the midst of the "cultures of death" with which we are surrounded. Christ offers Christians the possibility of transformation in our encounters with those of other faiths, opens up new possibilities for mutual understanding in the midst of religious diversity, and thrusts us out into the world to continue his mission of proclaiming the Good News of new life.

Deirdre King Hainsworth examines the way in which Christ is presented in the "ethical proclamation" of the UCC. Central to her argument is Christ's status as both an "example" and an "event." As "example," Christ stands as the model for the Christian way of life; while as "event," Christ is the utterly unique incarnation of God in the midst of the human experience. In this latter sense, Christ is beyond human capacity for imitation and is the vehicle for God's salvific work. In its public pronouncements, the UCC tends to focus on the prophetic character of Christ's identity and his teaching, rather than on his person, as the locus for social engagement. How Christ's identity as the incarnation of God factors into these matters is often left undeveloped. Hainsworth makes the case for the importance of developing this dimension of Christ's identity as "event" more fully in the church's public witness.

Theodore Trost brings the Christological conversation into the midst of a contemporary controversy, as he reflects on the meaning of Mel Gibson's movie *The Passion of the Christ* alongside the UCC's "Still Speaking" campaign. While *The Passion* represents a particularly militant, muscular, and aggressive brand of Christology, the UCC's "Still Speaking" campaign provides a more open-ended and "friendly" vision of Christ. Trost argues that each of these understandings is inadequate, and that the UCC would be better served by accenting elements of its history, particularly the theology of the Mercersburg movement and the theology implicit in several classic hymns. He ends with a discussion of Christ's transforming encounter in Tyre with a Syrophoenician woman, pointing out how Christ changes his mind in response to the woman's plea, extending his ministry to all, Gentiles and Jews alike.

In the final essay Stephen Ray addresses the idea of the "living Christology" of the United Church of Christ. Ray makes a distinction between Christology understood as "recovery" and Christology understood as "discernment." "Recovery," while an important dimension of the church's reflection, needs "discernment" in order to avoid the dangers of theological rigidity. A living Christology is predicated on the still-unfolding life of Christ in the midst of the common life of

Christ's people. It leads us out of concern with ourselves and into a concern for our neighbors and the world we inhabit.

This volume ends with four appendixes. Appendix A offers chapter-by-chapter discussion questions related to each essay, for use in classes and discussion groups. Our hope is that these questions will foster continuing discussion about these essays. Appendix B presents a number of classic Christological confessions, including the Nicene and Chalcedonian creeds, and the UCC Statement of Faith. We offer these as resources to those who would like to further explore how Christ has been spoken of in the church, and how he is spoken of today. Appendix C is a section of selected readings for those who wish to continue to delve into the questions raised here. Finally, Appendix D provides a selection of worship resources, compiled by Frederick Trost, who has long supplied these resources to members of the Confessing Christ mailing list.

CONCLUSION

The mystery of Christ's identity is central to Mark's Gospel, and it is central to the question of what it means to be a Christian today. If we are called upon to follow Jesus Christ, then a great deal depends on just *who* it is we are following. Yet, as in Mark's Gospel, there are no easy answers to that question. Indeed, the more deeply we probe the mystery of Christ's identity, the more questions emerge from the depths of our faith. Nevertheless, as a church we cannot cease to ask these questions, nor seek for answers. The nature of our answers, however provisional they are, ought to lead us to understand Christ more fully, not as an idea or a symbol, but as a living presence at work sustaining the church in its mission within the world.

To be a Christian is to stake one's life in the identity of Jesus Christ, to radically trust that, in Christ, we have come into an encounter with God. The identity of Jesus Christ is a multifaceted reality that frustrates and defeats our attempts to reduce it to simple slogans. In these essays, we have only illuminated a few of those many facets. May these offerings inspire further reflection, for the sake of the United Church of Christ, for the sake of all Christians, and most crucially, for the sake of the God whom we strive to follow and confess through our words and our deeds.

PART
ONE

HERITAGE

CHAPTER ONE

THE OFFICES OF CHRIST FROM EARLY CHURCH THROUGH THE REFORMERS

MAX L. STACKHOUSE

Others in this collection will doubtless address the person and work of Christ, the debates over the nature and character of the atonement, the relationship of the second Person to the first and third Persons of the Trinity, the classic questions about the nature of the incarnation and the resurrection, and the ways in which different New Testament authors and various theologians over the centuries have developed overlapping but distinctive Christologies. These are obviously important issues for Christian theology in a time of instability in the faith. They need further investigation because many today are uncertain about what we can and should believe, and more are uncertain about how God wants us to live.

But these issues also need attention because some of these views have at least indirect consequences for ethics, Further, while the theologians who take up these issues seek to state the truths of the gospel as clearly as possible, their efforts are often laden with contextually shaped themes and social presumptions. To recognize this is not, as some might suggest, a "sellout" to culture or contextualism, or to do a sociology of knowledge on the gospel, but it is to recognize that every serious Christology reveals that which transcends its context and simultaneously pertains to the context.

By offering an historical survey of how scripture and tradition have understood Christology, in regard to both the perennial truths of the gospel and their impact in changing contexts, we can see how Christian ethics seeks to address both personal and common social issues. This may allow us to develop new insights about faith's deepest dimensions, to reform our own views and ethos, and to engage in dialogue and debate, critique and learning, and mission and cooperation with nonbelievers.

Over the centuries as people confronted changing social constellations, they have had to find moral and spiritual guidance for their lives by drawing fresh insight from biblical and doctrinal resources. This approach presumes what I believe to be well-warranted by historical evidence: that religion, as institutionalized faith, influences personal behavior and social life, and that key understandings of doctrines can bend a religion in one way or another, thus changing behavior and society. Historically, doctrines have sometimes had unintended effect on ethical life, but once we learn to trace effects, the doctrines can be evaluated in terms of their ethical effects. Indeed, once we realize this, we become responsible not only for giving "an accounting for the hope that is in [us]" (1 Pet. 3:15), but also for the possible social and ethical consequences of how we formulate or reformulate our faith, and institutionalize it in our religious practices, our personal life, and our society.

With these things in mind, I want to investigate one strand of Christological thinking that has been present since biblical days and has been interpreted in several ways: "the three offices of Christ"—Prophet, Priest, and King. These are the three "anointed" ("christened") offices of leadership in the Old Testament, and they are all seen as culminating in Jesus, the Anointed One in the New. Various emphases in, or implications of, this biblical legacy and doctrinal strand of Christological understanding have been sometimes overshadowed by selective doctrinal accents prompted in part by perceived social urgencies, but it has never been entirely absent. Earlier, this strand was recovered, clarified, and recast from its previous early church and medieval Catholic developments by the Reformed tradition, adopted by many Lutheran and Catholic thinkers, and now may well be potentially critical, properly restated, for a faithful ethical response to our own age.

The term "office" is interesting in itself. It does not directly refer to a person, although persons in roles are presupposed. It instead refers to a defined place—a specific rank or status—in the organized body where particular qualified persons—either called, appointed, or elected—can fulfill a specific role. The office exists so that certain necessary tasks can be performed, tasks that people cannot accomplish by themselves. People, in fact, entrust themselves to those "set apart" to occupy the office and fulfill these roles. These positions are designed so that the right person can accomplish some indispensable functions in ways that command respect and evoke responsibility.

Today, in the context of complex societies, most people have many "offices." We are not "merely" a peasant or a knight or a mother or a princess. We are persons who may well have a "position" at work, in our church, as a spouse, parent, child, aunt, or friend, as a member (perhaps an "officer") in this and that civic organization or party, and as a citizen who follows the issues and votes in elections. People often become isolated or alienated if they do not have at least a couple of these; and as social pathology (alcoholism, drug use, criminal behavior, poverty, compulsive gambling, etc.) increases, the less people are socially embedded in a complex of "offices." Yet those who are engaged in many offices find it difficult to juggle the several roles and responsibilities and keep an integrated identity without the social institutions that support differentiated obligations. It becomes a complex personal and social issue. It also poses theological and ethical issues: How can we find a secure personal identity in the midst of such a variegated world? How ought we conduct ourselves with moral and spiritual coherence in the areas of our differentiated lives? What can hold the complex fabric of society together?

The model of how Christians are to live is generally to live as Christ lived, and he is portrayed in the Bible and the tradition in several roles. These are indicated by many titles given to Jesus in the New Testament: Son of God, Lord, Shepherd, Word, Friend, Master, Rabbi, etc. But the three titles of Prophet, Priest, and King, which gradually became specified as the "offices," came to be among the weightiest for a theologically based social ethics. In fact, some of the other titles are roles subordinated to or included in one or another of these three.

However, the idea was not perfectly clear in parts of church history. Evidently, in the early church, two offices of Christ tended to predominate, the Priest and the King. It is likely that this was related to the fact that the two centers of power in old Palestine at the time of Jesus were the religious and political, the temple and the palace, even though both were heavily contested. On the one side was the religious establishment, although there was tension between the Pharisees in the synagogues and the Sadducees in the Jerusalem temple—and both were challenged by and hostile to the Qumran sectarians of Dead Sea Scrolls' fame. And on the other was the tension between the ethnarch (the residues of former Judaic royalty) and the Roman Empire, and both were challenged by and struggled against bands of militant nationalist revolutionaries.

All of these opposed the nascent Christian movement. If Christ were understood as the true Priest and true King, the authority of these other claimants was relativized. By asserting loyalty to a higher authority in precisely these two realms, the early church embraced a streak of anti-authoritarianism. These believers held that Jesus was not only the highest of the High Priests, who subordinated all the authority of the temple priesthood, but also the final sacrificial lamb who put an end to the animal sacrifices—for a fee—to atone for breaches of the Law. Indeed, various ritual and legal obligations under the instruction and control of the competing religious officials became obsolete as well. Moreover, they held also that Christ was the King, indeed the King of Kings. Thus, the Herods, the Caesars, and the several revolutionary pretenders to nationalist sovereignty could not command their first loyalties. (Prophecy in this period was evidently primarily understood as a manifestation of the Holy Spirit that induced ecstatic utterances, largely incomprehensible to the community of faith or the larger society. It was present in the formation of the community of faith, but it was not seen as a dominant social force in the public spheres of life. In fact, it needed interpretation to make sense or be edifying to anyone, in or outside the church.)

As the church grew in the Roman Empire, in spite of much persecution, it became more confident of its own leaders and began to honor them as priestly officers, especially bishops, of the church. Further, in the face of wars, violence, and unrest, it saw the relative justice of the Roman Empire as something to be respected. The understanding of the two offices of Priest and King took a more positive rather than a merely negative turn. This trend culminated when the Emperor Constantine granted the church toleration and favor, and the church began to develop its own hierarchy of officials openly. The older anti-clerical and anti-political attitudes were inadequate, though many (the forerunners of the Anabaptists of the Reformation period and the still anti-Catholic and anti-Ecumenical "peace churches" today) resisted the acceptance of this new status and the new developments of the doctrine that Christ was Priest and King. They called it the "second Fall," a new plunge of the church into sinful worldliness. But the churches that became the Orthodox and Catholic wings of Christianity saw this development as a blessing from God, a fresh manifestation of the incarnate Lord of history now also shaping the larger civilization.

As is well known, Constantine called the Council of Nicaea and established a wider cosmopolitan peace than had been known for centuries. Constantine (sainted by the Orthodox tradition) was seen by some as Moses-like, the lawgiver and intercessor who had once learned the arts of war and governance in Pharaoh's palace but used them in the service of God. Others saw him as an echo of Melchizedek, the biblical priest-king who united the two offices in one person, or as the new King David, who also danced before the altar and composed psalms for worship, like a priest, and who inaugurated plans for the great temple in Jerusalem at royal expense. Bishop Eusebius, at that time, spoke of prophet, priest, and king in regard to the biblical text, but he was primarily interested in seeing Constantine as messiah-like leader of both church and regime. The role of prophet may have been exercised by such figures as Athanasius, who influenced the Nicene Creed more than Eusebius, and who subtly worked against such an exalted status for Constantine; but it was not called "prophecy" then.

But priests of Christ, ever more representing the sacerdotal authority of the church, and the Christian kings, representing the political-military authority of regime, did not blend so easily. When the Constantinian Empire fell apart, the old Roman Empire began its slow decline, and papal authority grew as the church centralized its hierarchical control. Regional kings became more and more powerful, seeing themselves in the image of David. The question became this: How, if sacerdotum and regnum are distinct, are they to be related? It was a practical question, but also a Christological issue, for they both claimed to represent the reign of Christ wherein the will of God could be done on earth as it is in heaven, at least in an anticipatory way. In a host of now obscure battles between popes and emperors, bishops and kings, pastors and princes—many fateful for the eventual development of a pluralistic society—the idea that there was more than one authoritative voice in society was established. But the boundaries were contentious. May the king appoint bishops and priests in his realm? May bishops crown kings or excommunicate them, de-legitimating them before the people? When a pious king donates land to a diocese and then dies, shall the bishop have legal authority over the peasants attached to the land? If a king invites an order to estab-lish a chapter as his chapel, is the abbot subordinate in authority to the ruler? May a king crown himself emperor without the blessings of the pope, and may a ruler dismiss an unruly pope? May the pope raise an army to depose a wicked monarch, since the Vatican is both the seat of the Church of Rome and a political realm in its service?

It was in this context that the understanding of Christ as Priest and King was given a second major interpretation. The resurrected Christ in medieval iconography, reflecting much theology of the pe-riod, is often portrayed sitting on a throne under God the Father in heaven, holding two swords, and attended by clerics and royalty. The one sword represents the sacramental realm of the Priest and the other the political realm of the King. What they represent are the necessary and complementary guides to life. The Protestant traditions followed this sense of duality, for the most part, but they more firmly stressed that the priestly and kingly offices are not entirely the same and that the one must not do the work of the other. One governs spir-itual life, the other material life; one deals with the soul, the other the body; one deals with the meanings of the Word, the other with the powers of the world; one administers canon law, the other civil law; one is dedicated to Christ's love, the other to the justice of God known in Christ. Here is the root of what, in Western civilization, is the distinction of "the two kingdoms" (particularly in Lutheran and Evangelical traditions) and the division of "church and state" (partic-ularly in Reformed and Baptist traditions), with other wings of Protes-tantism subordinating the church to the crown (as in the Anglican Church), or the subordination of the state to the church (as in Savonarola's Florence and Cromwell's England).

Such doctrinal and socio-political developments generated sev-eral models of the ways in which the "two swords" can maintain sepa-rate spheres of authority and still see the other as representatives of God's reign on earth, best known in Christ's offices as Priest and King. The legacy of the medieval Catholic tradition lasted well into the magisterial Protestant Reformation, and the idea of two fundamental spheres of authority, one religious and the other political, is not yet at an end. Yet it is clear to all that the fundamental domination of one by the other is neither faithful nor workable.

One can see the importance of this legacy in comparison and contrast with developments in other great religious traditions. In fact, we can see how parts of the Christian tradition veer into trajectories that make them roughly similar to several of the world's religions in this respect, for every civilization requires a religious (or quasi-religious) framework to provide spiritual and moral leadership, and a political framework to establish law and order. I think it is fair to say that the Confucian tradition, for example, accents the domination of the "priestly" functions by the "kingly" ones, in that it sees the Emperor at the center and peak of the society, with the learned and moral Mandarin literati serving the empire and being local representatives of virtue and commitment among the people. This pattern is perpetuated by the Maoists and, oddly enough, in the West by many post-Christian advocates of the secular Enlightenment (with party "ideologists" playing the role of "priestly" literati, in the one case, and "scientific advisors" playing the role in the other).

In contrast, the Hindu tradition has put the priestly Brahmans at the highest status level and at the moral center of society, with regional or local rulers under them in status and authority—even if the latter have greater political and economic power (classical India had regional dynasties, but never had a united Empire that could unify ritual duties, scriptures, script, moral virtues, or sense of national identity, until the Raj). Both of these contrast with the Islamic model in which, following the example of Mohammed, the Prophet who is also a Warrior-Ruler is the ideal. Interpreted from a biblical perspective, we can suggest that they aspired to have a new kind of Melchizedek as the leader of the Islamic world. However much this tradition preserved this ideal, it has broken into two distinct views of the relationship of "kingly" office, which rules by the pious use of the sword, and that of the "priestly" clerical "scholar," who rules by the use of the word, interpreting the prophecies. In actual practice, in the Sunni tradition "kings" have tended to control, by appointment, the "priestly" mullahs; and in the Shi'a traditions, "priestly" Ayatollahs have tended to control government officials—although some charismatic leaders have gathered followers as prophetically inclined spiritual-political leaders, some mystically oriented, some militantly oriented, and some both, as the contemporary world knows.

The twofold understanding of the offices of Christ can help us interpret the role of religion and politics of many societies, Christian and non-Christian, for wherever religion becomes dominant, there are fairly predictable consequences. The intrinsic character of the religion—whether it is the support system for the political regime, whether it expects the political regime to support it, or whether it sees itself as a parallel authority with the political regime—will bend the society in one or another direction, which is comparable cross-culturally. It will also shape the sense of personal duty among believers: Is their first duty to draw on their piety to support the common good of the political order? Or is it to seek spiritual awareness and fulfill the ritual duties of religion and expect the political authorities to support this end? Or is there some proper duality or necessary identity in these duties? At times, historically, the Christian dualism of authorities has pressed its adherents in directions almost indistinguishable from the world's other great civilization-forming religions, although it was believed in this long period of Christian history that the inner logic of a Christ-shaped civilization pressed toward a mutually supportive duality.

Yet this dualistic option did not, and does not, exhaust the implications of Christ for the form of society or for personal ethics in the Christian tradition. There is a lurking third office, one that does not let the matter rest. This is a point that is, in form and substance, similar to the development of another great doctrine of the faith: We can speak of the two natures of Christ, as true God and true human, but that acknowledgment leads one inevitably to the Trinity, if one thinks it through and follows the deeper implications of the scriptures. In regard to the offices, Christ is also understood to be the Prophet, the heir and fulfillment of the earlier biblical prophets. The recovery of that motif has deeply influenced Protestantism, and through it, modern religion, social views, and personal ethics in the Roman Catholic and parts of the Orthodox traditions and societies.

The Reformers took the scriptures very seriously and thought very hard in fresh ways about its implications for church, people, and society. They noted that, according to Genesis 1, God called humanity —male and female—into existence and commissioned them to be fruitful, to fill and subdue the earth; and, according to Genesis 2, God gave humanity the authority to give the names by which all the animals were to be called. Humans were given, in other words, a stewardly dominion over the creatures and a vocation to create culture.

Not only was all humanity called in a general sense, but a particular people, Israel, was called by name and "chosen" from all the peoples of the world to be witnesses to God's righteousness and faithfulness. Further, particular people in the community were called or "elected" to perform specific duties for the well-being of the people. From very early on, priests, for example, had a special role to play in conducting worship and offering sacrifices. Moses instructed the people in God's Law and pointed toward the promised land. Then, later, the prophet Samuel, in some ways following the example of Moses, was called to select the earliest kings of Israel; and later prophets, inspired by the spirit of God, chided both kings and the priests if they led the people in ways contrary to God's Law and way, and articulated the hope for a savior in times of trouble, a messiah who would bring a new age. By the time that David's rule was established (I Kings 1), prophets, priests, and kings were all "anointed" as those called to special responsibilities under the Laws of God, for the purposes of God, to guide the people in worship, ethics, and the formation of social life.

The Reformers saw that these ancient themes were adopted, adapted, developed, and refined in the Christian New Testament. Most importantly, Jesus was recognized as the Savior, the expected Messiah, the Christ, *the* anointed one—the one who was not only the incarnate Son of God, but also the fulfillment of the anointed offices of the previous biblical record. Matthew begins by tracing Jesus' legal lineage from the royal house of David and stresses the moral and spiritual illegitimacy of the ethnarch, Herod. Mark begins his Gospel by stressing the continuity of Jesus with John the Baptist, the last and greatest of the prophets until Christ. And Luke opens his Gospel by showing Jesus' continuity with the priestly family—Zechariah and Elizabeth. John begins his Gospel by speaking of the *Logos* and identifying the wisdom of the Word with the coming of Jesus. In a sense, John pointed to the deep coherence behind all historical roles of the Messiah. All of the Gospels are laden with other clues to the ways in which Christ fulfills and transforms, in unanticipated ways, all of the offices, as Robert Sherman has argued.[1] The "set-apart" three offices of the ancient tradition of special calling culminate in Christ's sacrifice.

As this doctrine—the *munus triplex*, as tradition named it—was discussed and developed, it took a variety of shapes, according to its relationship to other doctrines in the various streams of Christian thought. E. F. Karl Müller, for example, summarized the Thomistic and Lutheran adaptations of this motif some years ago. He pointed out that Thomas Aquinas had followed Eusebius at one point and had spoken of Christ as "legislator, sacerdos, *et rex*," presuming that the prophet was a lawgiver, but generally had not used the threefold division.

Further, Müller noted that the Lutheran tradition had to swim against the tradition of the "two swords," and it developed a tendency to resolve that tension by taking a view in which one of the offices was dominant.[2] He pointed out that the Lutheran theologian and pastor and coauthor of the Articles of Concord, Nikolaus Selnecker, was evidently the first scholar to speak about the threefold office, but tended to subordinate the offices of King and Prophet to the office of Priest. As a Wittenberg theologian and polemicist against Catholicism and Calvinism, Selnecker taught that the office of King was supreme and that it comprehended the other two functions. The medieval tensions, thus, remained for some time, but gradually the threefold office was accepted as a doctrine faithful to scripture and in accord with the best insights of historic experience by most Lutherans as well, even if other elements of Lutheran theology pressed in the direction of "two kingdoms" theories.

It was the Reformed tradition that most accented the three offices. Calvin was not the first or the only Reformer to stress this, but he gave the tradition a rather extensive and tight treatment of the three, arguing for the primal authority and work of Christ in these offices, overtly against the papal and Holy Roman Emperor sharing of power in the medieval period[3] and covertly against the early Lutheran view that one of the offices had priority, although he connects the messianic role primarily with the kingly office in one place.

Perhaps the most remarkable contribution of the Reformed traditions is not only reintroducing the prophetic office as co-equal with the other two, but putting it first. This is quite understandable, given the fact that in biblical history, the Prophet was, ordinarily, familiar with but not directly attached or indebted to either the traditional priestly or royal offices. It had a certain independence of established leadership. And although "schools" of prophets were to develop, there was no ordered pattern of succession. The Prophet had to have an extra-institutional charisma and to prove his (or her) legitimacy before the people (sometimes against the priests and royalty by the acuteness of inspired insights and the ability to interpret both the scriptures and the realities of the current religious, social, and political situations. The Prophet was believed to have been given, by divine inspiration, messages for the people of Israel, calling them to be what they were intended to be—a light to the nations. The oracular messages concerned true laws of righteous living, coming retribution for the betrayal of them, and the formation of just persons and covenanted social relations, as was dramatically the case with Moses. Later prophets lived in the shadow of Moses and reminded the people of the heritage of the covenant that could be obscured by human negligence, by the worship of false deities, by the betrayal of the Laws of God, by arrogance beyond proper confidence, and sensualism beyond genuine delight in God's gifts

In speaking of the prophetic office, Calvin particularly accents Isaiah's words:

> The Spirit of the Lord God is upon me, because the Lord has anointed me; he has sent me to bring good news to the oppressed, to bind up the brokenhearted, to proclaim liberty to the captives, and release to the prisoners; to proclaim the year of the Lord's favor. (Isa. 61:1–2)

The Prophet in this view is essentially the preacher and teacher, although not the same as the teachers of human wisdom only. The true Prophet does not teach to gain honor or standing for himself, but to edify the whole body of the faithful community. For this, he is anointed by the Holy Spirit to be a "herald and witness" of the Father's grace, and that Spirit is to be ever present and efficacious in valid preaching. The substance of Christ's inspired prophetic preaching is "treasures of wisdom," "perfect doctrine," and "the boundless immensity of heavenly blessings"—which cannot be surpassed by any further prophecy. This striking emphasis on the Prophet as preacher influenced much in the Reformed tradition, as can be seen even in church architecture in the reduced attention given to the Communion table and the obvious centrality of the pulpit, for example.

The duty to preach, teach, and testify in prophetic ways, however, are to be spread throughout the members of the body of Christ. Calvin cites Joel 2:28: "Your sons and your daughters shall prophesy, your old men shall dream dreams, and your young men shall see visions." This had unrecognized consequences, fully compatible with other themes in the Reformed tradition. As Luther's brief comments about the "priesthood of all believers," spread over the years to all Protestants, so did, more gradually, Calvin's suggestion that there should be a "prophethood of all believers." Both spread the offices of Christ to the laity.

The doctrine of the three offices of Christ was spread among the people in a number of ways, not the least of them were the catechisms of the Reformed tradition. We find a particularly compact formula in the Heidelberg Catechism (4.029–033):

> Q. *Why is he (Jesus) called CHRIST, that is, the ANOINTED ONE?*
> A. Because he is ordained by God the Father and anointed with the Holy Spirit to be our chief Prophet and Teacher, fully revealing to us the secret purpose and will of God concerning our redemption; to be our only High Priest, having redeemed us by the one sacrifice of his body and ever interceding for us with the Father; and to be our eternal King, governing us by his Word and Spirit, and defending and sustaining us in the redemption he has won for us.
>
> Q. *But why are you called Christian?*
> A. Because through faith I share in Christ and thus in his anointing, so that I may confess his name, offer myself (as) a living sacrifice of gratitude to him, and fight against sin and the devil with a free and good conscience throughout this life and hereafter rule with him in eternity over all creatures.

The themes of this doctrine appear also in a somewhat different, but also striking form in the Westminster Shorter Catechism and was learned by thousands and thousands of youth and young adults (Questions 24–26):

> *How doth Christ execute the office of a Prophet?*
> Christ executeth the office of a Prophet in revealing to us by his word and his Spirit the will of God for our salvation.
>
> *How doth Christ execute the office of a Priest?*
> Christ executeth the office of Priest in his once offering up of himself a sacrifice to satisfy divine justice and reconcile us to God and in making continual intercession for us.
>
> *How doth Christ execute the office of a King?*
> Christ executeth the office of a King in subduing us to himself in ruling and defending us, and in restraining and conquering all his and our enemies.

The Reformed tradition also generated a number of academic theologies that become more articulate about doctrinal matters in a new way as the Enlightenment gained a greater foothold in intellectual life, particularly where the link was made between right preaching and teaching and the understanding of the power of the word as rooted in the divine *Logos* that could interpret experience and produce theorems.

Indeed, in a number of places, Protestantism generated and guided the Enlightenment in the Reformed universities of Scotland, Hungary, Holland, Heidelberg, and in America—at Cambridge, New Haven, and Princeton. Perhaps the most famous theologian of this sort was Friedrich Schleiermacher, son of an Army chaplain, a student and later a professor at the University of Halle, which was the center of both Lutheran Pietism and the natural sciences of the day. He argued both that theology ought to have an honored place in the university because it was a genuine science based in Christian experience and in favor of the logical analysis of it, distinct from dogma. Still, he held that doctrine rightly "divides the whole activity of Christ into three offices."[4]

Regarding the first office, Schleiermacher argued that, as the ancient prophets felt it incumbent on them to preach out of the "impulse which [they] felt had come . . . from God" in times of crisis, so Christ's determination to "teach was the task of satisfying fully the powerful . . . (and creative) God-consciousness that took shape in (Him). . . . , and of so reproducing it that thereby the assumption of men into His fellowship might be effected." The meaning of the ancient prophets is often obscure, but the essence is that they spoke of a future in which God's true and final messenger would teach not with "limited concepts" but with "infallible perfection." That teaching points to the coming kingdom of God, already at work in the world. All apostolic prediction is only an interpretation or echo of Christ's prediction (First Theorem).[5]

Regarding the priestly and kingly offices, Schleiermacher claimed that the one is based in Jesus' active obedience to God's Law and his passive obedience in his atoning, sacrificial death, which made him the perfect intercessor between God and humanity, representing humanity before God and God to humanity (Second Theorem).[6] And the other "consists in the fact that everything which the community of believers requires for its well-being continually proceeds from Him." Schleiermacher insisted that Christ's kingdom is not of this world and must not be confused "with the disposal and arrangement of things of this world—which means that nothing remains as the immediate sphere of his kingship but the inner life of men individually and in their relation to each other." This is the "kingdom of grace," which sees such concepts as a worldly "kingdom of power" or an eschatological "kingdom of glory" as simply boundary matters, at the margins of the decisive kingdom of Christ in the fellowship of Christian believers (Third Theorem).[7]

One can discern a certain bias, perhaps loved by many Christian academics, that the accent decisively shifts from Old Testament prophetic preaching to New Testament teaching, and to the modeling of atonement by sacrificial good behavior and intercessory prayer. Even more, since Schleiermacher was teaching in a state-run university supervised by the Kaiser, the denial of real political implications of either prophecy or kingship seems too emphatic. Still, Schleiermacher's greatest contribution, one taken up by Karl Barth who taught in a similar setting a century later but who was sharply critical of Schleiermacher, is that all these three offices require one another.

Quite another strand of the Reformed tradition was developed in English and New England Puritanism, with certain parallels in the later Dutch theologian and Prime Minister, Abraham Kuyper. Several wings of the Puritan tradition took the notion of the "prophecy of all believers" as radically as they took the notion of the "priesthood of all believers," and they became sharply critical of the ecclesiastical and legal limitations on who could preach, teach, and publish on theological matters. Moreover, they saw these limitations increasingly imposed on Reformed pastors, preachers, and scholars by both the Catholic and the Anglican traditions. They rose up in the famous Puritan Revolution, prophetically denouncing both established Priest and established King offices, and raised an army—with help from the Presbyterian Scots who had been schooled by John Knox's struggle against the Catholic queen, and by the Covenanters, who fought against both "Romanism" and the Anglican episcopacy, who were backed by royal authority.

For a while these Puritans gained success, establishing a more representative parliamentary form of government, gaining religious tolerance, raising a "new model" army (in which the troops elected their chaplains to represent them with the command), and beheading the king. After all, if Christ is the true King, no one else could be. A limited kingship was later re-established in England when fighting came to an end, but the settlement involved religious toleration and a more democratic, constitutional order than the world had ever seen—one that took slightly different forms in England and America, with no royalty, a stronger separation of church and state as institutions, and stronger overt interaction of religion and politics in the latter. Most importantly, a fundamental new element had been introduced into the theology of the offices of Christ: the "kinghood of all believers." That is, the political opportunity, magisterial duty, and social responsibility of the citizen-believer, with definite rights for individuals and religious and civil groups to help determine the leadership and governance of *both* church *and* society.[8]

These themes have become more and more widely accepted. They were taught in the American Social Gospel and more recently in several forms of Latin America and minority Liberation Theologies. Indeed, the Roman Catholic Church has now made these accents part of their official teaching. The most recent authoritative Catechism of the Catholic Church (1992) ties the idea to baptism: "The whole People of God participates in these three offices of Christ and bears the responsibilities for mission and service that flow from them. . . . "(Art. 194) In fact, the great Catholic theologian Karl Rahner has been quoted as saying that "the doctrine of the three offices of Christ is one of the greatest gifts of the Calvinist tradition to the whole church," as J. L. Adams pointed out often in lectures.[9]

All of this sets the stage, I believe, on which we can take one more step. Or at least we can propose that the resources are at hand, from the biblical sources and the developments of doctrine, for an additional accent. Moreover, I think the case can be made that our problems today are not that we are dominated by ecclesiastical priests or political kings, who shape the ways in which the doctrine is interpreted and applied. If anything, people today distrust hierarchical power in religion and imperial pretenses in politics, at home or abroad. Yet there is very little accent on the prophetic critique of unrighteousness and injustice in many spheres of the common life, which are more decisive than church and state in people's lives.

Many churches do not teach or preach on these issues, and our seminaries do not prepare people to do so. True, some seem to think that calling for more "liberation," the ever greater maximization of liberty in the midst of a liberal society, is a kind of prophecy, but the world Catholic and ecumenical churches are disgusted with the fact that the Catholic and mainline Protestant churches in the West are beset by crises over child molestation and efforts to liberalize teaching about human sexuality. They see these events as contrary to scripturally based doctrine and ethics, and believe that greater issues are at hand (although, that many of their cultures are also beset by HIV/AIDS suggests moral laxity in sexuality as well). Meanwhile, the Evangelical and Pentecostal Churches are growing at a rapid rate around the world by ministering to the personal needs of seekers and believers as their societies modernize and seek to join the emerging global developments.

Very few Christian pastors and theologians have developed a sense of the importance and character of the globalization process that is presently sweeping the world and creating both many problems and the prospect of a very complex, highly technological, closely interdependent, enormously differentiated, and hotly contested global civilization. At the core of these developments is not only the obvious spread of economic capitalism, which many see as the central fact of the dynamic and read in a quasi-Marxist way, but the explosion of communications, engineering, legal, educational, medical, and transnational political interactions that make the economic interaction possible.[10] This globalization process has no common religion, no common government, and no common prophetic vision, yet many of the agents of this process are formed directly or indirectly by the indirect consequences of the Judeo-Christian understanding of the world and of life. What do we have to offer these leaders of globalization—and to the more who do not get it, and thus do not know how morally to react to it?

I would like to propose that it is one of the most important contributions that the churches of all traditions can make in this situation is to bring every believer to awareness of what we now know of the offices of Christ, and to equip them to carry these out: that is, to empower all those who are in Christ to become deputies, ambassadors, apostles of Christ's offices in every sphere of their lives. This, of course, can only be done if the several offices are held together by direct knowledge of the wisdom of the Word incarnate. This ministry to each person is also the indirect, but radiating ministry to all the spheres of civil society. Each person is "called" to be Christlike in the sense that he or she has a vocation, to undertake the "prophethood, priesthood, and political authority of all believers." We are to carry out ministries of justice and righteousness, pastoral care and liturgical proprieties with our neighbors, and political discernment and social "statecraft" in every sphere of institutional life where we live—in family life, in economic life, in cultural life, in political life, in education, law, medicine, management, ecology, and intercultural contact, as each of us has opportunity.

Seeing ourselves as members of Christ's body and participants in his ongoing life, and thus agents of his reality in the world, could make Christ—who, from the creation to the birth of Jesus was in principle the messianic Prophet, Priest, and King—more fully incarnate in the fabric of our common life and point more fully toward the consummation we hope for and he anticipated.

CHAPTER TWO

CHRISTOLOGY IN THE CONTINENTAL AND ENGLISH REFORMATION

LEE BARRETT

It has become a cliché that the most distinctive gift that the United Church of Christ has to offer the broader Christian community is the exemplary resolve of Christians who hail from different theological traditions to worship and work together. As with many platitudes, there is truth in the claim, or at least potential truth, especially when it comes to the understanding of Jesus Christ. The English Reformed tradition of Congregationalism, the more irenic Reformed heritage of the German Reformed Church, the unique amalgam of Lutheran and Reformed themes of the Evangelical Synod, and the noncreedalism of the Christian Connection all exhibit distinct emphases concerning the person and work of Jesus Christ. Moreover, within each of these individual heritages a wide spectrum of Christological views had emerged, a proliferation that has accelerated since the merger. Potentially, the interaction of these different perspectives could generate a richly textured, multidimensional Christology that reflects the wealth of things that God accomplishes for us and with us through Jesus Christ.

At times this variety may feel more like a curse than a blessing, leading to the suspicion that "Jesus Christ" has become nothing more than a blank screen upon which the proudly autonomous individual can project anything that tickles one's fancy. Frequently, it seems that the Christ who was supposed to be the center of the United Church has become the "wax nose" feared by Luther that could be twisted any way one wants, leaving the denomination centerless. Congregations and judicatories have been rent by disputes between those who insist that Jesus is only the gentle friend who walks with them in the garden and those who maintain that Jesus is the revolutionary who marches with them in the streets. Each perspective on Jesus in the vast array jostles for exclusive prominence, and unity in Christ seems to dissolve into Christological civil war. At the very least, this welter of perspectives makes it more difficult to specify the Christology of the United Church of Christ than is the case in more monolithically confessional traditions.

But in spite of the embarrassments and inconveniences, we must resist the temptation to reduce the multifaceted richness of Christ to a single theme. The church has wisely opposed efforts to amalgamate the pluriform witness of the New Testament into a sole one-dimensional gospel. It is significant that the canon includes four very different narrations of Jesus' life. *Reader's Digest*-style attempts to conflate their testimonies and eliminate their distinctive accents has always generated a lowest common-denominator rendition of the faith that lacks the thickness and depth to hold anyone's spiritual interest for more than a generation. The church should celebrate the fact that in Jesus Christ God saves us from so many different sorts of conundrums that Christ's work cannot be fully captured in a single narrative pattern. I shall argue that Jesus Christ can indeed mean a variety of different things, without meaning everything that anyone idiosyncratically happens to find congenial. We can embrace a range of understandings of the significance of Jesus Christ, without succumbing to unrestrained Christological relativism. In this endeavor the United Church of Christ is uniquely situated to do justice to the variety of perspectives on Christ reflected in scripture itself. The ancestor traditions that have contributed to the UCC all contain plausible and powerful elaborations of scriptural motifs that have been tested, enriched, and refined by generations of believers. If they are put in conversation with one another, they can both expand our appreciation of the multidimensional work of Christ, and provide sufficient focus and definition to counteract the vagaries of untrammeled individualism.

In order to preserve the fullness of the gospel, we would do well to follow the example of the Evangelical Synod's decision of 1848 to accept both the Augsburg Confession and Luther's Catechism from the Lutheran heritage, as well as the Heidelberg Catechism from the Reformed side. This irenic trajectory was continued in the formative decision of the United Church of Christ to heed the testimonies of the confessional documents of the ancestor denominations. In the language of "A Formula of Agreement" between the Evangelical Lutheran Church in America and three more Reformed denominations, including the UCC, even the areas of disagreement among the traditions can be embraced as fruitful opportunities for "mutual affirmation and admonition." Rather than viewing the areas of divergence as mutually exclusive incompatibilities, we can regard them as mutually enriching complementarities.

Accordingly, it is worth examining the Christological emphases in our respective traditions for the distinctive elements that each can add to the depth and richness of our witness to Jesus Christ. The historic confessions and representative thinkers of the ancestor denominations, particularly those such as Ursinus, Daniel Irion, Elmer Arndt, and Roger Shinn, who produced expositions of the confessions in particular or the theological heritage in general, and those such as John Nevin and Horace Bushnell, who exercised a pervasive influence on Christological reflection in their respective traditions, provide significant perspectives.

The UCC is indeed a living theological heritage, with a long and spiritually potent past. Its theological convictions did not spring newly and fully formed from the head of Zeus (or anyone else) in 1957. In a culture so inordinately enamored of novelty as to be "postcontemporary" (the current moniker for the era succeeding "postmodernity"), we must be exceedingly careful to avoid chronological imperialism and its nasty habit of disenfranchising that most powerless of constituencies, the dead. In exploring the Christology of the United Church of Christ, we must pay special attention to the voices of the ancestors. Only by doing so can we avoid the myopia of the present and the blandishments of the theological fad of the month.

The deepest interest in the significance of Jesus Christ is not spawned by detached academic curiosity but by Christians' most pervasive hopes and fears. The traditions that have contributed to the UCC have all been motivated by somewhat different (but often overlapping) concerns and passions, and therefore have articulated the significance of Jesus somewhat differently. Typically, they have indirectly described that significance by situating Jesus in their own version of the grand cosmic narrative of God's interactions with humanity. Jesus is given definition as the central character in a drama stretching from creation (or sometimes before creation) to the final consummation. The story concerns the ultimate origins, aspirations, tragedies, and destiny of humanity and the entire cosmos, and identifies the significance of Jesus in terms of them. The story has been told in a variety of ways, with strikingly different emphases. The different narrative variations highlight different human maladies and woes, and project somewhat different longed-for resolutions. Consequently, Jesus is presented as the answer to somewhat different questions. In our specific heritages, two distinctive plot lines are evident. One may be called the fall/restoration scenario, while the second may be termed the childhood/maturity pattern. Both of them occurred in all the traditions that contributed to the UCC and usually interacted in complex ways.

PLOT LINES

The first type of plot line, the fall/restoration scenario, may be the most prevalent and is dominant in the Reformation era confessions. In these foundational documents the problem that propels the plot is humanity's fall into sin and consequent forfeiture of bliss, liability to punishment, and loss of the capacities to grow in faith, hope, and love. For example, the Augsburg Confession (honored by the Evangelical Synod) introduces the discussion of Christ after its treatment of original sin and its deleterious effects. The Heidelberg Catechism follows suit, presenting the grace of God in Jesus Christ after the section on the guilt due to the failure to fulfill the Law. The Westminster Confession, which was presupposed by Congregationalism's Cambridge Platform and served as a model for a host of local congregational confessional documents, situated its Christological assertions in the context of the covenant of grace, which offers sinners salvation. The Evangelical Catechism follows the Lutheran pattern of presenting the gospel after the demands of the Law, and the impossibility of keeping them, have been made clear.

In all of these Jesus Christ is first and foremost defined as "the Mediator" whose mission of rescue and salvage is a response to the tragedy of the fall. It is a story that has given comfort and hope to those who recognize the dauntingly lofty nature of the commandment to love God and neighbor with all one's heart, mind, and strength, and candidly admit their own failure to even approximate the goal. Those who suffer from an appropriately deep moral and spiritual dissatisfaction with themselves continue to feel the power of this narrative pattern.

It is also crucial to note that in these confessional elaborations of the fall/restoration plot line, Jesus the Mediator is not a third party trying to change a vindictive God's mind. All too often, popular caricatures of the narrative portray Jesus as a benevolent older sibling protecting humanity from an irate parent. Rather, all the confessions insist that the work of redemption from sin is a continuation of God's enduring care and concern for humanity. The sending of the *Logos* is an expression of divine love, not an intervention by some outside referee designed to modify God's policies. It is appropriate that the *Logos*, the agent of God's original creative intention for humanity, should also be the agent of restoration. It is fitting that the light-bearing dimension of God should shine into sin's darkness and that God's primordial ordering principle should remedy sin's chaos. Only the power of God could have healed the alienation and restored the damaged creation. Consequently, most of the confessions make it clear that the whole Trinity is active in the work of redemption, with all three Persons functioning together. Far from being an aberration, Christ's saving work is rooted in the intra-Trinitarian life, in the love of the Father for the Son. The one who is a Son by nature makes us sons and daughters by grace.

A second narrative motif, the pattern of childhood/maturity, is also displayed in the traditions, although not originally with as much prevalence or visibility. Here the work of Jesus Christ is not primarily a response to sin but is rather the culmination of God's original plan for humanity, which predates the fall. In this scenario the problem, one even more basic than sin, is that human nature is incomplete. Jesus Christ is the conclusive chapter in the saga of the human race's maturation from the fledgling inception in the Garden to the spiritual fruition in the heavenly city. God's original intention was that the possibilities latent in the first Adam should be actualized in the second Adam, or even that new graces unimagined by the first Adam would be made available to humanity through the second. Organic metaphors abound, with Jesus described as the "seed" of a new humanity or the "flowering" of human potentialities. Consequently, in this version of the narrative, the themes of atonement and justification are less central than that of the incarnation itself.

John Nevin, the primary theological voice of the Mercersburg movement, frequently chastised evangelicals for focusing on the atonement apart from the incarnation, as if Christmas had occurred only so that there could be Good Friday. His ally Henry Harbaugh declared Christ's work of justification to be less central than the vivifying force objectively flowing from Christ's person.[1] This plot line was by no means restricted to the neighborhood of south central Pennsylvania. Throughout his career the Hartford Congregationalist minister Horace Bushnell described Jesus as the catalyst and pathway of humanity's spiritual ascent. Lyman Abbott, an influential late-nineteenth-century Congregationalist pastor, rejoiced that hidden forces in human history had evolved to the point where Jesus' human nature had been fully open to God's presence, and that now the rest of humanity was evolving into what Jesus was.[2] Elmer Arndt, attempting in 1960 to give expression to the theological heritage of the old Evangelical and Reformed Church, described Jesus as a new order of life that had become effective in humanity.[3] This narrative pattern in its various permutations speaks to the hearts of those who chafe at the prospect of spiritual stagnation, envision a richer, fuller life of love and service, and yearn for an infusion of religious energy to propel them on their journeys.

A subset of this plot line makes an even bolder claim concerning the state that is the goal of our growth. In some renditions the purpose of the incarnation was nothing less than to effect a wedding of the infinite and the finite, the supernatural and the natural, and eternity and time. Jesus offers more to humanity than the actualization of Adam's creaturely potentialities; Jesus offers participation in the very life of God. For John Nevin, the object of the incarnation was to couple human nature to the *Logos* as a permanent source of transcendent life. In Jesus, human nature was glorified and raised to the sphere of divinity, without becoming divine in its own right. Emanuel Gerhart, the late-nineteenth-century spokesperson of the Mercersburg heritage, would add that human nature has always possessed a capacity to participate in the life of God, a capacity actualized by God's extravagant self-communication to Jesus' receptive human nature.[4] For both Nevin and Gerhart, in some mysterious sense all of nature vicariously participates in the nuptials of the finite and the infinite. The entire cosmos becomes complete in the person of Christ through whom it is incorporated into the divine life.

In a more muted way, the 1931 revision of the Evangelical Catechism asserted that believers become partakers in Jesus' divine nature. In 1959 Elmer Arndt, a scion of the Evangelical Synod, repeated that through Jesus Christ God has given humanity a share in the divine life.[5] This variant of the grand narrative addresses the mysterious yearnings of those for whom the satisfactions of earthly life, even at its best, are inadequate and therefore hunger for a joy that finite existence simply cannot provide.

THE PERSON OF CHRIST

Both narrative patterns, the sin/restoration and the childhood/maturity variety, inevitably lead to reflection on Jesus' person. In both cases hearts wavering between fear and hope would need assurance that Jesus actually did possess the ability to accomplish his vital work. In order to ground the efficacy of Jesus' pivotal activity, both patterns require that Jesus be both divine and human. On the one hand, only God has the power to heal sin, bring human nature to completion, and marry the finite to the infinite. On the other hand, only human beings could be the site in which the healing, restoration, and marriage could occur. The sixteenth- and seventeenth-century confessions are all quite explicit about this dual character of Jesus' person. In the nineteenth century the Evangelical Catechism and the Congregational Creed of 1883 repeated the common claim that divinity and humanity were united in Jesus Christ.[6] Continuing the trajectory, the UCC Statement of Faith affirms that it is indeed God who comes to us in Jesus Christ, who nevertheless is the "man of Nazareth." As Roger Shinn explained, the statement makes it clear that Jesus is neither a mere human ambassador from God nor a disembodied divine apparition.[7] By these claims that echo the Definition of Chalcedon, we are assured that in Jesus Christ the power to heal and recreate has come into the most intimate contact with that which needs healing and recreation.

All of these confessional traditions share another common feature: They all stress the priority of the divine agency in Jesus. For example, both the Heidelberg Catechism and the Westminster Confession maintain that the Eternal Son took upon himself our nature. For many in the Reformed tradition, stretching from Ursinus and the Westminster divines through Nevin, this priority of the divine agency in Jesus was articulated through the technical vocabulary of the "anhypostasia" of the human nature and its "enhypostasia" in the divine person. In other words, the human body and soul of Jesus do not exist by themselves apart from the incarnation, but only became actual in the person of the *Logos*. The incarnation was not a union of the divine with a ready-made, self-subsistent human person. "Person" in this conceptuality suggests the principle of ongoing existence and continuing personal identity; consequently, the doctrines of anhypostasia and enhypostasia indicate that the basic uniqueness, fundamental identity, and personal unity of Jesus is grounded in God's life. The initiative comes from God and is affirmed by the receptive humanity.

Echoes of this sensibility, devoid of the complex metaphysics of natures and persons, can be heard in claims of Elmer Arndt, Roger Shinn, Robert Moss, and others of the founding generation of the UCC that Jesus' activity is that of God. Throughout the tradition the refrain recurs that the priority of the divine agency renders the union of the divine and the human indissoluble. This conviction undergirds the comforting assurance that Christ embraces his church just as tightly as the body that he assumed. The rhetorical force of the doctrinal focus on the divine person is to nurture the trust that both Jesus' humanity and our own are sustained by God.

However, in the early phases of the Reformed tradition, in both its German and English varieties, this priority of the divine nature in no way led to a compromising of the genuineness of Jesus' human nature. On the contrary, the Reformed traditions typically stressed the distinction of the divine and human natures through their denial of the *communicatio idiomatum*, the Lutheran doctrine that, because of the hypostatic union, the two natures communicate their properties to one another. As the Bremen Consensus of 1595 and most Reformed theologians of the seventeenth century maintained, the natures remain distinct in their properties; they are only indirectly united (*unio mediata*) by virtue of subsisting in the same person. The properties of each nature are ascribed to the person (the *Logos*), not to the other nature. The Westminster Confession similarly insisted on the distinction of the natures, claiming that each nature does what is proper to itself. The seventeenth-century consensus was that only the human nature suffered, needed to grow in wisdom, and underwent death.

This doctrinal point may seem like the sort of "idle curiosity" that Calvin decried, but it served crucial passional purposes. One reason for this differentiation was the pervasive Reformed conviction that finite creatures cannot contain the infinite Creator (*finitum incapax infiniti*). The eternal, omnipotent, omniscient, infinite God cannot be confined within the limitations of finitude. By stressing this, the Reformers were not motivated by an atavistic fondness for aloof monarchs or emotionally distant parental figures. Rather, they sought to safeguard the cosmic role of God as the foundation and sustainer of all things. That which is the foundation of all particulars cannot be a particular itself; that which undergirds space and time cannot be limited by space and time. The One who is the basis of our hope and assurance must be reliable, and not subject to fickle mood swings or diminution of power. In other words, the need for confidence required an emphasis on the dependability of God even in the incarnation. This inspired the distinctive doctrine of the "extra Calvinisticum," the belief that in the incarnation the *Logos* exists not only in the humanity of Christ but also beyond it. Although the human nature of Jesus is seated at the right hand of the Father, thus implying a specific heavenly location, the divine nature continues to be omnipresent and is never absent from us.

But concern to emphasize God's sovereign transcendence was only one of the motivations for the German and English Reformed traditions' denial of the *communicatio idiomatum*. Perhaps to an even greater degree they sought to protect the integrity of Jesus' human nature. Their theologians strenuously resisted the apparent deification of the human nature that seemed to be implied by the Lutheran contention that the divine attributes were communicated to it. For the Reformed, the humanity of Jesus does not become infinite; flesh does not become omnipotent. Jesus, through his finite human nature, experiences all the slings and arrows of outrageous fortune that afflict the rest of us. Reformed theologians on both sides of the English Channel, and later on both sides of the Atlantic Ocean, maintained that Jesus' body, like ours, developed in stages and was not intrinsically imbued with divine powers. He was susceptible to natural affections and weaknesses (but the weaknesses did not lead to sin), such as sorrow and anxiety. Moreover, the human nature remained truly human in its intellectual powers, which had to grow according to the laws of ordinary human cognitive development, and he did not know all the secrets of the universe.

From Ursinus through the Daniel Irion's influential exposition of the Evangelical Catechism runs the theme that as a man Jesus did have to observe the Law, although as God he had no need to.[8] Most significantly, the theologians agreed that the human dimension of Jesus was also vulnerable in spirit, capable of experiencing God's absence and even wrath. They uniformly maintained that the human nature underwent death, understood as the separation of the soul from the body (although the divine Person did not desert either aspect). It was important for both the heirs of Heidelberg and of Westminster to reiterate that Jesus possessed a genuine human will, distinct from the divine will, with its own potency. The work of the Mediator requires both natures, each doing that which is proper to it. The doctrine of the *communicatio operationum* explained that Jesus' actions are produced by the distinct effectiveness of both natures. The humanity cooperates with the divinity, agreeing to the initiatives of the divinity, and the divinity sustains and supports the humanity.

This persistent defense of the integrity of Jesus' human nature and its genuine identity with ours led to the distinctive Reformed doctrine of a "local" and "bodily" ascension of the humanity of Jesus. According to the Heidelberg Catechism and Ursinus's explanation, because human nature is never omnipresent, as a man Jesus must be somewhere in particular, namely, in heaven.[9] Minus these doctrinal intricacies, the emphasis of the genuineness of Jesus' humanity was continued in the nineteenth-century interest in the historical reality of Jesus and efforts to develop a "Christology from below," and in the UCC Statement of Faith's portrayal of Jesus as a specific "man of Nazareth."

This concentration on the genuine humanity of Jesus was motivated by a soteriological interest in the transformation of human nature. Jesus as archetypally human enters into the struggle against sin and develops obedient, righteous human nature as God intended it to be. In Jesus, human nature was sanctified, overcoming the defilement of sin. After the ascension, the exalted humanity of Jesus still does not participate in the divine metaphysical perfections, but does enjoy the highest gifts of the Spirit that a creature can receive. According to the doctrine of the *communicatio gratiarum*, Jesus as exalted human possesses creaturely wisdom and virtuous habits to a preeminent degree, and makes them available to those who are united to him. The battle against sin was won in a true human being; the ancient alienation from God had been healed in a real human nature so that Jesus' humanity could become the font of our own justification and sanctification. If he had not been a true human being, like us in all things except sin, he could not have been the firstborn of many brothers and sisters. This conviction accounts for the frequent reminders that Jesus possessed (and still possesses) a real, spatially circumscribed body, made human decisions, and suffered from human sorrows and fears.

A strikingly different pattern of relating the divine and human aspects of Christ developed in some circles of the UCC's ancestor denominations in the nineteenth century. In this alternative trajectory the intimate communion of the natures was emphasized, almost in Lutheran fashion. In the Congregationalist family Horace Bushnell, objecting to the scholastic distinction of person and natures, asserted that Jesus Christ was and is a single unified life expressing and communicating the Absolute Being.[10] In a different way the theme of the objective coming together of the finite and the infinite led John Nevin to stress the single, thoroughly unified "divine-human" life of Christ.[11] According to Nevin, in the organic union of divinity and humanity in Christ, the properties of one nature can indeed be predicated of the other, although they do not become intrinsic to the other nature apart from the union. Similarly, Emanuel Gerhart proposed that it is part of the very divinity of God the Son to be able to live and act according to a creaturely mode of existence.[12] Consequently, the divinity and the humanity of Christ are not distinct dimensions; rather, the divinity is immanent in the humanity. In fact, the form of a servant is an appropriate manifestation of divine life, for God's power can accomplish its purposes through human weakness. Gerhart goes so far as to deny explicitly the motto *finitum incapax infiniti*, for in Christ the infinite and the finite are not opposites. Only this Christological vision of the overcoming of earthly limitations could satisfy the yearnings of those for whom the world as we know it is not enough.

The Work of Christ

Both narrative patterns and both interpretations of the person of Christ as human and divine had to further specify the various ways in which Jesus Christ accomplishes the desired redemption from sin and finitude. Only a richly-textured recitation of the way the deeds, teachings, and passions of Jesus lead to the longed-for goal could have the power to shape the Christian life. Historically, the rubric of the threefold office of the Mediator, the *munus triplex*, has served to give expression to the diverse ways in which Jesus Christ accomplishes the redemption of humanity. Jesus exercises the three offices of Prophet,

Priest, and King because humanity needs illumination, reconciliation, and guidance as antidotes to ignorance, alienation, and waywardness. This threefold organizational conceptuality popularized by Calvin is found in the discussions of the work of Christ in the Heidelberg Catechism, the Westminster Confession, and the Evangelical Catechism. Ursinus explained that, as Prophet, Christ must reveal the will of God, illumine minds, and internally move hearts; as Priest, must offer sacrifice for sin, intercede with God the Father, and apply the benefits of salvation to the faithful; and as King, must sustain, guide, and protect the individual believer and the church.[13] More recently, UCC theologian Gabriel Fackre has continued this legacy by narrating God's provision of revelation, reconciliation, and liberation, and detecting echoes of these themes in the UCC Statement of Faith.[14]

The Prophetic Office
With the office of Prophet, the problem requiring remediation is located in us. Due to sin, we have lost the capacity to understand adequately our relationship with God, failing to grasp the essentials for human flourishing and blessedness. Our benightedness is so deep that we require not only outward proclamation of the truth but also inner illumination of the mind and enlivening of the heart. In most accounts we are oblivious both to the true righteousness that the Law requires and God's gracious offer of salvation. From Ursinus through Elmer Arndt and Roger Shinn, the theme recurs that our unaided fallen reason fails to teach us the truth about human nature and destiny, or the truth about God's identity and purposes.

Consequently, at the very least Jesus must function as the ultimate teacher of God's Law and as a model of the righteous life God desires. Jonathan Edwards hailed Jesus as the perfect exemplar of disinterested benevolence toward all creatures, and bequeathed this legacy to the influential proponents of the "New England theology." According to many Congregationalists of the late-nineteenth century, Jesus reveals the positive capacities resident in human nature that had been obscured by sin, a theme utilized by the Social Gospel movement. In the mid-twentieth century H. Richard Niebuhr interpreted Jesus as the revelation of a truly human life of trust and loyalty to God as the ground of being and value, manifesting the pattern of a totally God-centered life. More recently, the function of Jesus in revealing the Law has been redescribed as the revelation of God's vision of shalom or as the exemplar of the coming reign of God and the liberating praxis suited to it. In all its permutations, this theme is good news for those who know that they cannot discern the meaning and purpose of human life through their own unaided efforts.

Secondly, for most of the ancestor traditions, Jesus reveals the gracious, reconciling intentions of God. According to the seventeenth-century divines, some of the knowledge of God's Law should have been accessible to our natural capacities if we had not sinned, but the awareness of God's covenant of grace could not have been known at all unless it had been revealed. Through the pattern of Jesus' life, we are presented with a portrait of God's reconciling nature. In the older terminology, Jesus as the incarnate Son reveals the Father not only as sovereign power and justice, but also as forgiving love. In newer terminology, Jesus' enactment of shalom is said to render God's loving disposition visible in a human life. The common theme in all these diverse idioms is that God has not abandoned us to futile speculations about God's nature but has shown God's very self to be Christlike in nature.

The Priestly Office

With the priestly office of Christ, the locus of humanity's problem is not just in us but in the relationship of God and us. Although we should enjoy intimate fellowship with God, we have become alienated from God by sin and its consequent guilt. Jesus' prophetic role is not enough, for humanity needs forgiveness and healing, not just a good example. In spite of widespread agreement on the reality and severity of the problem of sin, no consensus concerning the way that the life, death, and resurrection of Jesus effect salvation from sin is evident in the heritages that contribute to the UCC. Rather, a multiplicity of root metaphors abound, which have given rise to a host of divergent atonement theories, each one emphasizing a different aspect of the problem of sin.

In the Reformation period and its aftermath, most theologians focused on the need to satisfy God's Law and articulated the work of Christ in forensic language. By breaking God's Law, we have become liable to the deserved punishment and the obligation to repay the owed obedience. Accordingly, the Westminster Confession could speak of the satisfaction of justice as that which purchases reconciliation. It is important to note that the Law must be maintained not because God has a penchant for rigid legalism or an implacable aversion to boundary transgressors, but rather because God must exclude violators of the Law from God's holy presence because sin is incompatible with God's righteousness and God's vision of an orderly, harmonious cosmos. Consequently, the Puritan theologians often spoke of the "offense" of sin to God's righteousness rather than employ Anselm's language of God's offended honor. God's requirement that sin be punished does not mean that God's attitude must be changed by Jesus from vindictive anger to merciful compassion. God's motive in maintaining retributive justice is God's care for a humanity threatened by the chaos of lawlessness and by God's desire to manifest God's glory in the order of creation. As the nineteenth century progressed, the conviction that God is not an enemy requiring placation was voiced with more vigor and frequency. In Congregational, German Reformed, and Evangelical Synod circles, it became increasingly common to insist that the requirement that the Law be satisfied is rooted in God's love as well as God's justice.

Given the focus on the need for sin to be punished, both the traditions of Heidelberg and Westminster spoke of Christ's substitutionary suffering of punishment as the satisfaction of God's righteousness. As the Heidelberg Catechism explains, we are set free from the judgment of God because the death of the Son of God makes reparation for us. The Evangelical Catechism and the revised version of 1929 agreed that Jesus accomplished redemption by suffering, dying, and experiencing the wrath of God. According to all the commentators on these confessions, by his suffering Christ has made it possible for God to justify the godless without injury to God's holiness. The substitution of Jesus for us was by no means an arbitrary strategy to satisfy the Law, for the punishment had to be visited upon a representative of humanity. In the technical language of theological schools, the passive obedience of the second Adam in accepting the punishment is the meritorious cause of salvation. Jesus' human voluntary submission to punishment achieves sufficient value to cover all the sins of humanity by virtue of its union to the infinitely valuable divinity.

This forensic model of submission to retributive punishment has often stressed the salutary nature of Jesus' suffering. According to the Heidelberg Catechism, Jesus underwent the misery of the curse, felt the full wrath of God over sin, and experienced extreme abandonment by God. The descent into hell was the unspeakable anguish that Jesus suffered in his soul both before and during the crucifixion. This extraordinary focus on Jesus' suffering does not suggest any divine sadistic delight in torment. Suffering is not an extrinsic imposition by a vindictive deity. Rather, suffering is the inevitable consequence of any honest admission of the extent and depth of human sinfulness. According to the Reformed theologians, Jesus contemplated all of humanity's sin and therefore experienced incalculable sorrow. Later, in the nineteenth century, Emanuel Gerhart would make explicit the role of Jesus as the representative penitent, claiming that Jesus perfects human nature by offering himself to God's wrath, as all of humanity should, and as all believers do through participation in Christ.[15] In the twentieth century, the tendency would become even more prevalent to view Jesus' suffering as the inevitable result of human nature's remedial and salutary confrontation with sinfulness rather than as the product of retribution.

The forensic model underwent modification in Congregational circles in the eighteenth century, moving from the theme of the vicarious satisfaction of retributive justice to the theme of the necessity to manifest the rule and dignity of Law that undergirds God's government of the universe. The shift in language was symptomatic of an increasing desire to portray God as a benevolent governor rather than as the arbitrary sovereign, which the rhetoric of the older Puritan tradition was taken (perhaps inaccurately) to suggest. Joseph Bellamy argued that by suffering punishment Jesus demonstrated that such punishment is the appropriate response to lawbreaking, for in a just society no violation of the public good should go unpunished. Similarly, Jonathan Edwards, Jr., Samuel Hopkins, and Charles Finney argued that the passion of Jesus was not a payment of debt imposing an obligation upon God. Rather, by accepting Jesus' death as punishment for humanity's infraction of the Law, God preserves the integrity of the legal system and public justice, thus making it safe for God to forgive sin without undermining the moral order.

Some theologians, such as Ursinus, were content to restrict the atoning work of Christ to Christ's vicarious punishment for sin, stressing Christ's "passive obedience" and regarding Christ's active fulfillment of God's Law as a mere precondition for the role of substitute. However, most other strands of Reformed theology stressed Jesus' active obedience as part of the satisfaction, a position that triumphed in the Helvetic Consensus Formula of 1675. Some theologians went so far as to claim that the cause of salvation is Christ's perfect obedience according to the Law, seeing the acceptance of punishment as one aspect of the fulfillment of the Law's requirements. The Westminster

Confession devotes unusual attention to Jesus' perfect fulfillment of the Law and sanctification, describing obedience as a legal debt owed to God that had to be discharged.

Through the nineteenth century, Congregationalist formulations of faith, such as the 1845 Articles of Faith of the Iowa Association, continued to echo the motif that Christ obeyed the Law and made atonement. The Evangelical Catechism agreed that Christ fulfilled Law in our stead, presenting his obedience to God as an all-sufficient offering. Implicitly, this focus on Christ's active righteousness drew attention to the centrality of a life of obedient righteousness as the ultimate *telos* of human nature. The second version of the grand narrative of the significance of Jesus Christ, the actualization of human nature in the second Adam, was making its presence felt.

The way in which the benefits of Christ's atoning work, both passive and active, were made available to humanity was also described in forensic terms by the early generations. The Heidelberg Catechism mentions the imputation of Christ's "righteousness and holiness" and the Westminster Confession speaks of the imputation of Christ's "obedience and satisfaction." Christ's satisfaction of the Law is ascribed to our account, effecting a change in our legal status. In the tradition of Westminster, the ground for the validity of the imputation of Christ's passion and righteousness to us was usually described in covenantal terms, as a promise made in eternity between the Father and the Son according to which the Father appointed Jesus as the head of the elect. The New England Congregationalists would elaborate this in the theme of Jesus as the federal representative of humanity. In all these cases, the emphasis falls on the external change in our judicial standing with God. The fact that Jesus is first and foremost our "alien righteousness," who secures forgiveness, served as an antidote to the temptation to regard reconciliation with God as the fruit of our own spiritual growth.

However, another trajectory, interwoven with the forensic theme, was always present in the ancestor traditions, one of which stressed the actual transformation of the sinner. According to this view, we are not only justified by Christ's atoning work, but also regenerated and sanctified. Here the problem is that we are more than culpable sinners who need a changed judicial status; we are corrupt sinners who need internal healing. All of the Reformed traditions maintained that the cross not only enacts God's judgment, but also breaks the power of sin in our hearts. This could be variously described as the enlivening power of Christ's righteousness graciously communicated to us by the Holy Spirit, or as the individual's insertion into the body of Christ, or both. In both instances some sort of spiritual union with Christ enables the righteousness of Christ to take root in the believer, producing not only pardon but also healing.

The Mercersburg theologians emphasized this union with Christ and the consequent transformation of the believer so much that they avoided the forensic rhetoric as much as possible. According to John Nevin, justification, the forgiveness of our sins, is not a legal declaration based on the imputation of Christ's external righteousness. Rather, the imputation of Christ's righteousness is mediated by the reality that Christ really does live in the believer's soul because of the believer's union with Christ.[16] The forensic conceptuality made justification seem like an arbitrary legal fiction that remained uselessly external to the church and the individual. Justification is not based upon a transaction with Christ as the federal head of the race, but rather upon the actual objective reality of Christ in the Christian's personal life. Consequently, the focus of attention was on the organic union with Christ and the life flowing from it rather than on the derivative pardon of sin. The objective, supernatural union with Christ is deeper than thought, will, or feeling, occurring at the basal level of our life force, and communicating to us a new living principle of righteousness. Moreover, this mystical union is with the whole Christ, the divinity as well as the humanity, which cannot be separated. Through the outpouring of Christ's vitality in the church, the divine life is flowing forth upon the world. Here sanctification reaches its apogee as glorified humanity shares in the priesthood and kingship of Christ, consecrating and governing all of nature.

Yet another understanding of Christ's priestly work, one which fades into his kingly office, is evident in the ancestor traditions. Here the locus of the problem is outside us, in the environing world. In this view sin is regarded not so much as moral culpability, nor as an internal spiritual malaise, but as an evil external force keeping humanity in bondage, in association with death and Satan. We are not so much the perpetrators of vice as its helpless victims. Militaristic images abound here, with sin, death, and the devil depicted as enemy forces that must be defeated so that humanity can be rescued from its oppression. This emphasis is rare in the tradition of Westminster, but more common in the theological strands influenced by Lutheranism. The Heidelberg Catechism does talk of sin as a sort of entity that must be destroyed and warns that we must be redeemed by Christ from the dominion of the devil. The Evangelical Catechism asserts that Christ had to descend into hell in order to triumph over the dominion of darkness, and Daniel Irion's exposition depicts Christ entering the sphere of death in order to free humanity from bondage to sin and Satan.[17]

The revised Catechism of 1929 continued this tendency to view the resurrection as Christ's victory over sin and death. On the German Reformed side, Nevin and Gerhart also employed the rhetoric of combat and victory, interpreting the cross as the crisis where the principle of healthy life overcame the principle of disease. More recently, Christ's struggle against evil has been cast in social and political terms, with the foe identified as the historical structures and dynamics that inhibit justice, peace, and ecological health. Whatever the preferred vocabulary, the force of these rhetorical devices is to give hope and comfort to those who feel trapped by forces beyond their control. Whether the forces be internal compulsions or external constraints, biological afflictions or social oppression, supernatural forces or historical dynamics, the common thread is the recognition that feeble humanity by itself lacks the resources to liberate itself from their clutches. We are reassured that in this struggle for emancipation we have not been left to our own puny devices.

A very different interpretation of Christ's atoning work once again locates the problem in us, but this time in our cold, self-absorbed hearts. This model shifts attention from the need for the spiritual adrenaline of sanctifying grace to the elicitation of human love by a manifestation of God's love. This interpretation grew in popularity in the nineteenth century, reaching its fullest expression in the work of Horace Bushnell.[18] Although Bushnell's theory of the atonement was complex, subtle, and underwent significant modifications, throughout its evolution it tended to concentrate on the contemplation of Christ's total self-giving. The atonement was not a function of God's righteous demand for punishment, nor of God's concern for public justice. Rather, the true vicarious sacrifice was and is the objective fact that Jesus identifies with sinners, suffers their anguish, and takes into himself their sins, pains, and burdens. The cross reveals Christ's inward nature, which in turn shows that there is a cross in the very heart of God. The self-sacrificial love manifested in the life and death of Jesus has the power to draw individuals away from sin, and therefore from its penalty, and to awaken the principle of love in them. "Liberal" theologians such as Lyman Abbott extended these themes, declaring Christ to be God's supreme entry into human life, whose example of self-giving and suffering for others draws people to him. In his 1946 attempt to summarize Congregational Christian theology, Walter Marshall Horton echoed this motif that God acts in Christ to offer forgiving, self-sacrificial love to the world in order to transform our hearts.[19]

A final interpretation of Christ's atoning work came to fruition in the twentieth century. Some of its roots lie in the previous tradition of the manifestation of love, some lie in certain Lutheran themes, and others lie in the influence of Karl Barth and later Dietrich Bonhoeffer. Like the heritage of Bushnell, this view employed the language of interpersonal relations, casting the atonement in terms of alienation and reconciliation, but it emphasized God's objective overcoming of the alienation rather than the human subjective response (which may actually have been Bushnell's intent). This theme had always been present in the Evangelical Synod, in which the Lutheran influence had engendered a tendency to focus on the cross as God's enactment of solidarity with fallen humanity. In the cross, and in the incarnation as a whole, God exposes God's own self to the anguish of life in fellowship with sinners. By mid-century this sensibility was prevalent throughout the traditions that formed the UCC. Roger Shinn, commenting on the UCC Statement of Faith, affirmed that through Christ God shares the cost of sin, risking the pain that inevitably results from the resolution to confront sin while nevertheless maintaining fellowship with sinners.[20] Gabriel Fackre has elaborated this motif in a manner reminiscent of Barth and Bonhoeffer, explaining that God overcomes alienation by taking into God's own broken heart the consequences of sin.[21] Suffering must be attributed to God because it costs God to accept that which righteousness must reject. The impassibility of the divine nature of Jesus, one of the themes associated with older rejection of the *communicatio idiomatum*, must be rejected, for God in Christ exercises sovereignty precisely through vulnerability and suffering.

The Royal Office

The royal office of Christ in many of the traditions is regarded as the telos of the other two. Most importantly, Christ guides, rules, and guards individual believers and the church as a corporate body. In the post-Reformation period, Christ's exercise of the kingly office after his exaltation was seen not as the divine nature's resumption of powers but rather as the elevation of the human nature to power and dignity. In regard to individuals, Christ as King administers the benefits of his saving work, providentially sending the Holy Spirit and guiding the Christian's rebirth, sanctification, and growth toward heavenly glory, and setting bounds to sin. According to the Reformed theologians of the seventeenth century, Christ in his royal office ensures that the believer's heart will cling to the faith, preserves and defends the believer from sin, and bestows spiritual gifts and graces. Often the oversight of the new life that will eventually blossom in our own ascension and glorification is ascribed to the royal office. The Christ who reigns in glory sends the Spirit as a pledge that we shall reign with him. The rhetorical force of these claims is to assure the individual that Christ has the power to keep his gracious promises to the believer and to reinforce the hope that ultimate felicity will become actual.

The royal office also has a corporate dimension, which the different traditions in the UCC family have treated differently. The Heidelberg heritage tends to restrict Christ's corporate lordship to a "spiritual" kingdom, that is, Christ's protection and guidance of the church during its earthly sojourn, his effectuation of its eventual elevation to a state of glory in eternity, and his governance of the heavenly realm where love is the supreme law. The exalted Christ rules heaven immediately, but now exercises his rule on earth indirectly through pastors and godly magistrates. This theme of guiding and protecting the church was present in the other traditions of the UCC as well. The early Congregationalists often described this in terms of Christ's guidance and protection of the body of the elect. On the Evangelical Synod side, the Evangelical Catechism also associated the kingship of Christ with his governance of the church.

Other trajectories in the UCC heritage have emphasized the extension of the kingly reign of Christ to all of human society, even the entire cosmos. The Congregationalists developed a tendency to view Christ's governance as including not only the church but also godly governments. By the later nineteenth century, this sensibility had evolved into the conviction that Jesus had come to establish among humanity as a whole the kingdom of God. Not only among the "liberals," who often saw Christ's kingdom spreading in an evolutionary manner, but also among more traditional postmillennial evangelicals, the rule of Christ was not restricted to heaven, a spiritual dimension, or the church, but was expected to extend over the entire world in all its dimensions. The Congregationalist Creed of 1883 asserted that "Jesus Christ came to establish among men the kingdom of God, the reign of truth and love, righteousness and peace," and the "ultimate prevalence of the kingdom of Christ over all the earth."[22]

In 1913 the Kansas City Statement of Faith would likewise exhort the faithful to "pray for the transformation of the world into the Kingdom of God."[23] On the German Reformed side, the theologians of the Mercersburg movement even more daringly proposed that the kingdom of Christ, actualized in Jesus and spreading from him, involves the glorification of our nature for the accomplishment of God's purposes throughout the cosmos. With the rise of the Social Gospel movement, the royal office of Christ was associated with the power of love and justice at work in the public square and in the marketplace, guaranteeing that one day swords will be beaten into plowshares. This conviction of Christ's sovereignty over history and culture was further popularized through the influence of H. Richard Niebuhr's description of the "Christ transforming culture" type of theological ethics.[24] In this vein Roger Shinn argued that the UCC Statement of Faith emphasizes Christ's claim on our public life in order to counteract privatized notions of faith and to nurture an understanding of the church as a missionary community that shares in Christ's ministry to the world.[25]

All of these expansions of Christ's royal office serve to give hope that, in spite of the tragedies of nature and the horrors of history, Christ's lordship will one day be manifest and complete. The thematic emphasis gives the church an imperative to be heralds and subjects of the reign of Christ, and functions as an assurance that our political, social, and economic struggles for earthly peace and justice are of significance and will have a future.

Conclusion

Our traditions present us with an embarrassment of Christological riches, bequeathing to the UCC a dizzying kaleidoscope of understandings of Jesus Christ. All of these interpretations of Jesus are scripturally rooted, all follow a plausible way of construing scripture, and all recur in different guises throughout our history. So what should we do with this somewhat bewildering variety? For the sake of a more cohesive identity, should we try to develop criteria to determine which portrayal of Jesus most closely approximates the real Jesus and then declare the others to be heretical?

Before rushing to that conclusion, we must first note that the variety in our traditions is not infinite. In fact, there are significant common threads. All of the trajectories agree that God Almighty was and is redemptively present in Jesus Christ in order to effect the blessedness of humanity. The spokespersons for the sundry traditions may conceptualize this presence differently, some describing it in terms of divine and human natures, some in terms of divine and human agencies, and some in terms of divine manifestation and human medium. But all agree that God takes the initiative in the life of Jesus. Also, all agree that Jesus was a real human being, participating in our common human lot, and that therefore we who share his humanity can also share God's work in him. Moreover, all agree that, to some extent, Jesus both enables us to recover from the disastrous derailment of human life of which we are both the perpetrators and the victims, and also to advance from our spiritual immaturity to the fulfillment God has intended for us. Finally, all employ, implicitly or explicitly, something like the schema of the threefold office (although some expand the roles beyond three) to suggest that God in Christ addresses more than one sort of human problem. At the very least, there is a convergence of conviction that we who dwell east of Eden are all benighted, alienated, and beleaguered, and require three different sorts of succor.

But it must be admitted that troubling discrepancies, or even contradictions, do seem to abound. Many of them pertain to the specific ways that the various offices of Christ are elaborated. Several of the theologians who developed distinctive motifs concerning the saving work of Christ presented them as being antithetical to alternative views. For example, the theme of the elicitation of love was proffered as being incompatible with the theme of the satisfaction of righteousness, and the doctrine of justification through the imputation of extrinsic righteousness as being incompatible with the doctrine of justification through the indwelling of Christ's righteousness. Similarly, Jesus the champion of social reform was often pitted against Jesus the atonement for sin. Most vitriolically, those who maintained the distinction of the properties of divinity and humanity saw themselves as being necessarily at odds with those who envisioned a wedding of the finite and the infinite.

Taken as exact descriptions of supernatural states of affairs, these Christological motifs seem incompatible. Ostensibly, it looks as if either the finite can contain the infinite or it cannot. However, taken as fallible human efforts to give voice to different aspects of God's elusive work among us mortals, they need not be mutually exclusive, they need not conflict. If we attend to their purposes in evoking our passions and commitments, we will find that the hopes and challenges they elicit are by no means incompatible. It is entirely possible to experience and live out simultaneously the existential imports of precisely those Christologies that seem to be in opposition.

For example, consider the dispute between those who posited a sharing of the divine and human attributes of Jesus and those who did not. Those who advocated the continuing sharp separation of the properties were attempting to reassure Christians that God's promises are utterly reliable and to foster the hope that our finite, creaturely human destiny will be fulfilled. Those who asserted a sharing of the divine and human properties did so in order to encourage an anticipation of a limitless joy that the world cannot give or take away. These concerns are not incompatible. It is possible to trust God's power, hope for a fulfillment of our creaturely lives, and long for a satisfaction beyond the confines of space and time.

In much the same way, the controversy between the advocates of intrinsic and extrinsic righteousness can be dissolved. It is possible to rejoice that we are reconciled to God quite independently of any transformation in ourselves, and also to fervently long for and expect such transformation. Furthermore, there is nothing at all contradictory about delighting in the forgiveness of personal sin and also struggling for corporate justice on earth. Similarly, honoring the importance of Law as a constituent of shalom and celebrating compassion for transgressors of shalom can certainly be integrated. Of course, the synthesis of all these elements occurs in the living of a complexly faithful life, not in the pages of a speculative theological system.

Our Christological traditions are more than complementary; they mutually require each other. The conversation with our ancestors in the faith has shown that the multidimensional richness of Christ cannot be captured in a single metaphor or theory. Each tradition by itself offers a less than full gospel and addresses less than the full range of human hopes and fears. God may have arranged a providential division of labor according to which each Christological strand in the UCC has a distinctive insight to offer the whole body. A conversation among them could serve as an antidote to the inherent tendency of each theological subculture to reduce the gospel to good news for its own particular range of concerns. The United Church of Christ, with its wide spectrum of Christological traditions, is uniquely poised to model such a conversation. Our danger is that the conversation partners may not candidly converse with one another, instead forming like-minded Christological conventicles; or that the respective traditions will be so forgotten that no party has anything distinctive to say. But if the cross-fertilization does occur, a more than four-square gospel may well be its fruit.

CHAPTER THREE

JESUS CHRIST IN THE TEXTS OF THE UNITED CHURCH OF CHRIST

GABRIEL FACKRE

TEXTS: WHY, WHAT, AND HOW?

The use of UCC "texts" as an approach to the subject of this volume prompts the questions why, what, and how. *Why* would we turn to inherited, written-down things? That may seem obvious to churches with clearly declared dogma, but not for those of us in the UCC with our eye fixed on the horizon rather than the heritage. If an answer is found, then the next logical query is, *what* are these documents? Again, this is a UCC pressure point, given our commitment to diversity and our openness to, in John Robinson's words, "more light and truth." Supposing that we do find them, *how* do we interpret them, considering that final doctrinal authority appears to be vested by our denomination's Constitution in local congregations? We take some time here, initially, to sort out these issues.

The *why* of the matter is tied up with our self-definition as a "church." When exploring what we believe about Jesus Christ in our denomination, we must take into account the decision made in our founding days to be the United *Church* of Christ, not just united *churches* of Christ. We came into existence, in some sense, as a common body and wrote a constitution to demonstrate it.

We have a corporate reality, and as such we resist the culture's individualistic ideology and attraction to that fragmentation in our own ecclesial history. Further, our very being, as in our name, is witness to our ecumenical search for life together—not life apart—a church "united and uniting," as it is often said. Indeed, we are still the only denomination in this country to have brought together four diverse streams of Christian history, not to mention the "hidden histories" included in our life together.[1]

If we are a common body, then common texts are significant for the subject at hand. These texts, in which the community as a whole through its designated representatives speaks, help to define what the United Church of Christ, collectively, believes about the fundaments. As a church, we have drawn on this lore in ecumenical negotiations. We cite our texts when asked to say what we believe, as in the UCC endorsement of the nine-church Consultation on Church Union (*The COCU Consensus*, now named, with language close to or own, "Churches Uniting in Christ"), our response to the World Council of Churches' study, "Baptism, Eucharist and Ministry," and our position in bilaterals establishing "full communion," such as the *Kirchengemeinschaft* with the Evangelical Church of the Union in Germany and "A Formula of Agreement" with the Evangelical Lutheran Church in America, the Presbyterian Church (USA), and the Reformed Church in America.[2] In the face of the occasional charges of UCC theological incoherence, it has regularly been said, "Please go by our texts, not by anecdotes."[3]

Acknowledging that we have a corporate reality with corporate texts—all of which speak about the meaning of Jesus Christ—just what are they? Implicit in the *what* are *where* and *when* issues.

The first answer to this question, one that enabled the UCC to come to be, was given by our founders when they struggled to produce a "Faith" statement in the Basis of Union of our church. Such a declaration is a short but significant primary text for discerning the corporate UCC faith in Jesus Christ. Its importance is underscored by its use as the framework for a second defining text, the United Church of Christ Statement of Faith, officially voted by the 1959 General Synod of the UCC. A third is the collection of authoritative postfounding texts in the United Church of Christ Constitution. Especially germane to our subject is its theological Preamble and the articles that define the pattern of belief in UCC congregations. A fourth text is the UCC *Book of Worship*. The product of widespread and lengthy testing, though not at the level of authority of the previous three, it includes orders of worship that manifest UCC Christological belief, as well as declarations of faith, ancient and modern, that entail perspectives on the subject of this volume.

In addition to these explicitly formative UCC texts are implicit ones referenced in those texts. If the former are ground-level documents, then the latter represent first, second, and third tiers of texts. The first tier is composed of standards cited in general terms in the Basis of Union as "the ecumenical creeds" and in the Preamble to the Constitution as "ancient creeds," appearing specifically in the *Book of Worship* as the Apostles Creed and the Nicene Creed, cited also in the Christological services, as is done, similarly, in the Services of Word and Sacrament in the *Hymnal* of the United Church of Christ and versions thereof in *The New Century Hymnal* produced by the United Church of Christ Board for Homeland Ministries.[4] A case could also be made that the shape of the creeds is reflected in the UCC Statement of Faith.

The second tier, further from ground level in authority, includes texts stated in general terms in the Basis of Union as the "evangelical confessions of the Reformation" and in the language of the Preamble to the Constitution as "the basic insights of the Protestant Reformers." The Constitution itself recognizes the role of the confessions and declarations of faith of the uniting denominations, stating that the uniting churches of 1957 join "without break in their respective historic continuities and traditions."[5] Thus the three symbols of the former Evangelical and Reformed Church (cited below) are given tacit constitutional recognition, as are comparable Congregational texts from the Cambridge Platform with its presupposed Westminster Confession to the Kansas City Statement of Faith. All, however, appear within the context of congregational polity.[6]

A third tier of texts, more distant in their claim to authority, but signed onto by General Synod vote after years of study and negotiation, is made up of ecumenical theological agreements. Prominent among them, as they bear on Christology, are *The COCU Consensus* on key doctrines and "A Formula of Agreement" with the ELCA, PCUSA, and RCA.[7]

If the foregoing are the *why* and *what* of the matter, the question of the *how*, the "hermeneutical" question, is yet to be faced. Traditionally, hermeneutics has to do with the interpretation of scripture, the principles employed in construing its meaning.[8] Here we are dealing with derivative theological documents, not scripture. But the *how* issue is still entailed as these received texts require interpretation. An organizing principle that functions in UCC interpretation of the texts offers recourse: Texts are to be taken seriously but not imperially.[9] This is to be understood in two senses.

One sense has to do with the ministerial, not magisterial, status of ecclesial texts. The distinction is often associated with "tradition" *vis-à-vis* scripture, the former serving the latter, and always accountable to it. Thus the UCC texts are always under the scrutiny of scripture and are corrigible in the light of it. The Evangelical and Reformed Church had three doctrinal "symbols" that defined its faith: the Heidelberg Catechism, the Augsburg Confession (1530), and Luther's Small Catechism. However, a constitutional qualifier was added declaring that where they may be seen to disagree, the norm of scripture was to be followed. Thus, even in a church with stated "doctrinal standards" found in discrete confessional texts, scripture was declared magisterial and the texts ministerial. This UCC tradition in textual interpretation judges them to be authoritative to the extent that they conform to scripture. They are a resource in developing a point of view on Christ, not the source; the locus of authority belongs to scripture alone.

The texts in question, on the other hand, are testimonial, not magisterial. This is stated quite explicitly in the Basis of Union regarding any formulation of faith: "Like the ampler statement called for in Article IV, Section F, it is designed to be a testimony, and not a test, of faith."[10] The "ampler statement" that did appear in 1959 was the aforementioned UCC Statement of Faith, also held regularly today to be a "testimony, not a test."

We should be clear about why the Basis of Union made this distinction, as it still applies to UCC polity and ecclesiology. Stipulated in the same footnote to its "Faith" section, regarding the status of any church-wide confession, the Basis of Union states: "It is not to be considered a substitute for any confession of faith which may be used in any congregation today."[11] Why so? The answer is that the UCC Constitution vests the final test for doctrinal authority in the congregation. However, the supraparochial declarations of faith do have significant weight, for the Constitution surrounds this paragraph with two others that assert congregational authority to be inseparable from a wider covenant with the larger church, making our polity a "covenantal congregationalism" in contrast to a pure congregational-ism of unaccountable local autonomy.[12]

This stance on the ministerial and testimonial status of received texts appears to separate us from other churches with presumed "binding" doctrinal standards, putting into question any ecumenical affiliations that depend on doctrinal controls charged by critics ex-ternal and internal. However, an honest look at the state of those standards in most "confessional," "creedal," and "connectional" churches will disclose a very similar situation, functionally. Current neo-Congregational tendencies, creedal and confessional illiteracy, and the inroads of current ideologies and individualisms are wide-spread in mainline churches—Protestant, Catholic, and Orthodox. Where such is the case, formally definitive church texts become, at best, ministerial or testimonial rather than determining church boundaries or serving as tests of membership. We are all in the same boat, and there is no "safe" ecclesiastical harbor.[13]

The Narrative Framework

Whatever we have to say about Christology in the UCC, textu-ally, must be placed in the narrative framework that characterizes UCC theology both "on the ground" and in its three tiers. In the first instance, the Statement of Faith is our own retelling of "the Great Story," as its primary drafter, Roger Shinn, describes it in his impor-tant book on the Statement.[14] The story movement of the Statement reflects the way "the faith" is set forth in the Basis of Union, as the for-mer was designed to express the latter. It is also found in the "Com-munion Prayer" in the Services for Word and Sacrament I and II in the *Book of Worship*. All embody a version of the narrative nature of the classical creeds from which they rise, whose account in three para-graphs of the deeds of God are often portrayed as a drama in three acts. The same structure appears in one way or another in the theo-logical documents of the Evangelical and Reformed Church, the "creeds and platforms of Congregationalism,"[15] and in our ecumenical agreements. Behind them all is the movement of the biblical narra-tive/drama from Genesis to Revelation, creation to consummation, with its centerpoint in Jesus Christ.[16] The understanding of UCC textual Christology requires its placement in the context of this "Great Story."

The narrative begins with its author and chief actor, the triune God. The three Persons are cited in the opening sentence of the Statement of Faith, in the first paragraph of the "confession" in the Basis of Union, in Article V, 10, in the Constitution on the beliefs of a UCC congregation, and in the formula for baptism in the Service for Baptism in the *Book of Worship*. Further, the flow of the Statement of Faith—reflecting that of the confession in the Basis of Union, the "ancient creeds" cited in the Preamble, the "evangelical confessions" of the Basis of Union, and the "basic insights of the Protestant Reformers" of the Preamble, the ecumenical agreements from *The COCU Consensus* to the WCC "Basis"—renders explicit what is implicit in scripture itself: the Trinitarian history of God. While employing various terms—Father/God, Son/Lord/Savior, Spirit/Holy Spirit—and stated tersely, both the immanent and economic Trinity are to be found in these grounding texts and all their tiers. The Trinitarian premises in UCC texts are no accident, given the denomination's prehistory: on the one hand, the strong Reformation *cum* classical roots of the Evangelical and Reformed tradition, and the same for the Congregational tradition with it specific controversy with Unitarianism in the nineteenth century as background.

Using the paradigmatic Statement of Faith, the "chapters" in the "Great Story" that follow the Trinitarian preface are:

- *Creation*, as God "calls the worlds into being, creates humankind in the divine image . . . " (Statement of Faith II)

- The *fall*, our response of "aimlessness and sin." (Statement of Faith, all versions)

- God's *persevering grace* (denominated sometimes as the covenant with Noah), which "seeks in holy love to save all people from aimlessness and sin" and "judges all people and all humanity." (Statement of Faith II)

- The special *covenant* with the Jewish people, with only passing reference in the Statement of Faith as in God's "righteous will declared through prophets . . . " (Statement of Faith I)

This reflects a missing piece in the ancient creeds themselves, but one retrieved from scripture in the UCC's 1987 General Synod resolution on the unbroken covenant with Israel, and its widely circulated 1990 interpretation developed after a two-year study by a select panel,[17] an accent anticipated in Communion Prayer 1 in both Services of Word and Sacrament in the *Book of Worship*.

- *Jesus Christ*, the center of the Story as "In Jesus Christ, the man of Nazareth, you [God] have come among us and shared our common lot conquering sin and death and reconciling the world to yourself." (Statement of Faith III)

- *The birth of the church* by the power of the Spirit, as "You bestow upon us your Holy Spirit, creating and renewing the church of Jesus Christ," calling us "to proclaim the gospel to all the world and resist the powers of evil, to share in Christ's baptism and eat at his table . . . " (Statement of Faith III)

- The gift and demands of *salvation*, as in "You promise to all who trust you forgiveness of sins and fullness of grace, courage in the struggle for justice and peace" calling us "to accept the cost and joy of discipleship, to be your servants in the service of others . . . " (Statement of Faith III)

- The *Last Things*, through which we look forward to "eternal life in your realm which has no end" with a joy able to declare, "Blessing and honor, glory and power be unto you!" (Statement of Faith III)

In the texts of the UCC, the meaning of who Jesus Christ is and what Jesus Christ does are inseparable from this Tale of God. To its center we now turn, examining it in terms of the classical dimensions of Christology: the person and work of Jesus Christ.

THE PERSON OF CHRIST

Who is Jesus Christ? Such are the circumstances in the UCC narrative as it moves to its centerpoint that only the Holy One can turn the Tale around. In doxological praise to the loving God we say in the Statement of Faith:

> In Jesus Christ . . . you have come to us and shared our common lot . . .

And why this arrival in our midst? Someone had to be about the task of:

> conquering sin and death. . . .

The narrative is about the radical action of divine enfleshment. Only by the entry of the Maker of history into that same history can the goal of God for us—a life together that reflects the triune Life Together—be pursued. Only God, firsthand, could and can deal with the opposition mounted by us to the divine purpose—our fall into "sin" and its consequence, "death" as estrangement from God. Here at the heart of the Story, we meet in Jesus "God reconciling" (2 Cor. 5:19). Thus the Statement takes up in narrative form the classical teaching of the deity of Christ, the incarnation of the second Person of the triune God.

Following Old Testament usage of the word "Lord" as a title for deity, the ascription of that title to Jesus in both scripture and tradition is an assertion of the same.[18] In that manner the deity of Christ is affirmed in the language of the Basis of Union:

> Jesus Christ . . . our Lord

And in Article V, 11, of the Constitution on the belief integral to a UCC congregation:

> profession of faith in Jesus Christ as Lord. . . .

And in the foundational rendering of the Statement of Faith (III):

> our Lord Jesus Christ. . . .

The same status is declared in the description of Jesus as upper-cased "Son," with its backdrop of Trinitarian language and pattern of thought, Christ being the Son of the Father, co-eternal and co-equal. So the Basis of Union reads:

> Jesus Christ, His Son. . . .

And likewise, the Preamble to the Constitution:

> Jesus Christ, Son of God. . . .

These current titles and formulations trace back not only to scripture but also to the "ancient/ecumenical creeds," "evangelical confessions of the Reformation," and the "basic insights of the Reformers" cited in the Basis of Union and Preamble to the Constitution. So:

> "I believe in Jesus Christ, his only Son, our Lord . . . " (the Apostles Creed, *Book of Worship*, 509)

> "We believe in one Lord, Jesus Christ, the only Son of God . . . " (the Nicene Creed, *Book of Worship*, 510)

> "Why is he called God's Only-begotten Son . . . ?" (Heidelberg Catechism, Question 33)

> "It pleased God . . . to choose and ordain the Lord Jesus. His only begotten Son . . . " (Chapter VIII, Westminster Confession/ Savoy Declaration)

> "We believe in . . . Jesus Christ, his Son, our Lord and Savior." (Kansas City Statement of Faith)

The ecumenical agreements that official representatives of the UCC have signed and General Synod has voted affirm the same status for Jesus Christ, as in the Consultation on Church Union's "Confessing the Faith":

> The Church lives and finds its identity in thankful confession of Jesus Christ as the one Lord and Savior . . . Christ is God's self-giving in the Holy Spirit . . . (*The COCU Consensus*, V)

So, too, declares the confession that unites national churches in the World Council of Churches: the belief in Jesus Christ as "God and Savior" (Basis, World Council of Churches).

The titles for Jesus Christ as "Lord" and "Son of God" have been judged patriarchal and hierarchical by some who have been eliminating these terms from hymnody, liturgy, and confessions of faith.[19] More's the pity concerning their censorship, as the attempts at equivalency by altering these biblical terms consistently fail, and also distance the UCC from the ecumenical relationships so central to our existence and professed intentions.[20] In the interest of inclusivity, it is better to use the lead end of the pencil rather than its eraser.[21]

Incarnation means, of course, the carnality of God, and thus the cruciality of the humanity of Jesus Christ. From the Council of Chalcedon forward, this companion theme has been integral to Christian teaching about who Jesus is—true human as well as true God—or in the fifth century Chalcedonian language, not only "very God" but also "very Man of reasonable soul and body . . . two natures, without confusion, without change, without distinction, without separation . . . together in one Person . . . "[22]

The humanity of Jesus becomes crystal clear in UCC Christological declarations:

> In Jesus Christ, the man of Nazareth . . . you have come to us and shared our common lot . . . You call us . . . to eat at his table . . . (Statement of Faith III)

The UCC Statement of Faith unambiguously asserts Jesus' real humanity not only by its explicit statement that Christ shares our "common lot" but also by refusing to eliminate the sexual identity integral to that humanity.[23]

The Basis of Union is less well-developed on the humanity, but echoes the earlier themes of the Apostles Creed ("He suffered under Pontius Pilate, was crucified, died, and was buried") and the Nicene Creed ("For us and our salvation . . . was made man . . . was crucified under Pontius Pilate, he suffered death and was buried"). The Kansas City Statement of Faith was, no doubt, influential in carrying forward the creedal language but rendering it more tersely:

> In Jesus Christ . . . who for us and our salvation lived and died . . .

The Heidelberg Catechism is more explicit about the humanity, reflecting also the Chalcedonian formula:

> The eternal Son of God . . . took upon himself our true manhood from the flesh and blood of the Virgin Mary . . . so that he might be the true seed of David like his fellow men in all things, except for sin. (Question 35)

The Westminster Confession/Savoy Declaration is even more explicit:

> The second Person in the Trinity . . . did, when the fullness of time was come, take upon him Man's nature, with all the essential properties and common infirmities thereof, yet without sin. . . . So that the two whole perfect and distinct natures, the Godhead and the Manhood, were inseparable joined together in one Person without conversion, composition or confusion . . . (Chapter VIII, 2)

The Evangelical Catechism puts it this way:

> Jesus Christ is true God and true man in one person. He thereby entered into human nature and became in all things as we are, yet without sin. (Questions 60, 62)

The ecumenical accords echo these assertions in their endorsement of the classical creeds.

The Person of Christ in UCC texts at all levels? Truly God, truly human, truly one. Only such an incarnation could do the at-one-ing work, to which we now turn.

THE WORK OF CHRIST

Pertinent to the question "Who is Jesus?" is this statement in the Preamble of the UCC Constitution: "The United Church of Christ acknowledges as its sole Head, Jesus Christ . . . Savior." Savior? Savior has to do with "salvation." In the long history of Christian thought, biblical teaching on this topic has been developed as "the doctrine of salvation," or "soteriology." And soteriology is further ramified as objective and subjective. The former has to do with the work of Christ done for us in his life, death, and resurrection. The latter refers to the work of Christ as it comes home to us, and in us. Sometimes the distinction is described as "redemption accomplished and applied."[24] Historically, the simple word "savior" is a weighty one.

To unpack its meaning, we begin with the obvious question: From what are we saved? As noted, The Statement of Faith uses the language of scripture and tradition by answering that Jesus Christ "has come to us . . . conquering sin and death." The twin enemies from which we are saved are (1) our "No!" to God's invitation—sin as our ego trip away from the divine purposes of life together with God, neighbor, and nature; and (2) "death" as the consequent alienation from our Maker and all that entails.

And just how does that happen? Here the distinction between objective and subjective soteriology emerges. Redemption is "accomplished" (the "objective" work) by "the man of Nazareth, our crucified and risen Savior" (Statement of Faith, all versions). We thank God for what has been done in Christ's life, death, and resurrection for "reconciling the world to yourself" (Statement of Faith III). Alienation—sin and its consequence, death—is over and reconciliation has begun. "Blessing and honor, glory and power be unto you!" (Statement of Faith III).

The triple reference—"man of Nazareth, . . . crucified, risen" —is no accident. It refers to the life, death, and resurrection of Christ, the three phases of Christ's saving career among us. In the Reformed tradition that shapes the UCC, this threesome has been expressed as the "threefold office of Christ": the prophetic, priestly, and royal roles Jesus played in the work of reconciliation. John Calvin was the premier expositor of this *munus triplex* that has had wide ecumenical impact.[25] The triple roles of Christ in his work are part of the confessional lore from both of the uniting streams that flowed into the UCC, as in the Heidelberg Catechism and the Westminster Confession that is presupposed in the Cambridge Platform of 1646.[26] The prophetic office is the disclosure in the teaching and example of Jesus of what God wills the world to be: a life together, not a life apart. The priestly office is God, on the cross of Jesus, taking into the divine heart the death we deserve for our sin. The royal office is God raising Jesus on Easter morning and thus validating and announcing that our estrangement is over, new life overcoming the old death.

The reconciliation accomplished for the world has to be received by the world, the objective joined by the subjective, the collective *pro nobis* moving to the personal *pro me*. Reconciliation reaches the "persons" created in the "divine image," and before whom is set "the ways of life and death" (Statement of Faith III), when what is accomplished in Galilee, Calvary, and on Easter morning comes home to "all who trust in the gospel" (Statement of Faith II) with "forgiveness of sin and fullness of grace" (Statement of Faith II). These are classical Reformation, but not only Reformation, formulations.[27] "Trust" is the term key to the Reformers' understanding of faith.[28] *Fiducia* is the trust of the heart in the gospel, the good news of God's saving work in Christ. Thus we are justified by faith, by grace through faith and not by works, first among the "basic insights of the Reformers" (Preamble to the Constitution). Hence, integral to the Services for Word and Sacrament is the call to confession:

> If we say we have not sin we deceive ourselves and the truth is not in us . . .
>
> . . . but if we confess our sins, God who is faithful and just will forgive our sins and cleanse us from all unrighteousness.

The confession itself:

> . . . we confess we are in bondage to sin and cannot free ourselves.

And the assurance of pardon:

> Through Jesus Christ we are forgiven of all our sins . . . (Service of Word and Sacrament 1)

Justification by grace through faith is a refrain, of course, in all the Reformation confessions and catechisms in our history, Heidelberg Catechism, Question 61 being representative:

> *Question 61.* Why do you say you are righteous by faith alone?
>
> *Answer.* Not because I please God by virtue of the worthiness of my faith, but because the satisfaction, righteousness, and holiness of Christ alone are my righteousness before God, and because I can accept it and make it mine in no other way than by faith alone.

The ecumenical documents to which we have signed echo that refrain, as in *The COCU Consensus:*

> Being justified by faith in Christ, we are reconciled to God and to one another through the faith and love which is bestowed in the Spirit.[29]

In our Reformed tradition, we insist upon the importance of "sanctification" as well as justification.[30] Hence the phrase "fullness of grace" (Statement of Faith, all versions) underscores the importance of works of love as the fruit of faith. This is echoed in the Service of Word and Sacrament 1 when, in the assurance of pardon, the words "and by the Holy Spirit we are empowered to new life" are added. For the Reformed tradition, and now for the UCC, such holiness has never been confined to the personal life but encompasses society as well. Why? Because its stress on the threefold office of Christ was not confined to the objective work, but continued into subjective soteriology, as in the Heidelberg Catechism's Question 32. Further, as Visser 't Hooft has shown, the third office has always been construed from Calvin forward as a warrant for Christians to hold the civil order accountable to Christ's royal rule, the latter not being confined to the church or the soul as in "two kingdom" interpretations.[31]

The social, economic, and political import of the royal office is reflected in the UCC Statement of Faith's elucidation of the sanctifying "fullness of grace" *vis-à-vis* these realms, as in the trust in Christ's giving us "courage in the struggle for justice and peace," and thus the UCC's history of involvement in justice and peace concerns.[32] And as doxology is theology, we hear the affirmation of the same in the leader's opening sentence of the Eucharist:

> Jesus came to preach good news to the poor
> to proclaim release to the captives

and recovery of sight to the blind
to liberate those who are oppressed
and to proclaim the year of God's favor.
(Service of Word and Sacrament 1)

Such is part of a Reformed trajectory found initially in the Heidelberg
Catechism as it stressed the imperative side of sanctification:

Why are you called a Christian? Because through faith I share in
Christ and thus in his anointing, so that I am to confess his
name, offer myself a living sacrifice of gratitude to him and fight
against sin and the devil with a free and good conscience
throughout this life . . . (Question 32)

And from Westminster/Savoy comes the chapter "Of Sanctification"
accenting the indicative side, the sanctifying gift given to those justified:

The whole body of sin is destroyed . . . and they more and more
quickened and strengthened in all saving graces, to the practice
of [all] true holiness, without which no man shall see the Lord.
(Chapter XIII)

New Light and Truth

"Well, so we have texts in the UCC. That was fine for folks *then*.
But what about *now*? Didn't one of our founding forebears say we
should be open to new light and truth?" Pastor John Robinson is part
of our lore, too. And even our Preamble picks up his concern with its
words about each new generation developing a relevant faith "in honesty of thought and expression." And in this twenty-first century we
have a national program that asserts God to be "still speaking," refusing to put a period where a comma belongs.[33] The UCC is a progres-
sive denomination, always open to new insights and not captive to the
old ones.

Let's look a little closer at these urgings and their roots. They do
represent important indicators of who we are, and what we believe
about Jesus Christ. Actually, they trace back to a long Reformed tradition of accent on the sovereignty of God. The free and majestic God
will not be bound by our formulations. As Karl Barth put it regarding
the Reformed confessions:

To our fathers the historical past was something which called
not for loving and devoted imagination but for careful and criti-

cal scrutiny. . . . There are documentary statements of their beliefs . . . but . . . our fathers had good reason for leaving us no Augsburg Confession authentically interpreting the word of God, no Formula of Concord, no Symbolic books which might later, like the Lutheran, come to possess an odor of sanctity. . . . It may be our doctrinal task to make a careful revision of the theology of Geneva or the Heidelberg Catechism or of the Synod of Dort or . . . it may be our task to draw up a new creed. . . . [34]

Barth counted the ancient creeds and the Reformation confessions as critical resources for his Reformed faith, but always under the Word of the sovereign God who is never confined to our past deposits of witness to the Word, Jesus Christ.

Yet it should be noted that Barth's call for ever-fresh listening to the Word was always done with the defining witness to that Word in hand, the biblical text in which God has spoken, and still speaks, authoritatively. That is exactly what John Robinson had in mind, as can be seen from his full original words on July 20, 1620: "The Lord hath more truth and light yet to break forth from his holy Word." The new Word spoken is always from the old Word written—and in like manner, touching on the past hearings of the Word as the creeds and confessions of our forebears, which were guides to Barth's own faith.[35] The Preamble to the UCC Constitution speaks about "this faith," specifically that of the "ancient creeds" and "the basic insights of the Protestant Reformers," not one we have created *de novo*, that is, to be put into the thought and language forms of each generation. So the UCC has sought to do in its Statement of Faith, in its Basis of Union, in its Constitution, and in the services of its *Book of Worship*. The "more light and truth" are always in continuity with the givens of scripture and tradition, the trajectory to which we connect and which we extend corporately into our own generation.[36]

Doing this necessitates identifying the textual trajectories that have made us who we are as a church. Conceived as rays, they are the extensions of the one "Sun of righteousness" that illumines scripture, with whatever "more light and truth" there is yet to be in continuity therewith. The person and work to which these texts witness give our name luster. May we always be faithful to that United Church of *Christ*.

PART TWO

ECUMENICAL CONNECTIONS

CHAPTER FOUR

JESUS IN GOD'S PLAN FOR SALVATION
LYDIA VELIKO

We hold the Church to be established for calling [people] to repentance and faith, for the public worship of God, for the confession of His name by word and deed, for the administration of the
sacraments, for witnessing to the saving grace of God in Christ,
for the upbuilding of the saints, and for the universal propagation of the Gospel; and in the power of the love of God in Christ
we labor for the progress of knowledge, the promotion of justice,
the reign of peace, and the realization of human [fellowship].
(Inclusive terminology added.)[1]

In 1943 these words, found in the Basis of Union of the Congregational Christian Churches and the Evangelical and Reformed
Church, became a platform from which both church bodies later
claimed their identity as the United Church of Christ in the context
of the church universal. This section of the Basis, with a focus on the
nature of the church, offers a glimpse into the faith of the leaders of
that generation and claims for both church bodies their place in the
historic stream of Christian witness. Along with Christians of every
time and in every place, it affirms the church as that place where
God's name is confessed, where God is worshiped and glorified, and
where the people of God receive the sacraments and hear God's holy
word preached.

It also reminds us that Christians through the generations have understood that the church is established *"for witnessing to the saving grace of God in Christ . . . and for the universal propagation of the Gospel."* Embedded in the faith and witness of our forebears, these words point to questions that are unavoidable for modern Christians: How do we understand God's saving activity in the particular person of Jesus Christ? How does our understanding of that saving activity shape who we understand Jesus to be?

There are few more vexing challenges for Christians at the dawn of the twenty-first century than how we will understand, and then proclaim, who Christ is in the context of a world whose religious diversity we can no longer avoid or deny. We are confronted daily with the ramifications of religious misunderstanding and bigotry throughout the world. We can sometimes feel confounded by the complex nature of the interface between religion and politics in our country and in other regions of the world. "Interfaith marriage" is no longer, in most places in the United States, an isolated or odd occurrence. We have siblings, children, and close friends who follow the tenets of other religions, and who are more assertive than earlier generations about their faith and its practices. It would be nearly impossible for Christians in the United States today to avoid facing these realities and their implications for understanding our faith.

Further, the final decades of the twentieth century saw the advent of deep and fruitful interfaith interaction in many communities. In some settings this is characterized by interfaith "cooperative efforts," where members of various faith traditions gather to work on behalf of their communities. In other places relationships have been built by means of "dialogue for understanding," where members from a variety of religious traditions discuss beliefs and share perspectives from faith commitments. It is no longer necessary, however, to engage in intentional activity to experience the interfaith nature of our communities. By simply entering an office building or participating in civic life, we encounter profound religious diversity.

My intent in these next few pages is to explore how some voices from Reformed theology can speak to our United Church of Christ context when discerning matters of salvation and, more specifically, who Jesus is in God's plan for salvation. In doing this, I hope to stimulate response and theological reflection among local pastors and lay members of congregations whose lives are touched by the interfaith nature of our communities. It is not my intent to provide a systematic or comprehensive review of the extensive academic literature written on the subject of interfaith relations, much less to give definitive response to these important questions. Theologians and academic experts in the UCC and beyond it have written extensively on these issues from a variety of perspectives, and serious consideration of this material is vital for our maturation as a community of faith. I strongly urge such study for all who wish to engage in interfaith relationships of any kind.

My goals here, however, are far more modest: to make some observations about the nature of the UCC and the implications for our understanding of who Christ is; to look at Reformed theological voices as one set of perspectives on these important questions; and to focus specifically on questions of salvation and who Jesus is in God's saving act.

THE UNITED CHURCH OF CHRIST—A WITNESS FROM A UNITED AND UNITING CHURCH

The United Church of Christ acknowledges as its sole Head, Jesus Christ, Son of God and Savior. It acknowledges as kindred in Christ all who share in this confession. It looks to the Word of God in the scriptures, and to the presence and power of the Holy Spirit, to prosper its creative and redemptive work in the world. It claims as its own the faith of the historic church expressed in the ancient creeds and reclaimed in the basic insights of the Protestant Reformers. It affirms the responsibility of the church in each generation to make this faith its own in reality of worship, in honesty of thought and expression, and in purity of heart before God. In accordance with the teaching of our Lord and the practice prevailing among evangelical Christians, it recognizes two sacraments: Baptism and the Lord's Supper or Holy Communion.

At its inception, the UCC claimed its identity as a "united and uniting" church. Though comprised of various church families, this united and uniting denomination understood itself to be a part of the church universal, claiming with others that Jesus Christ is the one through whom God came to earth and the one in whom we know our salvation.

Born in an era of ecumenical energy, and kindled by the flames of conviction that the church as the body of Christ on earth must embody God's reconciling love for and among all people, the UCC understood personal piety and work for justice and reconciliation in the world to be inseparable parts of one whole. Various theological and spiritual emphases flowed together in 1957 as the Evangelical, the Reformed, the Christian, and the Congregational traditions—joined very soon after by the African American congregations of the Convention of the South—committed to life together. The denomination's dedication to a community of justice and reconciliation was captured well by Louis Gunnemann as he wrote of one of our early ecumenical relationships. Describing our full communion agreement with the Evangelical Church of the Union (EKU) in Germany, he wrote, "*Kirchengemeinschaft* [full church communion] is essentially 'the reconciled and reconciling community.' It is, therefore, a way of life to be learned for the sake of God's *oikumene* in which nations, races, and oppressed people yearn for the hand of reconciliation and hope."[2]

Of that same relationship, Joachim Rogge, President of the Evangelical Church of the Union East, said:

> Certainly we [the UCC and EKU] come together with different understandings of the church and with different political convictions. Yet, nevertheless, we are all one. This unity is not true because we are so excellent or because we are so full of everlasting faith; but because Jesus Christ has prayed for us, that we may all be one . . .[3]

Rogge's words are crucial to understanding the character of a united and uniting church. Unity is not defined by uniform adherence to historic confessions or unanimity in interpretation of scripture or ecclesiology but rather as something God has given to us and Jesus prayed we might realize.

What felt like a wild and heady mix of traditions in the first few years of the union, however, has been surpassed many times in the decades since. No longer can the United Church of Christ be defined by these five initial streams of the larger church, varied as even they were! The United Church of Christ of the twenty-first century encompasses congregations that are both indigenous to the United States and from immigrant communities of countless traditions. American Indian, Samoan, Micronesian, South Indian, and Korean congregations are a part of the UCC. Our churches have characteristics born of the Reformation era but also increasingly carry accents that sound Baptist, plus characteristics whose specific strain of Christian tradition is hard to identify because the diversity within a given congregation is so wide. Members of the UCC bring as a part of their identity specific assumptions about what the church is and how it works; they bring emphases on a wide range of practices of piety. And, important for this discussion, they carry diverse perspectives about how the church should relate to the world beyond its borders. Because the unity of the church—that of our denomination or the church universal—is not something that we create but rather a gift we have received, we have learned to be grateful for these many accents.

Even within the context of the faith named in the Preamble to the Constitution, we face steep challenges as we seek to claim that unity for which Jesus prayed. Just as the church throughout the ages, we know Jesus to be the head of the church, and we rely upon the historic confessions as we seek to interpret God's word. We hold as a cherished conviction the responsibility that each generation is "to make this faith its own in reality of worship, in honesty of thought and expression, and in purity of heart before God." We believe the community of believers must stand in the presence of the witness of the historic church and make that faith its own in the context of today.

Posing a single answer to the question of how we in the UCC understand who Jesus is (and therefore how God acts in the world to save us) is not just a difficult question because of the diversity of religious expression in our world. It is also made difficult by the tremendous diversity *within* the UCC. If we are to take seriously the gifts of our various particularities, we are required to hear voices that, in some instances, contradict each other and, at other times, simply offer facets of questions that others do not see. Important for a united and uniting church—and critical to the recent "Formula of Agreement" full communion relationship among the Evangelical Lutheran Church in America and three Reformed bodies, including the United Church of Christ— is the principle of "mutual affirmation and admonition." This principle allows us to recognize that complementary positions do not necessarily point to church-dividing realities, and it provides a vehicle by which differing voices can speak affirming and sometimes corrective words to each other, all within the context of the one church.[4] "Mutual affirmation and admonition" not only enables us to cope with this struggle in a united and uniting church, but also allows us to practice the skill that is a gift of the very same nature: the capacity to hold diverging views without dissolving the union.

VOICES FROM THE REFORMED TRADITION

It is helpful to review the statements of a few Reformed voices, trusting that voices from other parts of the church family who have another word to speak will do so in dialogue with these. Even these Reformed voices, however, display both intentional diversity as befits the complicated task of giving testimony to the person of Jesus in a denomination comprised of a variety of traditions.

In an essay on Trinitarian theology in Reformed thought, Daniel Migliore writes:

> Equally emphasized within the Reformed theological tradition is to acknowledge the incompleteness and reform-ability of all confessional statements. While the confessional tradition of the church is to be approached with respect and even deference, it is not to be invested with absolute authority. In the Reformed view, the latter would be tantamount to idolatries . . . All confessions and practices are subordinate to the living Word of God and open to reform . . . Faithfulness to the gospel and openness to new insight from the living Word of God requires that the church make room for and learn from a diversity of receptions to the gospel.[5]

The diversity that characterizes the world beyond our denomination—and certainly beyond our Christian doors—can easily describe our own church as well. Edmund Za Bik, in an essay titled "The Challenge to Reformed Theology," seems to speak almost directly to the Preamble to the UCC Constitution when he writes:

> In the age of pluralism and relativism, pluriformity as the theological approach of the Reformed tradition is most blessed with the challenge and task of reconstructing and reinterpreting traditional theology in the context of the ever-growing multifaceted problems of today's world with a view to reorder our lives more meaningfully.[6]

Before focusing on "who Jesus is," it will be useful to begin with a brief treatment of the religious plurality of our communities and how various Reformed theologians view a Christian response to it.

The "challenge and the task" named by Edmund Za Bik requires that we not be sanguine about the reality of pluralism, either as we seek to articulate from within a diverse Christian body or, more pointedly, as we seek to name our Christian faith in the context of a religiously plural world. In the same essay noted above, Migliore writes:

Rightly understood, pluralism challenges the church to achieve greater clarity about Christian identity and the meaning of Christian life in community. This challenge is often missed by some familiar responses of the church to the pluralism of our time.[7]

He names three general responses of the church to pluralism: to withdraw in order to avoid corrupting influences; to adopt what he names as "authoritarian" constructs to bolster the identity of the church in the face of plurality; or to engage pluralism by encouraging the growth of the church to defend itself by sheer size against the growth of others. To these I would add a fourth for the UCC: the tendency to ignore concrete differences in the pursuit of harmonious community. Migliore's admonition related to the three responses apply to this fourth as well:

The church must learn to distinguish between forms of pluralism that enrich and enhance life in community and forms of pluralism that weaken and destroy community.[8]

In other words, it is critical for us in the United Church of Christ not simply to accept the reality of religious plurality, but also to ask ourselves how we will evaluate and relate to it. As inadequate a response as denial of religious pluralism is (not generally a tendency for the UCC!), so, too, is acknowledging it without assessing where we fit into it and how it affects our life of faith. While religious diversity is an undeniable part of our existence, is the resulting difference of beliefs and even values that attend this diversity always a good thing? Is it rarely or never a good thing? What criteria do we apply to determine what enriches or what weakens community? If we determine that religious diversity is not just a given but a good, what do we do with those aspects of our own faith that seem to foster discord?

Help from the Reformed tradition comes in understanding that God is always beyond our capacity to fully understand. Just as "the historical form of the church will never completely correspond to its destiny,"[9] so, too, our understanding of the gospel will always be tempered by our limitations and capacity for grasping the enormousness of God's saving work through Jesus. Migliore writes:

Communion in faith . . . knows that all confessional statements and theologies this side of the promised reign of God are *semper reformanda* . . . Unquestionably, there are boundaries that mark off the Christian communion of faith. Yet Reformed confessional sensibility, while unashamed and unapologetic about the specific content of the Gospel, remains teachable.[10]

The same can be said of the view of many Reformed theologians that we cannot know, on this side of the eschaton, who is saved. While one stream of Reformed theology emphasizes the doctrine of election, focusing on issues of regeneration and reprobation, another, in which stream many of the forebears of the UCC find themselves, argues that, in fact, we have no business trying to determine such things as election (particularly when understanding a theology of baptism), making appeal to scripture, especially Deuteronomy 29:29, which tells us that "secret things belong to the Lord." It is not for us to determine the secret things, but rather to teach the Law to our children.[11]

It is not, therefore, weak equivocation to say that there are things we simply do not know. To acknowledge this is to stand firmly in the stream of Protestant reformers who hold in balance, on the one hand, the confession that Jesus is the one through whom God offers salvation and, on the other hand, the humility to acknowledge that there are many things about the way in which God works that we cannot know.

JESUS AND SALVATION

Is Jesus the only path to salvation? Is there is salvation beyond the church? In order to consider the answers, we need to be careful to understand the scope of the questions. Too often separate questions become conflated into one without adequate analysis.

A first question: Can God, through Jesus Christ, effect salvation even to those who have not professed faith in Jesus, since scripture tells us that Jesus came that all might be saved? On this question Reformed theologians differ. Some believe that a profession of faith is necessary in order for the effects of salvation to operate. Others hold to a wide range of beliefs that God affects realities in ways that we do not, and never will, know. God's radical sovereignty (a strong Reformed theological concept in which God is not controlled by us or by circumstances) has meant for many Reformed theologians that while God's salvation is effected specifically through the person of Jesus Christ, the "how, when, where, and to whom" is often entirely unknown to us. Much has been written on this topic and is beyond the scope of this short review. I simply note it and urge careful study for all who wish to engage in interfaith relations and to deepen their own understanding of their Christian faith.

A second question: Is being "saved" a relevant concept for Christians considering who Christ is and whether it is Christ alone who saves? My purpose is not to answer the question, but rather to urge us not to answer one question when in fact we may be answering another. I suspect that when we respond negatively to the question "is Jesus the only path to salvation," we could pursue the matter more deeply in order to discover that in fact the entire concept of "being saved" is unclear and seems irrelevant to some Christians. If the understanding of "salvation," for example, is even unconsciously couched in theological constructs of a "physical" heaven and hell to which one does not subscribe, one might be disinclined to understand Jesus as the path to salvation because these theological assumptions seem irrelevant. It is very important to know what question we are actually answering.

A third question: Is belief in Jesus Christ *per se* the *only* path to salvation?[12] For the historic Reformed theologians and the confessions of the church, the response seems to be "yes." This is a profoundly complicated question, and in this limited space, we can only touch on a few of the critical issues.

Some Christians believe that there are, in fact, many paths to salvation, inclusive of but not exclusive to a belief in Jesus as Savior, and for them, this perspective is the result of theological exploration that has led them to a "common pool" or "common core" system of belief.

Still others, with Edmund Za Bik, believe that an openness to faith claims of other traditions does not have to be threatening both because a comprehensive understanding of worldviews, not randomly blended but more selectively compiled, can actually fortify Christianity in parts of the world where absolutism can no longer function. Christian faith is strengthened, rather than weakened, by the wisdom of other traditions.[13] An increasing number of Christians beyond the region of the North Atlantic hold to this view, and may be strongly influenced by the experience of living in a setting where Christianity is a minority culture.

A subquestion that often follows from this is whether *semper reformanda* stretches far enough in the twenty-first century to include revelation in which we understand that Christ is one among many (or at least one among several) routes to salvation.

There are others who believe that Jesus is the only path to salvation. (This view would comprise the majority of historic theologians and the historic confessions.) In 1865 theologian and professor Philip Schaff spoke of Jesus with these poetic words:

> True man in body soul and spirit, yet differing from all men; a character absolutely unique and original from tender childhood to ripe manhood . . . free from every sin and error; innocent and holy . . . and ever acknowledged since as the one and only perfect model of goodness and holiness . . . He is the great central miracle of the whole gospel-history.[14]

Though not, in this setting, specifically concerned with articulating Jesus' role in God's saving act, Schaff notes that there is no way for a human being fully to grasp the person of Jesus using human constructs, a perspective that has implications for the place of Jesus in salvation history. Jesus is completely other, infinitely greater than all we can imagine, and beyond any attempt to define or describe. Being fully human and fully divine ("moving in unbroken union with God"),[15] Jesus is beyond the scope of human reason to understand in completeness.

Jesus is at once with us and beyond us, and, for Schaff, literally incomparable. In this way, for Schaff and other Reformed theologians, Jesus is not simply an example of a "really, really good" human being. He is not on the human continuum at all, at least not as we generally understand it. For many of the reformers, there is no way to avoid the for-all-time, world-altering reality of God's coming in the specific person of Jesus Christ, and therefore it is foundational for them to what it means to be "Christian."

For many, however, who may be inclined to the perspective that Jesus is the only path to salvation, such a claim can still be profoundly uncomfortable in the face of interfaith relationships in our communities or immediate families, and in the face of history, which has given ample evidence of the evil perpetrated by exclusivist religious views, including from some Christians. It would be foolish to deny this discomfort in order simply to say, "It does not have to be so." For many—both within in the United Church of Christ and beyond it—the claim that Jesus is the only path to salvation seems laden with intolerance and fraught with potholes into which otherwise caring and generous-minded individuals can fall and get swallowed up. Further, it can feel to some that there is no difference between a claim that Jesus is the only path to salvation and a requirement to convert all who do not share this belief.

Again, to say "it need not be so" does not provide adequate resource for discernment. For those whose perspective tends toward a belief that Jesus is the path to salvation, I have a suspicion that these questions are difficult because, in fact, it is difficult to make Christocentric faith claims and not simultaneously load them with the overwhelming baggage to which history has made us heir. It is not necessary to frame questions of Christology in "inclusive-exclusive" constructs—in fact, I believe that it is profoundly unhelpful. But it is often the only framework we know unless other resources or constructs have been made more generally available. Twenty-first-century Christians must work far harder to explicate theologies where Jesus is the path to salvation without linking this claim to bad theology, bad practice, and reductionist assumptions. It will be important to the well-being of the communities in which we live together—and may be even more vital to the communities where we live apart—for us to move beyond simplistic Christologies.

INTO THE FUTURE

This sampling of Reformed voices is one set of lenses through which we can interpret important questions of who Jesus is in the context of a religiously plural world. Such voices remind us that the churches of the Reformation, of which the United Church of Christ is one, have a strong tradition of maintaining an openness to theology informed by context and confessions that are foundations of the faith but themselves not the ultimate authority. Here, the UCC finds not only a theological home but one where the strengths and sensibilities of a "united and uniting" church find easy repose.

The UCC is, however, more diverse than simply the Reformed tradition alone. It is also, as a united and uniting church, more than the sum of its parts. Our discernment as a church can never rest with only one part of our family. Recall if you will the words from Joachim Rogge in 1981: "Certainly we come together with different understandings of the church and with different political convictions. Yet, nevertheless, we are all one." Though he was speaking of the UCC and the EKU, those words certainly inform us within our own household as we seek to discern matters of the faith of utmost importance to how we relate to a complex world.

A critical task, as we seek "to make this faith [our] own," in every generation, is to engage matters of Christology in intentional dialogue with brothers and sisters in other parts of our church family, and, by virtue of our conviction as a united and uniting church, beyond our church family. Some perspectives will make us uncomfortable. Others will seem absurd. Still others will provide perspective that we did not even know we needed. As a church long engaged in mission efforts across the globe, we have no choice but to take seriously a wide variety of perspectives on who Christ is, how we name our faith as Christians working and living alongside those of other faith traditions, and how our profession of faith impacts those partners. Our local communities may be more self-consciously religiously diverse than in the past, but our mission activities always have been diverse. And who we are as a result of those engagements is another critical facet to our identity.

Further, if we are to continue to claim our vision, set forth in 1957 and given voice in many ways since then, of a church committed not only to the unity of the body of Christ but also to being agents of reconciliation and justice in God's world, holding in tension our piety and our action, it is imperative that we discern these matters rigorously. How we understand, and then live out, who Christ is for us will affect our relationships with each other and with partners in other faith traditions. And our relationships, both internal and external, have always mattered to us, because we cannot engage in reconciliation without them. I have suggested that voices from the Reformed side of our family can help us in that discernment, but all parts of the church must be engaged in the dialogue for the church to be healthy. This is "mutual affirmation and admonition" in the healthiest sense of those words.

Such a disposition toward discernment within community is indeed a reformed one its purest sense. It will not ever lend itself to simple answers, and in some cases, we as a church will need to be content with varying views, steadfastly maintaining our oneness in the face of our own diversity. But if we are to mature both as a church and as individuals within it, we must continue to take seriously the perspectives of the Word given us by God in the scriptures, of the faith of the ages in liturgy, the witness of the community of saints, the context in which we find ourselves, the lessons that history has taught us, and the partners with whom we share neighborhoods and nations. We do this encouraged by a church tradition that understands itself to be reformed and to always being reformed, making the faith of the ages our own in this day.

Who Jesus is has never been a static question for the church, but it has always been at the center of our lives, for it is what makes us who we are. How else are we to know what it is to "know Christ in the breaking of the bread?"[16]

CHAPTER FIVE

RECOGNITION AND THE PRESENCE OF CHRIST AT THE TABLE

JOHN H. THOMAS

The thing is there; not the name of the thing only, and not its sign or shadow; but the actual substance itself.
—John Williamson Nevin, *The Mystical Presence*

In those days Mary set out and went with haste to a Judean town in the hill country, where she entered the house of Zechariah and greeted Elizabeth. When Elizabeth heard Mary's greeting, the child leaped in her womb. And Elizabeth was filled with the Holy Spirit and exclaimed with a loud cry, "Blessed are you among women, and blessed is the fruit of your womb. And why has this happened to me, that the mother of my Lord comes to me? For as soon as I heard the sound of your greeting, the child in my womb leaped for joy. And blessed is she who believed that there would be a fulfillment of what was spoken to her by the Lord."
—Luke 1:39–45

The story of the "Visitation" in Luke's account of Jesus' birth places the question of Christ's presence before us in a striking narrative that serves multiple purposes. Elizabeth's greeting confirms the fact of Mary's miraculous conception of a child to be called "Lord." The relationship between Elizabeth's child, John, and Mary's child

Jesus anticipates their adult encounter at the Jordan. The vignette of the two pregnant women sharing a home for three months makes tangible the deep continuity between Israel's past—evoked by John's elderly parents serving at the Temple—and Israel's future—promised in the One who will reign over Jacob on the throne of his ancestor David. Structurally, the encounter sets up the canticle of joy and justice that Mary voices in the Magnificat, a song that names the salvific significance of Jesus in language recalling ancient longings while evoking contemporary oppressions. Finally, the wondrous leaping of John in Elizabeth's womb hints at his later ministry of preparation, much as generations before the wrestling of Rebekah's unborn twins, Jacob and Esau, foreshadowed their adult relationship.[1]

The Visitation is a narrative of recognition, the recognition of Christ's presence. While including interpretive words, at the center of the narrative is a physical sign, an action accompanied by the Holy Spirit. The movement of the unborn John transforms Mary's greeting into an encounter that makes plain to Elizabeth that she is dealing with more than theological concept, even with more than mere flesh and blood.

Interestingly, Luke's Gospel both opens and closes with recognition stories, each of which includes a significant physical action. The familiar Emmaus Road narrative involves two disciples who fail to recognize the presence of the risen Christ in their midst, even when he interprets to them the events of his passion in the context of the scriptures. Only the physical action of blessing and breaking and giving bread opens their eyes. Only then do they recognize Christ. Only then do words begin to take on significance and power: "Were not our hearts burning within us while he was talking to us?" (Luke 24:32).

It is not necessary to claim that Luke is intending to present a full-blown sacramental theology in his account, or to suggest that he is offering sacramental definitions relevant to our contemporary liturgical practices, to see that, for Luke, the presentation of the gospel necessarily includes accounts of physical action, that physical "things" are crucial complements to the stories of words spoken and heard. The final exchange between John and Jesus in Luke's account confirms this. The imprisoned John sends two of his disciples to ask Jesus, "Are you the one who is to come?" Jesus' response is to tell them, "Go and tell John what you have seen and heard." For John's disciples it is not just what they hear that will lead to recognition, but what they see: "the blind receive their sight, the lame walk, the lepers are cleansed, the deaf hear, the dead are raised, the poor have good news brought to them" (Luke 7:22).

However, for many members of the United Church of Christ today, the core text from Luke is probably neither the Visitation nor the Emmaus Road encounter. What often shapes our common witness is the story of the inauguration of Jesus' ministry in Nazareth as he reads from the scroll of Isaiah:

> The Spirit of the Lord is upon me, because he has anointed me to bring good news to the poor. He has sent me to proclaim release to the captives and recovery of sight to the blind, to let the oppressed go free, to proclaim the year of the Lord's favor. (Luke 4:18–19)

Here the scriptures are fulfilled in their—our?—hearing. Yet these other Lucan texts remind us that a close reading of even this one Gospel narrative challenges us to notions of presence and recognition that require more than words from and about—or memories of or reflection upon—Jesus. We are called to a ministry of word and sacrament; we are invited to liturgies where the pattern of word and sacrament is normative rather than occasional, where the rational is joined by mystery.

In the past twenty-five years, much of the Christological reflection taking place in the United Church of Christ has been shaped by a number of ecumenical dialogues and initiatives, including the Ecumenical Partnership between the United Church of Christ and the Christian Church (Disciples of Christ), the nine-church union effort called Churches Uniting in Christ (formerly the Consultation on Church Union), the process of responding to the convergence document of the World Council of Churches, "Baptism, Eucharist and Ministry," and the dialogues leading toward full communion between the Evangelical Lutheran Church in America and three Reformed Churches: the Presbyterian Church (USA), the Reformed Church in America, and the United Church of Christ. While much passionate debate has centered on the question of the ordering of ministry and the nature of episcope, equally foundational has been the question of the nature and significance of Christ's presence at the Table of the Eucharist.

The ultimate purpose of these dialogues, of course, is a fuller and richer visible expression of the unity of the church. But the dialogues have also forced the UCC to engage the "affirmations and admonitions"[2] of its partners, affirmations and admonitions that have roots in disputes rising out of the Reformation era between Catholic and Evangelical Christians, and then between Lutheran and Reformed Christians. Attentiveness to these affirmations and, in particular, to these admonitions has led to significant Christological reflection that has begun to shape liturgical practice and, through that, the piety of the UCC. At the same time, it has exposed aspects of our contemporary life and witness that lead to some of the caricatures and stereotypes we often find so offensive. As we explore those ecumenical encounters that have revolved around Christological questions, particularly in the Eucharist and the issue of the presence of Christ at the Table, they can help us, like Elizabeth, experience a deeper recognition, and with Mary, utter in word and deed a more profound song of justice and joy.

These questions are not, of course, new to the modern ecumenical movement or to the present members of the UCC. One finds them most prominently in our distinctive heritage in the theology of the Mercersburg movement founded at the Reformed Church's seminary in Mercersburg, Pennsylvania, in the middle of the nineteenth century. In his classic, *The Mystical Presence*, John Williamson Nevin describes on the first page of his treatise what was and remains at stake:

> As the Eucharist forms the very heart of the whole Christian worship, so it is clear that the entire question of the church, which all are compelled to acknowledge, the great life problem of the age—centers ultimately in the sacramental question as its inmost heart and core. Our view of the Lord's Supper must ever condition and rule in the end our view of Christ's person and the conception we form of the church.[3]

The Mercersburg theology of Nevin and his colleague Phillip Schaff, and the controversy that ensued, had much to do with the meaning of sacraments, the shape of the liturgy, and the nature of the church. For our purposes, it is important to note that the "evangelical catholicity" espoused by these theologians, and their liturgical reforms, was always in service to Christological concerns that lay at the core. As Nevin put it,

> We communicate—in the Lord's Supper—not with the divine promise merely, not with the thought of Christ only, not with the recollection simply of what he has done and suffered for us, not with the lively present sense alone of his all-sufficient, all-glorious salvation; but with the living Savior himself, in the

fullness of his glorified person, made present to us for the purpose by the power of the Holy Spirit . . . As such it is a real communion with the Word made flesh; not simply with the divinity of Christ, but with his humanity also . . . In the Lord's Supper, accordingly, the believer communicates not only with the spirit of Christ, or with his divine nature, but with Christ himself in his whole living person; so that he may be said to be fed and nourished by his very flesh and blood.[4]

For Nevin, this sacramental understanding is crucial for both Christology and ecclesiology: "Low views of the sacrament," he believed, "betray invariably a low view of the mystery of the incarnation itself, and a low view of the church also, as that new and higher order of life, in which the power of this mystery continues to reveal itself through all ages."[5] These "low views" associated with Zwinglian understandings of the sacrament, along with Nevin's interpretation of so-called Roman and Lutheran views, are to be avoided in favor of a "mystical" union:

[It] is not a corporal union, nor a mixture of substances . . . but spiritual and mystical; not merely mental, but including the real presence of Christ's whole life under an objective character, and reaching on our side also through the soul into the body; arising from the indwelling of the Spirit, not as the proxy only of an absent Christ, but as the supernatural bond of a true life connection, by which his very flesh is joined to ours, more intimately far than the trunk to is branches.[6]

Why is this sacramental understanding critical for salvation? Because for Nevin, salvation in Christ "is a new life." It is "not a doctrine merely for the mind to embrace. Not an event simply to be remembered with faith . . . Not the constitution only of a new order of spiritual relations . . . But a new life introduced into the very center of humanity itself."[7] And it is the sacrament that "certifies and makes good the grace it represents, as actually communicated at the time. So it is said to exhibit also the thing signified. *The thing is there*; not the name of the thing only, and not its sign or shadow; but the actual substance itself."[8]

To read Nevin is to be drawn back into the Reformation debates about the sacraments and, more importantly, the way they convey the saving grace of Christ's redemptive work. How is it that, to use Nevin's wonderful phrase, "the thing is there"? To read Nevin is also to anticipate ecumenical dialogues that continue to wrestle with the question of Christ's real or, as Nevin proposed, Christ's "true presence."[9] In 1982, the Faith and Order Commission of the World Council of Churches published the landmark study "Baptism, Eucharist and Ministry," culminating decades of ecumenical research and dialogue by Protestants, Orthodox, and Roman Catholics that began in Lausanne in 1927 at the inaugural Faith and Order Conference.[10] Central to the section on Eucharist is a recovery of the full meaning of the term anamnesis, or memorial as involving more than mere historical recollection. Thus, BEM states, "Christ himself with all that he has accomplished for us and for all creation (in his incarnation, servanthood, ministry, teaching, suffering, sacrifice, resurrection, ascension, and sending of the Spirit) is present in this anamnesis, granting us communion with himself."[11] BEM asserts, "The Church confesses Christ's real, living and active presence in the eucharist."[12]

In a commentary to the text the authors acknowledge continuing areas of debate where the "convergence" achieved still remains far removed from "consensus." Thus in a commentary on paragraph thirteen cited above, BEM says:

> Many churches believe that by the words of Jesus and by the power of the Holy Spirit, the bread and wine of the eucharist become, in a real though mysterious manner, the body and blood of the risen Christ, i.e., of the living Christ present in all his fullness. Under the signs of bread and wine the deepest reality is the total being of Christ who comes to us in order to feed us and transform our entire being. Some other churches, while affirming a real presence of Christ at the eucharist, do not link that presence so definitely with the signs of bread and wine. The decision remains for the churches whether this difference can be accommodated within the convergence formulated in the text itself.[13]

Each of the member churches of the World Council of Churches was asked to respond to BEM, stating "the extent to which your church can recognize in this text the faith of the church through the ages."[14] The United Church of Christ responded in 1985 by action of its Fifteenth General Synod in 1985.

On the key issue of Christ's presence, the United Church of Christ response addresses the continuing ambiguity of the meaning of "presence," affirming the "breadth of interpretation concerning 'the real, living, and active presence' of Christ," while at the same time acknowledging "the diversity . . . already experience[d] within the United Church of Christ." The response further cautions about too narrow an understanding of the way Christ's presence is manifest in the sacrament:

> We are concerned that this presence neither be identified exclusively with the elements of bread and wine nor associated rigidly with any one particular moment in the celebration, but that Christ's presence be understood in relation to the entire eucharistic action.[15]

In these few deft phrases, we can see the multiple traditions found in a church that brings together various expressions of the Reformed tradition (German, Swiss, Hungarian, English), along with Lutheran traditions, as well as Calvinist and Zwinglian streams in each. Even more, we can see the struggle with cultural influences, such as those Nevin was combating in his book *The Anxious Bench,* which tend to relegate presence to memory and salvation to the subjective experience of the converted, a presence and salvation to be conjured up through emotion rather than to be received in faith. How "the thing is there" was the key question for Nevin, and it remains an unresolved question in the UCC.

While the 1986 *Book of Worship: United Church of Christ* was not prepared in response to BEM, the ecumenical project is everywhere apparent in the introductions and the liturgical texts, as is the more distant horizon of the Mercersburg movement. Thus we read in the introduction to the Service of Word and Sacrament I:

> The invitation and call [to the supper] celebrate not only the memory of a meal that is past, but an actual meal with the risen Christ that is a foretaste of the heavenly banquet at which Christ will preside at the end of history.[16]

A variety of options provide for diverse convictions about the manner and mode and even "location" of Christ's presence in the sacrament. For example, when distributing the elements, one may say,

> "Take and eat, this is the body of Christ, broken for you";

or

> "The body of Christ, the bread of heaven" (Word and Sacrament I);

or

> "The body of Christ, the living bread," (Word and Sacrament II).

In the Communion prayer at the invocation of the Spirit, the prayers alternately ask God to:

> "send your Holy Spirit on this bread and wine, on our gifts, and on us";

or to

> "show forth among us the presence of your life-giving Word and Holy Spirit to sanctify us and your entire church through these holy mysteries, [granting] that all who share the communion of the body and blood of our risen Savior may be one in Jesus Christ" (Word and Sacrament I);

or to

> "bless this bread and cup and all of us with the outpouring of your Holy Spirit [and] through this meal make us the body of Christ, the church" (Word and Sacrament II).

Finally, the prayers of thanksgiving include:

> "unite us with all who are fed by Christ's body and blood";

and

> "we give you thanks that you have refreshed us at your table by granting us the presence of Christ" (Word and Sacrament I);

and

> "we thank you for Christ's presence and for the spiritual food of Christ's body and blood" (Word and Sacrament II).

If prayer both reflects and shapes belief, then great care has been taken to reflect diverse views about how Christ's presence is recognized at the Table, as well as to shape a Eucharistic piety. If the objective nature of the gift is affirmed—faith recognizes what is given, rather than effecting the gift itself—present practice in the United Church of Christ is not all that different from that of the old Prussian Union of the nineteenth century in Germany (transplanted to American soil in the Evangelical Synod of North America). This approach glossed over the differences between Reformed and Lutheran doctrines of the Eucharist by offering as the formula of distribution the simple words, "Our Lord Jesus Christ says, 'This is my body,'" a formula that leaves the meaning of presence open to the communicant's convictions.[17]

While the United Church of Christ was receiving a new *Book of Worship* and was in the midst of reflection on, and response to, the ecumenical convergence document "Baptism, Eucharist and Ministry," the church was also engaged in a thirty-year process of ecumenical dialogue bringing together several Lutheran and Reformed Churches in North America, which ultimately led to a declaration of "full communion" in 1998 between the Evangelical Lutheran Church in America, the Presbyterian Church (USA), the Reformed Church in America, and the United Church of Christ. Topics addressed during these years included diverse approaches to confessional commitment, ethics, ministry, and, of course, real presence. However, it was this last that dominated, as signaled unmistakably in the title of the report of the first round of dialogue in 1966: "Marburg Revisited: Lutheran-Reformed Consultation Series, 1962–1966," recalling the famous Colloquy in 1529 where Luther and Zwingli found themselves unable to agree on a formula for describing Christ's presence in the sacrament.

"Marburg Revisited" acknowledged that, while during the Reformation both traditions "exhibited an evangelical intention when they understood the Lord's Supper in the light of the saving act of God in Christ," "different terms and concept were employed which not only shared in the inadequacy of all human thought and language but also led to mutual misunderstanding and misrepresentation." It further suggested that "one-sided" teaching and practice in the churches over the intervening four centuries had the result of presenting the positions of Lutheran and Reformed as "contradictory" when, in fact, they were "often complementary."[18]

On the key issue the participants, including those from the UCC, were able to affirm:

> The sacrament is a form of visible, enacted word through which Christ and his saving benefits are effectively offered to men . . .
> The assurance of his presence is given in the self-witness of Christ in the instituting rite: This is my body, this is my blood. The realization of his presence in the sacrament is effected by the Holy Spirit through the word . . . The significance of Christology for the Lord's Supper is that it provides assurance that it is the total Christ, the divine-human person, who is present in the sacrament, but it does not explain how he is present.[19]

The report concluded with an admission that "a number of differing views and emphases remain to be resolved," but also affirmed that "we see no insuperable obstacles to pulpit and altar fellowship."[20]

A second series of dialogues held between 1972 and 1974 made little headway. It restated the conviction that

> there has existed and still exists a consensus among Lutheran and Reformed Churches concerning the following doctrinal points: The Lord's Supper is (1) a sacrament; (2) a means of grace, in which (3) the true (proper) body and blood of Jesus Christ are present and are eaten and drunk. Disagreement remains . . . concerning the mode of Christ's presence.[21]

Sensitivity to the volatile social and political context of the day—such as the Vietnam War and the Civil Rights movement—can be seen in a note of frustration that, for some in the dialogue,

> The basis of church fellowship cannot be in the settlement of sixteenth-century disputes about the Lord's Supper but in a common confessing of Jesus Christ in the face of contemporary issues facing our churches in America.[22]

A new element in the Lutheran-Reformed relationship was contributed by European churches with the signing of "The Leuenberg Agreement" in 1973 by Lutheran, Reformed, and United Churches. In the key sections on the Lord's Supper and Christology, Leuenberg states:

> In the Lord's Supper the risen Jesus Christ imparts himself in his body and blood, given up for all, through his word of promise with bread and wine. He thus gives himself unreservedly to all who receive the bread and wine; faith receives the Lord's Supper for salvation, unfaith for judgment. We cannot separate communion with Jesus Christ in his body and blood from the act of eating and drinking.[23]

The Christological consequences follow as Leuenberg affirms:

> In the true man Jesus Christ, the eternal Son, and so God himself, has bestowed himself upon lost mankind for its salvation. In the word of the promise and in the sacraments, the Holy Spirit, and so God himself, makes the crucified and risen Jesus present to us.[24]

In a commentary on the text of the Agreement, Marc Leinhard points out that two possible distortions are avoided:

On the one hand, the concept that would isolate the body and blood of Christ from the person of Christ and would make him a sort of 'celestial matter'; on the other hand, a spiritualist or docetist concept that would reduce the person to his spirit.[25]

Further, as Leuenberg itself affirms, the goal is to "give renewed and effective expression to the special insights of the Reformed tradition," described as a "concern to maintain unimpaired the divinity and humanity of Jesus, and those of the Lutheran tradition," described as a "concern to maintain the unity of Jesus as a person."[26]

None of the Lutheran or Reformed Churches involved in the North American dialogues were parties to Leuenberg and were, therefore, not asked to formally respond to it. Nevertheless, the third round of dialogue between 1981 and 1983 took place very consciously in the context of Leuenberg and in light of the question of whether "pulpit and altar fellowship" or "full communion" might be declared on the basis of the European achievement. The report of the third dialogue, "Invitation to Action," reaffirmed the agreements on "Marburg Revisited" and "The Leuenberg Agreement." While denying that "all differences in eucharistic doctrine between (and within) our two communions have thereby disappeared or become negligible," "Invitation to Action" maintained that "the remaining differences should be recognized as acceptable diversities within one Christian faith."[27]

In 1989 the General Synod of the United Church of Christ approved an extended response to "Invitation to Action" and, on the basis of that, "recognized" the several participating churches as "churches in which the Gospel is proclaimed and the sacraments administered according to the ordinance of Christ; recognized as both valid and effective the ordained ministry" of the participating churches; and "recognized the celebration of the Lord's Supper" in each of the participating churches "as a means of grace in which Christ grants communion with himself, assures us of the forgiveness of sin, and pledges life eternal . . ."[28]

One section of the UCC response reveals the continuing diversity of the church's convictions around the question of Christ's presence at the Table. Reporting on the work of several local study groups, the Response stated:

Some of our congregations and people do embrace Luther's understanding [of the real presence]. This is especially true for some rooted in the Evangelical Synod of North America. [Another] group highlighted the following: "The Mercersburg tradition brought a recovery of Reformed Eucharistic faith and advocated the sacramental unity and balance while affirming the mystical real presence of Christ in the whole sacramental act through the power of the Holy Spirit." [Yet another group] said, "Yankee Congregationalists desire to teach many different understandings of the meal and to build on all of them, rather than to exclude any." They continued, "For us, it is not simply a memorial feast, but an occasion of re-membering,' of joining ourselves to past, present, and future in the sacred feast. 'Then' becomes 'now' when the Church breaks the bread and pours the wine."[29]

While the UCC demonstrated its readiness to move toward full communion of pulpit and altar fellowship, decisions by the predecessor bodies of the newly formed Evangelical Lutheran Church in America—especially questions raised by the Lutheran Church in America given over to the new church—required an additional process of "theological conversations," which included detailed attention to issues of Christology and the presence of Christ. The report of this theological conversation was published in 1993 as "A Common Calling: The Witness of our Reformation Churches in North America Today."

The authors of "A Common Calling" carefully articulated Lutheran and Reformed emphases. Lutheran emphases included "the notion of the Lord's corporeal presence in the Supper through the Word," the "link between the Lord's true body and blood in the elements," the assertion "that even unbelievers or unworthy recipients eat and drink the true body and blood of Christ," "the ancient Christian teaching about the interchange of properties between the two natures of Christ," and the teaching of the "ubiquity of Christ's human and divine natures after the resurrection and the ascension." Reformed emphases included "the notion of the presence of the Lord in the Spirit as the mode of the presence of his body," "the distinction between the Lord's body and blood and the elements," saying that "bread and wine are signs of the presence," the role of "the Holy Spirit providing the bridge for faith between 'sign' and 'thing' in the Supper," the assertion of "the need for the distinction of Christ's human nature from his divine nature," and the "local circumscription of Christ's body in heaven."[30] Seeing these emphases as "complementary," the dialogue participants admonished both sides:

> Lutheran Christians need to understand and uphold the Reformed emphasis on the Spirit, the Trinitarian work of God, and

the assembly of the faithful. Reformed Christians need to understand and uphold the Lutheran insistence on the incarnational
paradox, the real Christ in bread and wine, and the objectivity of
God's gift in Word and Sacrament. Both sides must heed the
concerns of the partners, if not as a guide to their own formulations, then at least as no trespassing signs for the common forms
of the churches' witness to the reality of God's action in the Supper. It should be clear to everyone that Lutheran Christians do
not want to end up asserting a simple identity of the elements
with the body and blood of the risen Lord, and that Reformed
Christians do not want to be seen as celebrating the Supper
merely as a memorial.[31]

After four years of debate and discussion, in which both substantive issues as well as considerable caricature, stereotype, and simple resistance to move beyond Reformation era judgments surfaced,[32]
the four churches involved approved in 1997 a document titled "A
Formula of Agreement,"[33] which summarized the thirty years of dialogue, citing relevant portions of "Marburg Revisited," "Invitation to
Action," "A Common Calling," and particularly the key paragraphs
on Christology from "The Leuenberg Agreement." In 1998 representatives of each of the churches gathered in Chicago for a festive service of worship in which the formal acts of recognition were
accomplished and full communion declared.

While ecumenical agreements and declarations of full communion are important in themselves, the processes of theological dialogue, response, and reception that lead to these agreements are at
least as significant. Such has been the case in the Lutheran-Reformed
dialogues described above, their wider context in "Baptism, Eucharist
and Ministry," and the reception process that has accompanied this
landmark document. For the UCC, these dialogues and their reception processes have led to a renewed interest in the meaning and practice of the sacraments, to a deeper appreciation for the subtler
meanings of "memorial" and "remembrance" aided by the ecumenical
use of the term "anamnesis," and to a recovery of distinctive Reformed Christological understandings, now additionally read through
the complementary lens of Lutheran convictions and correctives.

One concrete illustration of this impact is found in worship
practice. In 1995 the United Church of Christ published *The New
Century Hymnal*. Included in this hymnal are the orders for Word and
Sacrament found in the *Book of Worship*, as well as a substantial in-
crease in the number of Communion hymns over predecessor hym-

nals. In addition to traditional and familiar texts, new texts were included that reflected converging ecumenical understandings of presence. For example, we find the hymn of the Iona Community, "The Time Was Early Evening."[34] Remembered events in each verse are made "present" in a refrain acknowledging the work of the baker and the winegrower as joined by the Savior's promise to meet disciples in the bread and wine. Or, in the compact text of the hymn "Jesus Is Here Right Now" by contemporary African American composer Leon C. Roberts, the peace of Jesus is here with the bread and wine.[35]

Classic Reformed themes articulated by the Mercersburg theologians are also present as in the post-Communion prayer of Henry Harbaugh, originally published in his confirmation resource, *The Golden Censer*, in 1860 and now recovered in the hymnal's section of liturgical resources:

> O God, who is eternal salvation and inestimable blessedness: grant to all your servants, we pray you, that we who have received things holy and blessed may be enabled to be holy and blessed evermore.[36]

As United Church of Christ theologian Lee Barrett puts it in an essay on the Lutheran-Reformed full-communion proposal:

> For Calvin the focus falls on the elevation of the soul, its spiritualization, rather than on the descent of God. It is God's plan to lift us up to God's self. Christ descended to earth so that we might ascend to heaven.[37]

As Harbaugh's prayer suggests, Christ's presence is intimately related to the communicant's sanctification.

If understandings of Christ's presence are reflected in and shaped by hymnody and prayer, so they are also acknowledged in confession. For United Church of Christ members, the most commonly used confessional statement about Christ is found in the UCC Statement of Faith:

> In Jesus Christ, the man of Nazareth, our crucified and risen Lord, God has come to us and shared our common lot, conquering sin and death and reconciling the whole creation to its Creator.[38]

Here the incarnational language of the Statement of Faith has us, to borrow Barrett's terms, looking through a characteristically Lutheran lens. "In the incarnation, God has descended—abased God's self—in order to establish solidarity"—shared our common lot—with sinful human beings."[39] In this case, ecumenical dialogue helps dissect the intentions of the authors of the Statement of Faith while giving greater "substance" or "content" to the believer's confession.

Gabriel Fackre, a UCC participant in the final round of theological conversations, identifies classic Lutheran and Reformed voices in the Lutheran accent of "Christ's continuing solidarity with us in ecclesial tangibilities," and the Reformed accent of "Christ's continuing sovereignty over us in both church and world."[40] Fackre calls attention to the old Reformation phrases that had been so determinative in the Lutheran and Reformed sacramental debates: *finitum capax infiniti* (the finite is capable of receiving the infinite) and *finitum non capax infiniti* (the finite is not capable of receiving or encompassing the infinite). In so doing, he helps enrich our understanding of "shared our common lot" with Dietrich Bonhoeffer's concept of "God's haveability," provisionally set forth in his 1931 book, *Act and Being*:

> In revelation it is not so much a question of the freedom of God—eternally remaining within the divine self-aseity—on the other side of revelation, as it is of God's coming out of God's own self in revelation. It is a matter of God's given Word, the covenant in which God is bound by God's own action. It is a question of the freedom of God, which finds its strongest evidence precisely in that God freely chose to be bound to historical human beings and to be placed at the disposal of human beings. God is free not from human beings but for them. Christ is the word of God's freedom. God is present, that is, not in eternal nonobjectivity but—to put it quite provisionally for now—"haveable," graspable in the Word within the Church.[41]

Few UCC members saying the Statement of Faith in congregational worship would be aware that their Christological confession was shaped at this point by a "Lutheran lens," let alone by the interpretation of the young Bonhoeffer. Nevertheless, the concept of God's solidarity is clear and ought to nurture a sympathy for sacramental understandings that are capable of bearing the weight of this incarnational reality. Or, as Nevin would say, "the thing is there."

UCC theologians, shaped by both Lutheran and Reformed heritage, would not want to ignore Christ's sovereignty in a full articulation of core Christological themes. So it is that Barrett encourages a complementary attentiveness to "a shift from trust in the reconciling solidarity of God with humanity to participation in Christ's life," and thereby reminds us that the Eucharist is not only "the presence of the incarnate God" but also "the vehicle of spiritual transformation."[42] Fackre, while conscious of the seductions of human arrogance inherent in a Reformed desire to transform society, nevertheless cautions Lutherans with a characteristic Reformed admonition:

> God is the Sovereign to whom we are accountable in society as well as in the church and the soul. Indeed, the regency of Jesus Christ extends over the marketplace and the counting house. As such, the systems and structures of this world must answer to Christ's own rule, not to lesser or more accommodating norms.[43]

So UCC members will join their confession in the Statement of Faith of God's promise of "forgiveness of sins and fullness of grace" with the accompanying and equally compelling promise of "courage in the struggle for justice and peace."

Decades of ecumenical engagement and encounter have encouraged many parts of the United Church of Christ to discover dormant elements of its sacramental practice and to fresh articulations of Christological understandings. Weekly Communion, desired by Calvin and encouraged by BEM, is still the exception rather than the rule in UCC congregations where the spoken Word prevails over the enacted Word. Nevertheless, official responses to BEM and to the Lutheran-Reformed dialogues have all expressed appreciation for the admonition regarding Communion frequency, and that appreciation is echoed by the prominence of the services of Word and Sacrament in the *Book of Worship*. More importantly, the liturgies of the *Book of Worship*, which increasingly serve as the norm by which local UCC congregations exercise their liturgical freedom and responsibility, have helped to reclaim the concept of anamnesis, which rescues the idea of presence from mere intellectual recollection and restores classic Lutheran and Reformed themes. As Barrett and Fackre show, the mixed theological heritage of the UCC is particularly receptive to a "bifocal" vision[44] that perceives God's solidarity and Christ's sovereignty as complementary elements of an adequate Christology, themes presented with fresh urgency in the several Lutheran Reformed dialogues.

This essay began with a reflection on Luke's account of the Visitation, and on the importance of "spirited" acts for conveying the reality of presence. It was the physical movement of John in Elizabeth's womb that led to recognition of the "presence" of Christ in Mary's womb. Likewise, it was the physical breaking of bread at Emmaus that led to recognition for the disciples who had clearly not recognized the risen Christ through words alone. Analogously, it has been ecumenical dialogue, even harsh debate, on the meaning of Christ's presence in sacramental acts that has opened up new or recovered understandings of the nature of Christ—who he is with and for us—thus deepening the import of our recognition and the power of our witness and confession. In part, this can be seen as vindication for the ecumenical work that is so often viewed as arcane and detached. Even more, it asks of the UCC to continue its attentiveness to Eucharistic practice, not for the sake of ecumenical accommodation, but for the faithfulness of its witness to the One who came to live among us, sharing our common lot.

In the end, of course, faithful recognition *of* implies a recognition *for*, and here the story of the Visitation is also suggestive. In the midst of the encounter between the mothers of John and Jesus, Luke inserts the Magnificat, a song of joy and of justice, both of which are evoked by Elizabeth's recognition of Christ's presence. For a tradition such as that of the United Church of Christ, which so identifies itself with the "lifting up of the lowly," with "filling the hungry with good things" and the attendant reversal of the world's categories of power, privilege, and prestige, faithful prophetic witness finds greater nourishment in the sacrament of Christ's real presence than in wordy imperatives sounding more of duty than of joy. The "scattering of the proud" and the "humiliation of the powerful from their thrones" requires far more than "the name of the thing" or "its sign and shadow," as if we might contend with the world or "resist the powers of evil" (Statement of Faith) armed only with the memory of Christ's words and deeds once upon a time in a place far away. No, such witness requires that "the thing is there," as it was for Mary and Elizabeth and the disciples and all who have followed—a recognizable presence of the crucified and risen Christ who is God come in solidarity to share our common lot, conquering sin and death, and reconciling the world to God's self, thus opening up dimensions of sovereignty and sanctification through "the presence of the Holy Spirit in trial and rejoicing, and eternal life in that kingdom which has no end."[45]

PART THREE

CONTEMPORARY ISSUES AND PRACTICES

CHAPTER SIX
PLURALISM AND MISSION
MARY SCHALLER BLAUFUSS

PLURALISM, MISSION, AND CHRISTOLOGY

"Mission is the Mother of Theology."[1] New Testament scholar
Martin Kähler's assertion is quoted often by missiologists trying to discern the nature of mission and to articulate the reality of God's interaction with the world. Kähler was not necessarily trying to assert the
primacy of one theological discipline over another, but was exploring
the nature of New Testament writings as living interactions with God
and God's action in the world. He claimed that New Testament writers "wrote in a context of an 'emergency situation' of a church which,
because of its missionary encounter with the world, was forced to
theologize."[2] This "missionary encounter" occurred as the writers interacted with the diversities of their world in trying to discern and witness to the nature, action, and purpose of God in the midst of that
pluralism.

Kähler's assertion reminds us that our articulations of God's
presence and action in the world (theology) take place in the midst of
our own participation in God's interaction with the diversities of the
world. In today's world, pluralism is a given. Our interaction with diversity is necessary. The way in which we negotiate this encounter
can be destructive, dominating, isolating. Or we can participate in
processes that lead to the creation of new possibilities for life that are
available for all, possibilities that are participatory and relation-

ship-building. The latter is the action of Christian mission. It is mission, as David Bosch articulates, that "gives expression to the dynamic relationship between God and the world."[3] It is mission that draws us and the world into that relationship.

This dynamic missionary discernment is particularly true in the articulation of Christology in which the pluralism of human and divine meet in the person of Jesus, in which Jesus historically interacts with the world in all of its complexities. The content and style of the encounter, the nature of the Christ discerned, and the mission enacted by Christ and in which Christ sends us are all wrapped up in a symbiotic relationship. This meeting with Jesus the Christ is a missiological encounter. It is an encounter that leads to mission.

Christological discernment always has taken place in the context of pluralism, but it has not always been mutually relational. Often our Christological discernment has been articulated in the midst of domination. It has been the outcome of encounters in which those with power in the church, in the society, and in government tried to determine and enforce a normative nature of Christ. Those who dominated were able to decide for all. Bosch reflects:

> The various church councils were intent on producing definitive statements of faith; their formulations were conclusive and final rather than references to the ineffable. The unity of the church was regulated by scrutinizing people according to whether or not they subscribed to these formulas. Those who did not were excluded by means of anathemas.[4]

Mission became an effort to bring uniformity and adherence, directed as much toward heretics "within the church" as to relating Christ with those outside the church.

But different kinds of interaction with diversity lead to a much different Christological discernment and to participation in a different kind of mission. Jesus' encounter with Martha in John 11 gives us another framework in which to explore an encounter with Jesus that is not dominating, but engaging; not propositional, but relational. Like other stories in John's Gospel, the story of Martha's confession of faith and Jesus' raising of Lazarus from the dead shows, rather than simply tells, the challenges and possibilities that arise from encountering Jesus.[5] The context of the encounter in Martha's social location on the periphery of society, her dialogical style of interacting, and Jesus' action in response to the encounter shape the nature of Christ discerned and the mission in which we are called to participate. It is an encounter that emerges from a Christ of interactive relationship. It is a Christ who brings about mutual relationships with one another and communion with God. It is a Christ who puts possibilities into practice for the purpose of a radical newness for all; that is, resurrection life. It is a Christ who "came that they may have life, and have it abundantly" (John 10:10) and involves us in the work for that transformation of life. As Marlene Perera, Franciscan Missionary of Mary, affirms from her experience as a Sri Lankan:

> The mission of the church and also ours is rooted in the mission of Jesus, who inaugurated the reign of God in the world among us human beings and from which we draw inspiration. The good news that Jesus entrusted to us is none other than participating in the saving action of God in history, bringing the whole of creation to fulfillment and the joyous proclamation and celebration of it.[6]

CHRISTOLOGICAL ENCOUNTER IN THE MIDST OF CULTURES OF DEATH

At the United Theological College in Bangalore, India, where I worked as a faculty member through the support of the Common Global Ministries Board of the United Church of Christ and Christian Church (Disciples of Christ), we asked students finishing their theological education to reflect on Christological questions in light of their emerging ministries in the church and society: "Who do people say that I am?" And then as they contemplated their anticipated ministries, "But who do you say that I am?" and "Do you believe this?"

Such questions of Christological discernment are especially important in India in the midst of situations of social stratification where people are excluded and discriminated against because of who they were born. Christological questions intersect with real life in a changing global economy that vanishes people who already are struggling for survival and who are left out of opportunities to experience an abundance of life. They are the questions to ask in the midst of religious pluralism where people experience different beliefs and where forces of religious nationalism cement certain forms of faith as the only acceptable identity for people, thus aligning them with a particular political power. They are the questions that are significant in the midst of cultural pluralism where people of different backgrounds might complement each other, coexist, or be in competition with one another.

These Christological questions, however, are not only for theological students in India. Nor is this pluralism the context only in India. All over the world and in each of our local contexts, we negotiate diversity and pluralism on a daily basis. Global issues are not abstract but are *local* issues somewhere, affecting people's lives. And local issues are global issues because we are all interconnected, especially in today's context of globalization in which time and space are compressed, and the interaction among different peoples, times and places is not only inevitable, but intensified.[7] This context for discerning the nature of Christ is our context, too.

In John 11, as Martha encounters Jesus and makes her confession of faith, the context is complex, revolving around despair and death. Many kinds of death comprise Jesus' return to Bethany. Lazarus had been sick for some time and now has died. Mary and Martha are grieving, and friends have come out from Jerusalem to console them—though Jesus delayed. Jesus' own life has been threatened if he goes back to Jerusalem, and yet he continues to head that way. The disciples, led by Thomas, the Twin, have decided to accompany him, realizing, that this act may mean they need to die with him.

Death defines the context of the encounter, but it is not just the suffering and death of an individual. Mary and Martha are grieving in the midst of the community that also has been affected by Lazarus' death. They grieve together. When Martha and Mary and the people encounter Jesus, he becomes part of a whole community of suffering, living in the shadow of death. Though Jesus' later encounter with Martha is face-to-face and personal, even that encounter is not individualized because Martha's situation is intimately connected to Mary's grief.

The suffering that sets the scene for Martha's confession of faith is present in the contexts of death that define so much of our world today: in the utter hopelessness of the young woman who takes her own life because she cannot face returning to her parents' home and she cannot stand the violence she endures with her husband; in the destruction of the lives of children and young women who are trafficked from villages or across national boundaries and put to commercial sex work; in the despair of the three-year-old girl who is infected with the HIV virus passed on by her mother, who has now developed AIDS, and her father, who already has died of the disease; in the genocide and obliteration of whole populations as others consolidate their own power; in the militarization in which people live as refugees within their own homeland; in those who watch their babies starve because resources have been used for guns instead of food. Contexts of death allow discrimination, exclusion, and powerlessness to be the norms of societies' structures rather than their exceptions. The world knows this context of death all too well.

Encounter in the Peripheries that Transcends Social Limitations

The missiological question, then, is what is our interaction with this context of death: acceptance, embrace, passivity, apathy, resignation? Or can our very style of relating, as Martha's, make this a life-giving missiological moment? The style of Martha's encounter with Jesus corresponds to the nature of the Christ she discerns and confesses.[8] It is dialogical in that each listens and speaks. It is reciprocal in that both are engaged and even changed. We often think of dialogue as a formal discussion with well-formulated questions and responses. Martha's dialogue with Jesus here is much more part of an informal "dialogue of life," full of commitment, passion, and expectation.

Martha has set out with a commitment to encounter Jesus. She is disturbed by the death that surrounds her. She is ready to confront Jesus with the promises of faith and what they mean for her life and the world. She is willing to transgress the social limitations placed on her and to encounter a radical newness.

As a woman, Martha's gender—and the resulting social limitations of her time and place—are significant for her encounter with Jesus and who she discerns the Christ to be and to do. In a culture, like so many others, where women are praised for their silence and passivity, Martha exercises none of those characteristics. Martha moves outside of the familiar surroundings of home. She goes out beyond the boundaries of friendship circles that have gathered to console her. She moves beyond comfort zones that insist she conform to social norms. She goes *out* to meet Jesus.

And when she does meet him, Martha has a few things to say: "Lord, if you had been here, my brother would not have died" (John 11:21). Her passion is unmistakable. Her commitment to Jesus' ministry that brings life is certain. But things have not worked out as she would have liked, and she is going to let Jesus know that she will not take this turn of events passively. She will fight against death with all that she is. "But even now," she continues, "I know that God will give you whatever you ask" (John 11:22).

The location of this Christological encounter—on a road outside Bethany, outside Jerusalem—is symbolic of the stratifications present within any society. The proximity to Jerusalem places the events close to the seat of power and, therefore, in a dangerous place for Jesus. But it is clear that this is a village on the periphery, not a place where the center of the world's action is located. It is not in Washington, Nairobi, Baghdad, or Delhi, but a village outside the city—actually on the path outside the village. It is here that Martha encounters Jesus and discerns the Christ, on the peripheries of the Hebrew community's stratification.

Intracultural stratifications exist within any society, dividing people into hierarchies, hiding certain people at the peripheries. Those people on the periphery are often the ones who discern most clearly the Christological encounter as a relationship with the one coming into the world to bring fullness of life to all. Mercy Amba Oduyoye from Ghana articulates this in her reflection on the way that members of the Women's Commission of Ecumenical Association of Third World Theologians (EATWOT) responded to the question, "Who is Jesus?" She observes the power of the peripheries: "The theology starts from the peoples' struggle for justice, fullness of life, and loving, caring relationships."[9]

This peripheral location of the encounter is often a difficult thing for middle-class Christians to admit. It is easier to relate to others of the middle class cross-culturally than to relate to someone across the stratifications of class within a single culture. Bosch reflects,

> The historical gap of two millennia between our time and the time of Jesus may turn out to be of less importance than the social gap that separates today's middle-class elite from the first Christians or, for that matter, from many marginalized people today.[10]

Locating Christ in the peripheries of those who are marginalized causes us to understand fullness of life and abundance of life in light of those are the most vulnerable. During my years of living in the Indian context, I came to realize that life "in the style to which I am accustomed" was actually harmful and life-taking for others. What made my life easier was not necessarily life-giving for others. The criteria of "life" for those who were most vulnerable meant that my life needed to be wrapped up with the well-being of those who suffer. This meant judging the criterion of "life" by how a Dalit woman working in the unorganized sector of Indian society as domestic help was treated. This meant that the well-being of the child who must beg in the street determined my own.

The Jesus whom Martha encounters, and the nature of the Christ she confesses, is the Christ who makes possible a "fullness of life." He is the one working to make people and places no longer pe-ripheral. Jesus began his earthly ministry with an announcement of his purpose:

> The Spirit of the Lord is upon me, because he has anointed me to bring good news to the poor. He has sent me to proclaim release to the captives and recovery of sight to the blind, to let the op-pressed go free, to proclaim the year of the Lord's favor. (Luke 4:18–19)

David Bosch suggests that much of Jesus' ministry took place in the way he broke through and rearranged many of its internal social stratifications. "Jesus' 'self-definition' was such that he consistently challenged the attitudes, practices, and structures which tended arbi-trarily to exclude certain categories of people from the Jewish commu-nity."[11] Bosch calls mission the "provocative, boundary-breaking nature of Jesus' own ministry."[12]

John Dominic Crossan's work on discerning the historical Jesus in the New Testament has an extended discussion about the role of commensality in Jesus' ministry that complements Bosch's assertion. "Commensality" says Crossan, is "not just almsgiving but a shared ta-ble."[13] In other words, Jesus and his disciples engaged in a ministry of mutuality that broke through many local hierarchies that stratified people into givers and receivers, agents and objects of mission. In a context in which food was a major way of marking social groups, Crossan observes that "They [Jesus and the disciples] share a miracle and a kingdom, and they receive in return a table and a house."[14] He reminds us of Jesus' primary focus in his earthly ministry in the local community and notes how the most difficult thing to do (and one that Jesus did with great regularity) is to cross the threshold of a peasant—to break those stratifications within our own cultures:

The mission we are talking about is not, like Paul's, a dramatic thrust along major trade routes to urban centers hundreds of miles apart. Yet, it concerns the longest journey in the Greco-Roman world, maybe in any world, the step across the threshold of a peasant stranger's home.[15]

The Christological starting point, therefore, is not the certainty of the center, but the ambiguity of the periphery. People who are on the periphery of society are the ones who lead in this encounter of discernment and mission. Jesus announces that ministry in the peripheries, and then embodies it in all he says and does. He embodies that boundary-challenging mission by taking Martha's confrontation so seriously that he engages her in theological dialogue that results in Martha's confession of faith and Jesus' action that transforms life.

Jesus' Self-Identification Transforms Our Relation to Religious Pluralism

It is in the midst of this dialogue that Jesus articulates his identity and purpose.

"Your brother will rise again," Jesus tells Martha.

"Yes," she agrees, repeating all of the foundational theological ideas of her time and tradition: "I know that he will rise again in the resurrection on the last day."

But the reinforcement of old ideas is not what Jesus intends, not "someday he will rise again" as an abstract theological adage. Instead, he translates that assumption into personal identity and immediate action: "I am the resurrection and the life," he announces. Jesus takes what Martha knows, her experiences, her religious-cultural tradition, and transforms it by translating it into the complexity of the concrete and the personal—himself and his relation with the world.

This new, concrete, and personal type of relationship that has life as its reason for being is also the basis for a new type of relationship of Christians with people of other faiths. It is a missiological question because it deals with how we meet diversity. It is a Christological question because the relation of Christians with those of other faiths emerges from our encounter with Jesus and the nature of Christ we confess. A Christian theology of religious pluralism is one of the most important challenges of our day. As cultures, economies, and polities come into closer and more intense contact with one another through the forces of globalization, we are more aware than ever of the reality of religious pluralism. Those encounters are often competitive and destructive, more about building walls than building relationships. But this self-identification of Jesus the Christ leads us to a different type of encounter with others: one that takes old ideas that have become abstract and doctrinal, and transforms them into interactive relationships that operate within the complexities of actual situations of life.

It is interesting to note that three broad categories of Christian attitude to those of other faiths—exclusivism, inclusivism, and pluralism—have all used Jesus' self-identification in John 11:25–26 to represent their point of view. Exclusivists, who hold that the truth of Christ excludes all others, claim that this identity statement excludes from life all who do not intentionally profess a belief in Christ. Inclusivists, who leave room for the mystery of God to work in other religions, utilize this identification to advocate interfaith cooperation on particular issues. In the final analysis, they believe the fullness of life comes through Christ. Pluralists, who say that God cannot be limited or encircled by any one tradition, recognize this as a faith claim for Christians but contend that it is not necessarily normative for others.[16]

Typologies, however, rarely describe the complexity of perspectives. The story in John 11 addresses different questions than we are asking of it in these contemporary Christological controversies.[17] Jesus does not seem to be making a comparison with other faiths, but affirming a type of new relationship with God and one another. Jesus says nothing about what might happen to others; he makes only the affirmative statement of "the new and the now"—the resurrection and the life.[18] It is an affirmation that Jesus' purpose of life is more powerful even than contexts of death.

In light of Jesus' affirmation of the power of life over death, the most life-giving Christological formulations are those that do not fit neatly into any of the three broad typologies, but keep several things in tension. Stanley Samartha, S. Mark Heim, and O. V. Jathanna offer three such perspectives.

Stanley Samartha, first director of the World Council of Churches' Sub-Unit on Dialogue, articulates a Christology that situates itself in the midst of these tensions. He suggests that Christians move from a "normative exclusivism" toward an understanding of the "relational distinctiveness" of Christ. His view takes seriously the difference in religions and the particular identity of Christ, but does not require a negative attitude toward people of other religions. Neither does it turn dialogue into a means by which to convince others of the normativeness of Christ for all. Samartha emphasizes the relational possibilities of a theocentric Christology that does not try to figure out the mystery of how God is working in multiple ways and by multiple means. He says,

> It is relational because Christ does not remain unrelated to neighbors of other faiths, and distinctive because without recognizing the distinctiveness of the great religious traditions as different responses to the Mystery of God, no mutual enrichment is possible.[19]

Samartha's Christological articulation of "relational distinctiveness" emphasizes an open and mutual Christology that works well in situations where Christians are in a position of power. It does not, however, do as well in addressing situations where people of other faiths are not in favor of that openness or mutuality, or where "the playing field is not equal" in terms of power. Whereas for Samartha himself, one's Christological understanding leads to this type of relation with others, in the actual interaction, that overt Christological confession is moved to the background.

To this concern, Mark Heim suggests an "Inclusivist Pluralism" that takes seriously the difference between religions in terms of their religious ends and does not try to force a Christian understanding of salvation on others. He does, however, take the overt Christological confession as important for Christians in their interaction with others:

> The decisive and universal significance of Christ is for Christians both the necessary ground for particularistic witness and the basis for recognizing in other religious traditions their own particularistic integrity.[20]

O. V. Jathanna articulates an attitude toward people of other religions he names "critical inclusiveness." Like those of Samartha and Heim, this approach takes seriously the real diversity of religions, "stressing the need to take seriously cultures, religions and ideologies other than one's own by being in direct living and listening touch with them."[21] Because the embrace of all takes place in the midst of real-life complexities of the relation between living faiths, it avoids sweeping generalizations, good or bad, about people of any religion. Instead, it makes ongoing relationship and mutual interaction important means and goals of the Christological intention identified by Jathanna as *agape* love. Jathanna insists on a critical element in "embracing one and all while rejecting all theoretical and praxial elements that go against the *agapeic* lifestyle and thought pattern, in the light of the Christ-event."[22] Although Jathanna's articulation of inclusiveness still relies on an implicit attitude of Christian superiority, "critical inclusiveness" becomes a way to affirm our identity as Christians in Christ and the importance of Christ's work without cutting off or truncating the very relationships Christ's work tries to make real in the world. "It helps us to be rooted in faith and to remain/become open in hope in the unity of the all-embracing self-giving love of the triune God."[23]

I believe that a Christian theology of religious pluralism necessitates an articulated Christological commitment. Religions are different and a realization of that diversity needs to be affirmed as part of the Christological discernment and confession. Diversity then can create opportunities for openness to substantive change in our understanding about what that Christological identity means for ourselves and the world. The mutuality in this kind of committed interaction includes honest and open witness, as well as critique and encouragement of one another. It is a reciprocal dialogue that includes cooperation on issues of justice, the understanding of which is discerned in that interaction. Such Christological commitment is the possibility to participate in God's transformation of the world toward life. Jesus as "the resurrection and the life" is the one who makes the new relationships of life concrete and personal, real and immediate.

Martha's Confession Leads to Jesus' Action

Martha hears Jesus' self-identification, but it is not enough only to listen to Jesus. The interaction requires a commitment. And so it is that Martha responds to Jesus' articulation of his purpose for life with a confession of faith of her own.

"Martha, do you believe this?"

Martha replies, "Yes, Lord, I believe that you are the Messiah, the Son of God, the one coming into the world."

Hers is a confession in the midst of difficult circumstances. It is a confession of faith in a life that is qualitatively different from anything people have experienced before. Often, Christian missiology speaks of "uplift" of people, a betterment of their condition, a measure of progress in people's lives. This is all well and good, but with this model of progress there will always be stagnation. There will always be relapse. Instead, Martha is confessing that the one standing before her, whom she has just confronted, is the Messiah—the one who enacts the new. He is the one who actually recasts death with life.

It is in the wake of this confession that Jesus acts his identity into being. He goes to the tomb of Lazarus, orders the stone taken away, and says in a loud voice, "Lazarus, come out!" It is an impossible situation. Lazarus has been dead four days. Martha points out that the stench is there to prove the finality of this death. Although Martha just has made an astounding confession of Jesus as the one who embodies and enacts the newness of God, she still does not completely understand the implications of that newness.

The reality of death and the newness of life are always comingled in the reality of our world. Sometimes even though we believe in "the new and the now," it is difficult to see those glimpses of life in the midst of death. And yet, in response to Jesus' power of the newness, the fullness of life, Lazarus emerges from the tomb.

Today, struggle and death continue to define our world, and yet, from the perspective of the poor in Latin America, Elsa Tamez identifies glimpses of this radical newness when she confesses her experience of the reign of God in their midst:

> The situation cannot continue as it is, impoverishment and exploitation are not God's will, but now there is hope, resurrection, life, change. The reign of God, which is the reign of justice, is at hand.[24]

Lazarus' resurrection becomes a prefigurement of what Jesus makes possible for all in his own death and resurrection. This abundant life is not just a future hope, but today's possibility. The new becomes reality in our midst now. Jesus Christ universalizes and eternalizes that specific action of life-giving transformation. The "one coming into the world" works in the midst of the hopelessness and death of static peripheries. The Son of God makes those limitations incompatible with the reality he acts into being.

MISSION IS THE MEANS OF THE ENCOUNTER AND ITS CONTINUATION

Mission has been taking place all along in this text. Jesus' entry into situations of death as the "one coming into the world" is mission. Martha transcending limitations of social expectations to go out to meet Jesus on the peripheries of society is mission. Jesus' self-identification as the one who embodies traditional theological formulas and transforms them into the catalyst for interfaith relationship and cooperation that embodies the "fullness of life" is mission. Martha's confession that commits her to this vision and gives her a glimpse of this newness is mission. The dramatic raising of Lazarus through which Jesus acts his identity into being is mission. And the means of this encounter are mission because all of these aspects are drawing people into communion with God and closer to one another in new and life-giving ways.

Even as Lazarus is raised, mission continues. Communion is extended as Jesus draws us into participating in the very creation of that newness. Jesus draws Martha into closer communion with God as she sees the glory of God in this act. Resurrection enacts and embodies the promises of abundant life and eternal life for all humanity. Relation with Christ is now a continuing possibility and that relation can be unending.[25] And in that continuing relationship, we all are given the opportunity to see the glory of God.

Jesus also draws the crowd into the significance of the encounter as Martha makes her confession and Lazarus is raised. In Jesus, they, too, have connected with God. Jesus looks upward as he raises Lazarus and says, "Father, I thank you for having heard me. I knew that you always hear me, but I have said this for the sake of the crowd standing here, so that they may believe that you sent me."

Jesus can identify himself as the one who makes real relationships of life for the world because of his divine identity in relation to the Trinity. Christ is not Christ alone, but within the relationships of the Trinity. The very nature of God is diverse persons interacting with one another in mutual relationships that are a communion of love. Constance Tarasar, member of the Orthodox Church in America says,

> All three persons are fully and completely united, acting as one, with one will, always together and freely cooperating with one

another. And yet, each acts differently in relation to human persons and to the world.[26]

Christ as the incarnation of these divine relationships is their embodiment as well as the catalyst for their extension into the world. This is what Mark Heim speaks about as salvation. Christ is constitutive of salvation as an expression of the triune life of God. "Christ is one who comes from the triune life into human life but also one who brings human life into its fullest participation in the triune life."[27] In announcing his identity as the one who is the "resurrection and the life," and embodying and enacting that identity through the raising of Lazarus and finally his own death and resurrection, Jesus draws the crowd into the experience of that communion: "*so that they may believe that you sent me.*" Jesus gives them the opportunity to live that communion in relation with one another and the wider world.

Jesus also draws the people into this communion by making them integral to the action itself. "Unbind him. Let him go," commands Jesus. Just so, Jesus sends us to get our hands dirty; to work in the nitty-gritty of people's lives in particular situations. And in doing that we participate in the new life Christ brings.

Martha's confession helps inform our own by living the interrelationship between how we encounter Jesus and who we discern the Christ to be. Her confession gives us the framework in which to articulate the nature of Christ we encounter as the one who embodies radical relationships of dialogue and mutuality. This Christ is the one who will not "settle" for the powers of death and despair nor only talk about them. In his self-declaration, "I am the resurrection and the life," Jesus acts that identity into being by raising Lazarus from the dead. He universalizes and immortalizes resurrection life through his own death and resurrection. And it is this Christ who sends us out in mission to embody the continuation of that mission. We are sent to make the good news of that new life real in the world today—"the new and the now."

CHAPTER SEVEN

IDENTITY AND ETHICAL PROCLAMATION
DEIRDRE KING HAINSWORTH

"God is still speaking." This simple claim has become the slogan for our denomination's identity and outreach efforts as the twenty-first century begins. Throughout our history as a denomination, the conviction that God is indeed still speaking and active in this world, calling us to raise our voices to speak for justice, has been a hallmark of our public witness.

"God has spoken decisively in Jesus Christ." This claim, as well, is part of our heritage. The Preamble to the Constitution of the United Church of Christ clearly proclaims this as the cornerstone of our UCC identity: "The United Church of Christ acknowledges as its sole Head, Jesus Christ, Son of God and Savior." From this basis, the UCC Constitution acknowledges kinship with the faith of the "historic Church," from the earliest creeds to the work of the Protestant Reformers. The church's self-appointed task was also clearly laid out in this uniting document in 1957:

> [The UCC] affirms the responsibility of the Church in each generation to make this faith its own in reality of worship, in honesty of thought and expression, and in purity of heart before God.[1]

How do we connect these claims in the UCC today? How does our denomination's passionate, public work for justice and emphasis on inclusion today stand in living relationship with this historic faith and, more importantly, in a living relationship with the church's cornerstone and head, Jesus Christ? How are our stances on ethical and social issues rooted in the practice of Christology, in sustained theo-logical reflection on the person and work of Jesus Christ? How well do we open that process of faithful reflection to our members and to the ecumenical community, particularly in this time when "Christian" public discourse is often either narrowly conceived or reduced to increasingly conservative and socially exclusive agendas?

Renewed attention to Christology is a necessary starting point for our ethical reflection and a necessary grounding for our prophetic task in this world. Recent UCC public statements on ethical issues re-fer to Jesus as a prophet and Jesus as an example, but largely overlook the powerful implications of Jesus as the Christ, as God incarnate. Only reflection on the fullness of God's work in Jesus Christ, con-fronting us with both a moral example and a decisive event in history, can connect the call to justice with the real hope for transformation, and can reveal the bridge between our lives and the restoration of community and creation.

THE BIBLICAL ROOTS OF CHRISTOLOGY

The starting point for Christian reflection and faith is what has been revealed to us. We are hearers, discerners, people who reflect upon God's being and action. Although in our relationship of faith we have personal experience of God, we have no secret knowledge of God, nor some additional source of information. Rather, we must rely for knowledge of God on God's own gracious self-revelation to us: through our experience, through our discerning reading of God's work in our hearts and in the world, and through the attestation of our historical human experience of God's self-revelation, recorded in the witness of scripture. In Christian theology this knowledge has rested on an affirmation that in scripture we have received a reliable and trustworthy witness to what God is really like.[2] Scripture offers a witness to God persistently in relationship with us, with humankind: reaching out through creation, through speech, through Law, through prophets and the call to justice; in Jesus Christ, engaging in direct, warm human relationship and acting on our behalf; through the intimacy of the Holy Spirit with human hearts and minds.

Within this witness Jesus Christ stands as the fullest revelation of God's character. Jesus Christ is the center of Christian life and history. And so Christian theological and ethical reflection turns to the New Testament and begins with the Gospel accounts of the life of Jesus of Nazareth. On one level, these texts offer a selective historical narrative: an account of three years of the life of a young Galilean Jew, a carpenter who emerged as an itinerant interpreter of Jewish Law and attracted followers through his performance of healings and other apparent miracles, as well as his willingness to serve and minister to others, regardless of their perceived social worth. He was perceived as a threat by religious and civil leaders in Roman-ruled Jerusalem, was killed by crucifixion, and was claimed to be resurrected and to be the Messiah by his followers. On another level, the events told by the Gospel texts have been redacted to illustrate a central claim that pervades the New Testament writings: that the itinerant Jew of Nazareth was in reality the Son of God, sent by the God of creation and covenant to offer a clear revelation of God's character and purposes, to the point of accepting death as a human as part of overcoming death's power over creation.

In the Gospel accounts Jesus is presented not as a new God, but as living in a complex relationship with the God Israel already knew through covenant, Law, and prophecy. Throughout the Gospels, Jesus refers to God intimately as "Father" and describes himself as a representative sent by God the Father, a means to knowledge of God, sharing in God's power and in the work of creation and salvation. The Gospels attest to the particular divine activity of Jesus Christ, who declares himself "the resurrection and the life," and "the way and the truth and the life," and refers to his particular tasks of preaching and salvation as well as his return in the future consummation. Jesus places this self-revelation historically in the context of God's ongoing covenant with Israel, through the fulfillment of prophecy concerning the expectation of the coming of a Christ or a Messiah, as well as in ongoing relationship with the church and world through the coming of the Spirit as God's continuing presence after his death and resurrection.

The Gospel writers and early Christian missionaries, including the Apostle Paul, developed the first Christological reflections in the very drafting and redacting of their texts. They sought to explain Jesus' identity and significance, both within the context of the religious convictions and assumptions of first-century Judaism and within the complex philosophical worlds of Greek and Roman society. Just as each Gospel writer emphasized a slightly different aspect of Jesus' ministry and significance, Paul and other apostles emphasized Jesus as the "new covenant," amplifying and relativizing the Law and opening up relationship with God and salvation on the basis of faith, rather than membership in the covenant people of Israel.

CHRISTOLOGY:
JESUS AS BOTH "EXAMPLE" AND "EVENT"

Today, we stand as heirs to this early Christological work, with its multifaceted picture of Jesus Christ. This is the starting point for our consideration of faith and action, the window through which we view and experience both God and world. Taken together, the New Testament accounts confront us with Jesus Christ as both "example" and "event."

The example of Jesus shines through the Gospel accounts. The incarnation has been described as a revelation "fitted" to humanity: God's purposes and character expressed in a way human beings could perceive and understand. The revelation in Jesus Christ has this comprehensible character as an example for human beings because it is God's self-disclosure through the basic events of human life. In Jesus' encounters with the Pharisees and others who questioned his interpretation of Torah Law, he repeatedly returned to the connection between adherence to the Law and attention to the basic needs of all in the community. Rather than an account of Jesus concerned only with spiritual matters, the Gospels portray a Jesus who amplified an earlier prophetic tradition in which spiritual health and relationship with God was embodied and expressed in remarkably concrete ways. The discourse of Jesus in the Gospels is similarly revealing in a way fitted to his hearers' understanding. The stories told by Jesus pertain to events and examples hearers would have understood: fishing, farming, and family.

Yet because of the very particularity of person and location, Christians have wrestled with difficult questions of the relevance of Jesus' "example," debating over "the scandal of particularity": issues raised by the fact that the Gospels show a Jesus, God incarnate, as male rather than female, Jewish rather than Gentile, and so on. In Christian theology the incarnation located in Jesus of Nazareth has at times been read very narrowly as privileging male over female as a more complete reflection of the image of God and Christ. In the twentieth century, the insights of feminist and other liberation theologians have highlighted aspects of the Gospels that emphasize other views of Jesus Christ—Jesus as the founder of a new community, for example, and Jesus as a model of egalitarian, inclusive human action—while downplaying Christian ascriptions such as "Lord" as too liable to promote hierarchical arrangements among humans.[3] Other interpretive issues have been raised by the distance in time and place between the Gospel accounts and contemporary events. Cultural and social differences abound between first-century Palestine and the world in the twenty-first century.[4]

Because of these challenges raised by the very particularity of Jesus' identity, it is tempting to avoid them by focusing not on the person but on the earthly acts of Jesus, acts that illumine a life of moral integrity and solidarity with the vulnerable—a life and example that, in embodying obedience to the calls of the prophets, becomes prophetic itself. Yet these acts are only part of God's self-revelation and action in Jesus Christ. A faithful Christology must take account of both the actions of the incarnate God in Jesus Christ and the fact of the incarnation itself: moving beyond Jesus as "example" to Jesus as "event." The "event" of Jesus Christ is, simply, the fact of incarnation, crucifixion, and resurrection within salvation history. Our reading of history of human aims must be done within the understanding that we live in a creation and sweep of time that God not only created, but also has chosen to redeem through Jesus Christ. Through this particularity and fact of incarnation, God did not merely provide another example for our actions, but rather caught up all of human embodied existence in God's life for God's own purposes of judgment and restoration.

Since the early centuries of the church, the event of the incarnation, crucifixion, and resurrection in Jesus Christ has raised a series of controversies. In the first few centuries, doctrinal controversies centered on the common divine identity of father and son, highlighting not just the particularities of location and gender, but the "scandal of the incarnation" itself. Resting on a presumed essential opposition of spirit and matter, proponents of various forms of docetism rejected the idea that Jesus could be truly human. This had implications for the reality of the resurrection as a less-than-truly human Jesus could not have truly died. Others resolved the difficulties of spirit versus matter, and the implications of incarnation within an imperfect world, by positing two distinct Gods: a God of creation, attested to in the Hebrew scriptures and responsible for now decaying physical existence, and the God of Jesus of Nazareth, a separate God with a distinct purpose. In this view Jesus was detached from the larger sweep of divine history, only apparently human, and actually representative of the new, good God, the severing the connection between old and new covenant.[5]

The early church correctly resisted attempts to "protect" the divine identity of Jesus from being sullied by contact with the physical realm, emphasizing Jesus Christ as truly human and truly divine in the ecumenical creeds of the fourth century. Indeed, the act of choosing incarnation through Jesus reveals God to us as much as do the events of that incarnate witness itself. God chose to take on human form, risk human rejection, and face human death as a way of restoring relationship with humanity; incarnation was not incidental but central and necessary to the work of salvation. Christian churches have traditionally affirmed that in the incarnation, rather than God's divinity being harmed by the encounter with the physical and human, human embodied existence was itself hallowed and reclaimed by God.

The UCC and the Challenge of a Common Identity

It is precisely this gracious action of God to inhabit and reclaim creation and human life that makes attention to social and ethical matters a central task of Christian faith. The United Church of Christ, throughout its history, has taken on this task, and, indeed, the foregoing account of Christology is drawn from the historical theological resources that are our heritage in the UCC. In our founding documents as a denomination, we have more particularly located ourselves within the Reformed tradition, a tradition committed to the truth of the historic ecumenical creeds, the central and authoritative role of scripture, and the responsibility and privilege of each believer to engage in his or her own discernment of right action and right belief before God.[6] Our UCC Statement of Faith recognizes Jesus Christ as divine and human, the locus of salvation for us and central to God's overall work of salvation and restoration in creation.[7] A focus on public prophetic speech and action for justice, common to each of the constituent UCC denominations, has been a mark of our common life and witness since 1957, and remains central to our denominational self-identity.

However, while the United Church of Christ has a definite public identity, and shares a common theological heritage, in practice it has no requirement that an individual congregation adhere to a given doctrine or support a particular social or ethical position. Individual churches in the UCC exist in covenantal relationship with one another. Each, by virtue of its continued membership in the UCC, assents to remain in continued covenantal relationship under the Constitution of the UCC. Each congregation, as well, finds its own way of connecting its theological principles somehow with the most basic confessions and texts shared by the larger denomination, whether in its current practices or in its historical traditions. The denomination's web site, for example, leads those interested in UCC theology to a compilation of historic church creeds and statements that are described as "testimonies, not tests" of faith.[8]

This approach allows significant diversity among the practices of individual congregations. One example of this diversity can be found in the conduct of worship. In my own experience in the local churches of the United Church of Christ across the United States, the Sunday morning worship services I have attended in New England UCC churches, Pennsylvania UCC churches, California UCC churches, and Kansas UCC churches have each been quite different. Each has been shaped by different theological and sacramental histories, resulting in quite different worship formats and sacramental celebrations. A visitor familiar with Communion in a historically Congregational Church, for example, must learn to adjust to the sacrament as celebrated in a historically German Reformed congregation. Indeed, this variation is consistent with the denomination's founding expectations. Our UCC *Book of Worship* describes itself as "intended to be a resource for the public worship of God," rather than a central, magisterial authority that defines our mandatory liturgical or sacramental forms for ministers and congregations.[9] Aware of our diversity, the crafters of the *Book of Worship* allowed for our differences while identifying the common core of what worship is about.

Our shared self-governance must also encompass similar diversity. The UCC's biannual General Synods stop short of mandating particular ethical practices or stances. While General Synods ratify organizational decisions that affect the denomination as a whole, the resolutions and pronouncements adopted by General Synods are words spoken "to the church, not for the church." While individual churches and associations usually are involved in drafting and proposing such statements, once approved by the General Synod, these statements are commended to individual churches for their consideration. While the decision to approve or disapprove resolutions reflects the mind of a gathered Synod—women and men representing the regions of the church—the resolutions themselves are without binding authority over the decisions or actions of individual congregations or their members

As a snapshot of the mind of the gathered church at a given time, our General Synod resolutions, pronouncements, and other public ethical statements reveal something about the ethical and social issues important to the denomination, as well as the biblical and theological grounding for our reflection on ethical and social issues. Where do we turn for guidance in determining how to live out an ancient faith in a new time? What beliefs do we hold in common? How do we think together about the implications of our common beliefs? And which of those beliefs take priority as living and relevant for our lives and our denominational identity?

JESUS CHRIST AND OUR PROPHETIC VOICE

An examination of recent resolutions and pronouncements approved by General Synods offers a picture of our ethical and theological reflection. First, in their description of their biblical and theological rationale, our public ethical reflections and resolutions overwhelmingly cite and rely upon the prophetic texts found in the Hebrew scriptures. Second, where Jesus Christ is mentioned in the theological justification of resolutions and public statements, he is most often presented as simply a moral example for us, or narrowly referred to as speaking specific moral injunctions. Third, larger questions of Christology—the implications of Jesus Christ as "event," God breaking into history in a new and decisive way—are largely invisible in our public ethical pronouncements and reflection.[10]

These patterns are evident in a range of statements. In the biblical and theological rationales of various resolutions considered by recent General Synods, references to Jesus and the Gospels refer primarily to the example of Jesus in very general terms: particularly Jesus as an example of mercy or inclusivity in his willingness to heal and feed others, and his willingness to eat with and associate with those considered outcasts or ritually unclean within prevailing society.

Of Jesus' statements and teachings as recorded in the Gospels, three appear most frequently as biblical rationales for ethical or social positions in recent General Synod statements. The first of these is part of a statement summarizing "the whole of the law": "You shall love your neighbor as yourself" (Matt. 22:39). Throughout recent General Synod resolutions, this is used as an injunction taken in isolation, which then is used to support inclusion of, or support for, a particular "neighbor." For example, this passage is used as a basis for offering assistance, rather than punitive measures, to those struggling with drug addiction, for urging the Boy Scouts of America to refrain from discrimination against gay and bisexual persons, for confessing and renouncing the sin of anti-Semitism, and for relationship with other churches.

Resolutions also make repeated reference to Jesus' teaching in Matthew 25, listing examples of care for the vulnerable—feeding the hungry, tending the sick—and concluding with the statement, "Just as you did it to one of the least of these who are members of my family, you did it to me" (25:40). Again, the broader context of the text, or the theological import of doing such things for Jesus, is absent, and the text is taken as an injunction to do good things generally for others. Resolutions incorporating this passage as a major theological basis include those promoting reflection and education on dietary choices, supporting micro-credit lending organizations in developing nations, redistributing individual tax rebates to the poor, advocating reform of the juvenile justice system, and reaffirming Constitutional protections against search and seizure in the aftermath of the police shooting of an unarmed immigrant man, Amadou Diallo, in New York City.

A third, often repeated, reference from Jesus' words in the Gospels is a familiar one in our broader United Church of Christ history. This is Jesus' prayer to God before his disciples, found in John 17:21: "that they may all be one." This prayer appears in the biblical and theological rationale of a variety of resolutions, and is used as a basis for promoting unity across a variety of divides. For example, this passage is used as a basis for arguing against discrimination in the Boy Scouts of America, for urging work for peace and justice in the Korean peninsula, and for forming and continuing partnerships with churches in other countries.

Other references from Jesus' teachings and Jesus' example appear in the biblical rationale of resolutions in more general ways, consistent with the specific teachings detailed here. Occasionally, Jesus' teachings in the Sermon in the Mount are referenced—particularly the Beatitude statement "Blessed are the peacemakers"—in addition to other general claims about Jesus: Jesus as being generally opposed to greed, committed to working for healing, as well as examples of what Jesus ate. Overall, however, the biblical and theological rationales for our recent General Synod resolutions draw especially upon the prophetic books of scripture and the overall theme that God is a God of justice. In most cases the references to Jesus Christ, described above, are prefaced by references to calls for just treatment of others and God's vision of a just world, taken often from the prophets Micah, Isaiah, Amos, and the covenantal requirements detailed in Deuteronomy. Rather than connecting these stories of Jesus to any larger theological account, wherever Jesus is cited as an example, these stories tend to be used as supporting evidence for the relevance of the prophets' call.

This call can be found, as well, in the UCC's broader grounding and guidance for justice advocacy. In the *2003 Briefing Book*, written annually as a resource for UCC congregations and individuals engaging in public advocacy, the opening description of the "Biblical call to advocacy" locates this call firmly within the prophetic tradition, a tradition in which "justice in human community is inextricably linked to being in right relationship with God."[11] These roots in biblical prophecy are further developed with reference to the prophet Isaiah and the emphasis in Isaiah 10 on the importance of just laws and structures, as a further basis for public policy advocacy as an expression of faith. In this description of the biblical call to advocacy, Jesus appears as an example, one who served to "remind us of the call to compassion and justice, showing special care and concern for those who in his day were considered 'expendables.' "[12]

More detailed discussions of Jesus Christ's relevance for our lives can be found in pronouncements or longer statements summarizing focused study undertaken at the Synod's request. During the twenty-fourth General Synod in 2003, delegates approved a pronouncement on globalization, "A Faithful Response: Calling for a More Just, Humane Direction for Economic Globalization." In their summary the authors concluded that, while "economic globalization has yielded some positive outcomes . . . seen through the lens of faith, it has also produced great economic and social injustice. The rules and institutions that shape economic globalization must be fundamentally changed" in order for all to benefit.

In the section detailing the pronouncement's biblical and theological perspective, the authors state that they "take our primary guidance from the wisdom of Jesus as revealed in the Gospels." These teachings of Jesus pertaining to economic justice are presented as threefold. First, "Jesus acknowledges God the Creator as the giver of all that is good," thus pointing to a responsibility of stewardship. Second, "Jesus understands God to have a 'preferential option for the poor,'" as illustrated by Jesus' invocation of Isaiah 61 to describe himself as bringing good news to the oppressed, as well as Jesus' use of parables describing the kingdom of God as an inclusive banquet. These teachings are used to connect Jesus to the larger prophetic tradition of the Hebrew Scriptures. The final biblical perspective offered is that of a "theology of abundance": "our faith as exemplified in Jesus calls us to see the world as a place wherein God's provision for our needs is total." Jesus is offered as a teacher and example here, in his insistence on feeding the multitudes (Mark 6), as well as in his warnings not to hoard for ourselves out of fear.

Each of these points highlights the wisdom of Jesus rather than the action or function or significance of Jesus. This emphasis on Jesus as example and teacher continues in the pronouncement's "Proposal for Action," which states that "God has chosen to reveal the divine will for justice especially through the one we confess to be the Christ for us, Jesus of Nazareth. In this One we see incarnated the way of justice and peace for all creation." While these are profoundly Christological claims, they are never fully developed, as the pronouncement immediately moves to more narrowly focus on Jesus as example: "In particular Jesus taught and manifested in his ways a concern for how we use material possessions, the economic life of individuals and society."

THE NEED FOR BROADER CHRISTOLOGICAL REFLECTION

The relations between ethical action and Christological doctrine, and between prophetic action and personal belief, have been challenging ones for the UCC to navigate since its initial steps toward union and early life as a denomination. Louis Gunnemann, UCC theologian and historian, has written of those early decades that the imperative to show Christian unity after World War II resulted in a subordination of doctrinal differences, a subordination that marked the ecumenical movements in general as well as the uniting process that formed the United Church of Christ in particular. One of the consequences of this subordination of doctrinal focus and difference, he writes, was "the increasing dominance of a social activism that often lacked clearly articulated theological grounding and consistent development."[13]

The *2003 Briefing Book* also offers a clue into the choices that the UCC has perceived as necessary in shaping its emphasis on prophetic public witness. As an inset in its section describing the biblical call to advocacy, the *2003 Briefing Book* reminds readers of the "Resolution on Political Education and Sensitivity," from General Synod 11 in 1977:

> Whereas many people have committed to memory John 3:16—'For God so loved the world that God gave God's only-begotten child' and though this verse has become one of the best-known and often-quoted verses in the Scripture, we have failed to take cognizance of one of the key elements of this verse—'world.' We have believed, rather, that God so loved the church, or the well-behaved people or the Christians, but not really the world; i.e. the whole people. The church is people, people who are called in every time and every place to the task of continuing the essential ministry of Christ. We in the UCC need to understand that ministry and responsibly appropriate it in the world . . . [14]

Here, the role of incarnation and God's grace in the work of salvation, as well as the personal impact of faith and salvation, are seemingly set in opposition to the prophetic, justice-oriented work of the church. Yet these cannot be divided. The larger work of Jesus Christ in salvation, and the breadth of God's invitation to us and vision for this world, are the heart of what Christology offers us as a resource for our theological and ethical reflection. Christological reflection reminds us that Jesus was not simply a moral example, but also God incarnate, willing to participate fully in creation and human life in order to restore and save it. In our consideration of the incarnation, we find the clearest possible evidence that God's love for this world persists, and that questions of how we sustain and order our material, physical lives are central to theology and faith.

The example of Jesus is a gift that we have through the Gospel record. Yet focusing solely on the example of Jesus, or the wisdom of Jesus, tells only part of the story. For what we find in the Gospel accounts of Jesus, again, is the example of one concerned not simply with just treatment, or equal provision, or even solidarity, but also with transformation. In our reflection on the Gospels and the New Testament witness as a whole, this transformation becomes visible precisely as the work of Jesus Christ in salvation: for us, for others, and for the world. Without reflection on this larger work of Jesus Christ, the call to pursue and create justice may be seen simply as a command, an injunction, or rule, disconnected from our own transformation and thus invisible as the invitation that has been offered to us through Jesus Christ.

A focus on the prophetic materials in scripture to emphasize God's concern for justice is also important, and should continue to be a central part of our reflection. The prophets lay out God's expectations, God's vision for human life lived fairly in community. The call of the prophets to the people of Israel is a call to return to the covenant relationship they formed with God through God's initiative and grace. Certainly the example of Jesus on earth gives us a window into life lived obediently with God and the demands of the covenant as an expression of relationship with God.

Yet within the Christian tradition, reflection on the meaning of such prophetic texts cannot be separated from the breadth of Christological reflection. Our hearing the words of the prophets necessarily takes place with the knowledge offered in the Gospels and the testimony of the early church and the apostles. The covenant to which the prophets recall the people is now a covenant that has been broken open through Jesus Christ. Rather than a particular covenant relationship with one people, one nation, saving relationship with God is open to all through faith in Jesus Christ, who serves as not simply a moral example, but also as the "new covenant."

Attention to a broader Christology does not negate our prophetic task or make the example of Jesus irrelevant to our lives. Instead, Christology reminds us of our place in the divine story. Christological reflection on the cross and resurrection reminds us that the salvation and restoration of the world is a work that is beyond us in its totality. While we imitate God's character as revealed in the earthly example of Jesus Christ in our work for justice, our work in and of itself does not inaugurate or equal the kingdom of God. Our reflection on the fact of the cross calls us to consider our tendency to sin, our inertia and apathy, and our resistance to God's justice in this world. Our work must always be accompanied by self-examination and repentance. As theologian Douglas Ottati claims in his description of theological ethics in the Reformed tradition:

> Reformed theological ethics is theocentric in the sense that it
> tries to put God's reign and glory at the center of faithful living
> rather than our needs, wants desires or interests . . . God's reign
> cannot be equated with the way things are. God's purposes do
> not simply ratify our cherished projects and commitments. On
> the other hand, God is not loveless, thoughtless power. God is
> faithful. Human life is not separate from God, it is life in the
> arena of God's presence and purpose.[15]

Our words of reconciliation and justice are thus never simply
words to governments or organizations or to others, but always words
to ourselves as well. At the same time, a Christian ethic that takes
Christology seriously understands that we need to view our human
projects with the humility that comes with our awareness of our need
for God's forgiveness and salvation, and the continued persistence of
sin.

This understanding is not the last word Christology has to offer
ethics. If it were, Christian ethics could easily remain analytical, safe,
and private, focused only on promoting our inner personal restoration
and relationship with God, simply venturing judgments on the world
beyond. This is not a choice that we can faithfully make in light of
what God has done. Christological reflection on Jesus as example and
event calls us to move from the safety of ethics as analysis of self and
world, of motive and structure, even beyond the speaking of words of
prophecy to those in power, to go further and to embrace ethics as
practice and action without fear. Through faith we are caught up and
transformed by the redeeming event of Jesus Christ, and through this
event we are called to take profoundly seriously the reality of life now
made possible through Jesus Christ: life lived within a being-restored
creation.

Taking this transformation and call seriously, but with humility,
requires us to take up the challenge of moral imagination in our time
and place. This practice of moral imagination is something different
from claiming "Christ's ministry as our own." It is, as well, distinct
from reducing the ethical task to the question of "what would Jesus
do?" Christology reminds us that we are not Christ, not our own sav-
iors, but recipients of God's grace before we can act as signs and instruments of God's grace. The question for us is not "what would
Jesus do?" nor solely a matter of "what example does Jesus offer?" but
rather "how can we live fully and justly in light of what God has done
in Jesus?" Moral imagination requires reading the world around us

and its needs, creatively considering responses and solutions to promote justice and wholeness that go beyond the "conventional wisdom," and especially requires our willingness to relate our experience
of transformed life in Christ to equal possibility and hope for the
world.

CHRISTOLOGY AND OUR PROPHETIC FUTURE

Christology thus points us to an essential bridge in our ethical
reflection, a bridge between the prophetic call to work for justice and
inclusion for all and the basis for our individual participation in that
work. Through faith in Christ, we are able to give ourselves to this
work, and imagine the world differently, precisely because we have
the assurance that we cannot lose God's love and care for us. Even if
we risk our safety or comfort, or even our lives on behalf of others, we
cannot lose our lives in any ultimate sense, for we have been claimed
by God through Jesus Christ.

We need to be reminded of our place in this larger story of divine
grace by reflection on Christology. And our future will be determined
by our ability as a denomination to consciously engage in this reflection—deeply, persistently, transparently—and to find ways to articulate the connection between God's larger work in Jesus Christ and our
call to faithful, risky response. Our commitment to theological and
biblical reflection, independent of particular ethical issues and
stances (rather than as an effort to justify them), will shape how fully
we are able to invite all our members to participate in work for justice
and inclusion as their own work, part of their lived response to what
God has done for them. Without finding ways to engage in more rigor-
ous, more widespread Christological theological reflection on all levels of our denominational life, we stand to lose the opportunity to
participate in a common conversation with others in the broader
Christian tradition. We will simply ignore the resources available to
us in the recorded discernment of the faithful who have gone before
us. We will lose the ability to model faithful ethical discernment that
wrestles both with the moral clarity and the moral ambiguities that we
inevitably confront in bringing today's questions to reflection on
scripture. In the end, we will inevitably marginalize ourselves further
in the public eye, ceding the label "Christian" to those who would reduce scripture to simple answers, moral safety, and hope for a limited
few. As our gift to the world in the last century was taking the risk of

unity and prophecy, let our gift to the world in this time become a renewed witness to the example and event of Jesus Christ, in whom God has already decisively defeated the power of death and calls us to work and live to make that visible.

CHAPTER EIGHT

THE PASSION AND THE COMPASSION OF THE CHRIST

THEODORE LOUIS TROST

The Passion of the Christ, a film by Mel Gibson, officially opened on movie screens across the United States on Ash Wednesday, 2004. Actually, the film was available for viewing a few days earlier in certain regions of the country where potential moviegoers had expressed a predisposition to support Mr. Gibson's cinematic enterprise. In Tuscaloosa, Alabama, where I live, *The Passion* appeared on the Monday and Tuesday before the start of Lent. Numerous churches and other religious organizations that play such a dominant role in the culture of this region had purchased all the available seats in advance. In a secondary promotional venture, the local Baptist Student Fellowship sponsored a "two-for-one night." Members were encouraged to buy tickets at ten dollars apiece and to bring an "unsaved friend" to the show—a friend who could then share the experience and the message of *The Passion* for free (or for half price, depending on the deal that was cut with the one who was to be saved). Many, including some who had not yet seen it, believed the movie would have prophetic qualities, such as the power to convert. But then again: "Blessed are those who have not seen and yet have come to believe" (John 20:29). If box office sales are any indication, at the very least the film's power to convert to profit should not be underestimated. Produced for a mere $35 million, *The Passion of the Christ* became the eighth largest domestic grossing movie of all time, having amassed over $370 million in sales by August 2004.[1] When the DVD version of the film appeared on September 1, 2004, it sold 4.1 million copies on the first day of release.[2]

The Passion offers a significant example of theology performed in the marketplace. Interestingly, the film appeared at the same time that the United Church of Christ was embracing the commercial tactics associated with Hollywood and Madison Avenue as it launched an unprecedented advertising campaign called "God is Still Speaking," [sic]. The comma is central to the purposes of the campaign. Using a variety of media, including television, this promotional venture endeavors to establish name recognition for, and attract new members to, the UCC. Unlike the excruciating torture and death sequences in The Passion, the UCC's self-promotion features the friendly slogan (attributed to the comedian Gracie Allen), "Never place a period where God has placed a comma." This openness to the future is captured in a kind of Christological affirmation that brings closure to the denomination's first nationally broadcast television ad with the words, "Jesus didn't keep people out; neither do we."

While the messages are different, the methods employed by Mel Gibson and the United Church of Christ are similar. Both The Passion of the Christ movie and the "God is Still Speaking," ad campaign endeavor to affirm Christian identity and to engage the larger culture in a conversation about what this identity means in the twenty-first century. Moreover, both the movie and the commercial respond to the climate of conflict characteristic of American culture in the aftermath of September 11, 2001. As such, they offer a starting point for these reflections on the importance of articulating a Christology for the twenty-first century in the UCC.

Under the heading "The Responsibility of the Church in Each Generation"—a phrase drawn from the Preamble to the UCC Constitution—the first section of this chapter looks at both The Passion and, more briefly, the "God Is Still Speaking," campaign as consumer products and in the context of the protracted war on terrorism and the ongoing war in Iraq. In this extraordinary moment in American culture, people are wanting a particular Christ-figure. One version is offered in the movie, and inklings of another are offered in the UCC's ad campaign.

The second section, "The Faith of the Historic Church," turns to the insights of the Mercersburg movement, an important theological critique of popular religious trends in mid-nineteenth-century

America. Arising in the German Reformed Church, one of the UCC's predecessor denominations, the Mercersburg movement offers one instance where God placed a comma. Now is the propitious moment to return to that resting place in order to advance the theological work of our forbears in the faith. Mercersburg also has something to say about both the Christ of *The Passion* and the resort to slogan-making characteristic of our media-saturated era.

The final section, "The Word of God in the Scriptures," returns to a particular moment in the Gospel narrative that *The Passion* inevitably left out: the story of the Syrophoenician woman. A review of this story, with insights gained from the witness of the Mercersburg movement, sketches a preliminary outline for a UCC Christology in this day and time.

THE RESPONSIBILITY OF THE CHURCH IN EACH GENERATION

When it comes to films about Jesus, the trend in Hollywood has been to present at least a few scenes from Christ's early ministry before the inevitable turn to Jerusalem where suffering and death await. For example, of the thirteen films listed in his book *Jesus at the Movies: A Guide to the First Hundred Years*, W. Barnes Tatum notes that only one, *Jesus Christ Superstar*, "confines its onscreen story to events related to Jesus' last week."[3] Even here, Tatum notes, *Superstar* makes use of the flashback technique to recall instances of healing and exorcism that occurred some time before the showdown in Jerusalem. *The Passion of the Christ*, like *Superstar*, is an exception to the general rule. In the tradition of the medieval passion plays, Mel Gibson's movie zeroes in on Jesus' arrest, trial, and execution. As with *Superstar*, the technique of the flashback is used to recall particular moments in the life of Christ. However, the emphasis is not so much on the ministry of Christ to others as it is on the mystery of Christ's identity—especially in relation to the sacrament of his body and blood as signaled in Holy Communion. This is true even in the case of the somewhat whimsical and perhaps perplexing (and extra-canonical) scene in which Jesus, as a youthful carpenter, creates an anachronistic waist-high table instead of a low table for reclining on pillows, as was custom. "It might catch on," Jesus says in the movie.

Theologically, the connection between Christ's suffering and death is explicated in the doctrine of *substitutionary* atonement:

Christ acts as worthy substitute, suffering on behalf of sinful humanity the penalty due to all on account of sin. Precisely this understanding, often associated with the Reformer John Calvin (1509–64), is suggested at the beginning of the film with the quotation from Isaiah (53.4): "Surely he has borne our grief and carried our sorrows . . . "[4] Another traditional understanding of atonement that emerges from the film can be derived from the medieval Roman Catholic theologian Anselm (1033–1109). He argued that humanity's general sin, and the particular sins of human beings, dishonored the perfect God. For the sake of justice, an act of reparation was required to undo this injury to God. Christ's death, then, becomes a sufficient vicarious *satisfaction* for sin because, as a human being, Jesus is sinless, and as God (in the second Person of the Trinity), his payment is of infinite worth.[5]

The emphasis on Christ's blood that dominates this film, then, can be accounted for with reference to these twin understandings of atonement. The suffering that is depicted is extreme; so much so, that at one point the character who carries Jesus' cross tells the Lord that he need only endure the brutality a little longer on the way to Golgotha; then relief will come in the form of actual crucifixion and death. Only a divine person, it seems, could endure this much suffering. The relentless nature of the torture, meanwhile—the brutal scourging, for example, and the apparent delight most of the crowd seems to take in the violence—suggests the pervasiveness of the sin that Jesus carries away. This infinite offense requires infinite satisfaction.

Both of these understandings of atonement play a central role in the liturgy or worship life of certain Christian communities. The Eucharist, particularly in the pre-Vatican II sense of the sacrament favored by filmmaker Gibson, serves as a reenactment, as it were, of Christ's death while the communicant ingests the transubstantiated body and blood of the sacrificed Christ in the bread and wine. From another point of view, the key feature of the film is its depiction of what amounts to a "bloodbath"—as one commentator from the Evangelical Church in the Rhineland called it.[6] But although the German critic intended "*Blutbad*" as a negative assessment, the profusion of bloodletting depicted on the screen resonates with certain emphases in American evangelical Protestantism, as seen especially in those hymns that focus on Christ's savage death and the supposed salvific power of spilt blood. The refrain "Are you washed in the blood of the

Lamb?" is typical of a kind of theology that appreciates the bloodfest *The Passion* displays.[7]

This combination of Roman Catholic and evangelical Protestant appeal in the film led theologian Harvey Cox to remark, "I'm terribly disconcerted to see an alliance forming on the American religious scene between the Protestant evangelical, fundamentalist right and the far right of Roman Catholicism." Cox continues, perhaps ironically: "In the good old days, these were people who hated one another."[8] More generously, Julie Ingersoll has critically assessed the mainly positive reception of the film by certain groups of evangelicals and Catholics through evidence gathered on the Internet. She does note the negative critiques of some fundamentalists who would otherwise appreciate the "straightforward albeit graphic depiction of the role of crucifixion in the atonement"; these folk accept the bloodletting as absolutely necessary but absent themselves from the Catholic and Evangelical coalition of the killing, as it were, on account of the central role Mary plays in the film. In other words, for these fundamentalists, the film is simply too Catholic.[9]

Key to all Christian witness is an articulation of the meaning of salvation. To the extent that *The Passion* does this, it encourages ecumenical conversation about the meaning of Christian identity. While the film could be commended in this regard, it should also be subjected to passionate as well as compassionate critique. In the first place, I would suggest that the portrait of Christ presented in the film is not sufficiently well-rounded; he is significant only inasmuch as he dies. This thought is not unprecedented in Christian history. Calvin framed the matter in the fifty-fifth question of the Geneva Catechism, which refers to the passage in the Apostle's Creed that declares Christ as "born of the Virgin Mary, suffered under Pontius Pilate, was crucified, dead, and buried." The Catechism asks, "Why do you leap at once from his birth to his death, passing over the whole history of his life?" The Catechism answers, "Because nothing is said here about what belongs properly to the substance of our redemption."[10] This separation of Christ's life from the purpose of "our" redemption is unfortunate, for reasons that will be discussed in the next section.

But *The Passion* does not simply participate in a theological conversation about the nature and the work of Christ. It is also a product of contemporary culture, of Hollywood conventions. It is characteristic, in this regard, of the kinds of stories Americans like to tell themselves (if box office success is any indication). And so, although this is an extremely brutal film, Americans are accustomed to brutality on screen, particularly when it is related to a Christlike figure engaged in some kind of mission to save humanity. Consider, for example, the torture Neo endures in the third Matrix film, *Revolutions*; or the extended battle between the Terminator and his nemesis in *Terminator 2: Judgment Day*. This is particularly so in any number of Mel Gibson's movies, especially *Mad Max Beyond Thunderdome*, in which postapocalyptic gladiators endure ungodly punishment in an arena for the entertainment of a perverse crowd. (Instead of "Crucify him!"—as Pilate's audience implored—this crowd recites the simple, cruel truth: "Two men enter, one man leaves.") As expected, after the hero has withstood more violence than the average person could possibly endure, he rises up as if from the dead and obliterates the enemy. "I'll be back" is the Terminator's recurring refrain.

This expectation of return, it seems to me, is one way to understand the last scene of *The Passion*: as an homage to the Hollywood revenge narrative. In the tomb is no young man, as Mark would have it, directing the perplexed women to Galilee. Instead, a scarred Christ prepares to exit the tomb naked (in much the same manner as the Terminator entered the world in *Terminator 2*), ready to confront his enemies and—if currently operative notions of justice are entertained—to do away with them before they ever have a chance to inflict harm.[11]

In Mel Gibson's movie, Jesus becomes the central figure in a battle against an axis of evil that includes his former colleague, Judas (whose hanging serves as a warning and as a portent of revenge to come), his Roman torturers, his Jewish accusers, and most significantly, the devil, who is portrayed as an androgyn (or at least a person of dubious gender and uncertain sexual orientation). The battle against evil began in the Garden of Gethsemane when Jesus, in what might be termed a preemptive first strike, crushed the head of an albino serpent, thereby undoing the original sin that led to humanity's fall in the Garden of Eden. The battle is about to be raised to the next level as Jesus prepares his exodus from the tomb. No doubt he will retrieve his "Enemies List," then amass his armies of righteousness on the field of Armageddon—as the popular imagination, educated by the *Left Behind* series, would expect.

Gibson's is a malleable—but ultimately a warrior—Christ. It is perhaps all too obvious why a Christ like this would be wanted at a time like this, when the heterosexual household is somehow threatened by the prospect of gay marriage; when the United States and its allies in the "coalition of the willing" encounter the insurgent citizenry and "enemies of freedom" in the streets and deserts of Iraq. Young women and men can be called upon in this terror-framed context to lay down their lives for the forces of Good, to endure war and to sacrifice for an eternal reward—heaven or freedom—believing they are on the side of the good. After all, what is their suffering compared to the ordeal Christ has already undergone on their behalf? While it can be hoped that Christ is present with these people as they traverse Iraqi roads in their inadequately armored vehicles, a fully-rounded Christology would have to point to Christ's presence also among those who suffer torture unjustly at the hands of brutes and sadists—the prisoners in Abu Ghraib, for example.

In contrast to Mel Gibson's singular Christ, the UCC has recently offered a kinder and gentler sketch of its titular head. On December 1, 2004, the denomination launched its first-ever, nationwide television advertising campaign. The inaugural thirty-second spot, dubbed "the bouncer ad," features two muscle-bound security guards stationed at the entryway to a tall-steepled church. As church bells ring in the background, with ominous synthesized bass notes providing an undertone of foreboding, the bouncers decide whom to admit into the church and whom to exclude. Allowed in are two blond teenage girls and a young, white, middle class, seemingly married, heterosexual couple. Among those kept out are two males holding hands, an Hispanic man, an African American girl, and a white man in a wheelchair. The cold gazes of the bouncers collide with looks of disappointment on the faces of those denied entry with words such as, "Not you"; "No"; "No way." A sharp clang like the sound of a slammed gate echoes as the picture fades to black.

Then the music ascends to the treble clef and two sentences appear on the screen: "Jesus didn't turn people away. Neither do we." Congas kick up a kind of world beat; a single voice in an unrecognizable tongue starts singing; soon a whole choir joins in sympathetic and celebratory tones. An ecumenical gathering of humanity appears on the screen: old people; young people; red, yellow, black, brown, and white people. The announcer says, "The United Church of Christ: No matter who you are or where you are on life's journey, you're welcome here." The advertisement ends with a still shot of the UCC's logo in black against a band of red. Above the church's name appears the identity campaign's slogan, "God Is Still Speaking," and below it in bold letters is the denomination's web site address. The comma at the end of the slogan is of particular significance. Taking their cue from a remark made by sage comedienne Gracie Allen, the overseers of the overall identity campaign have advised—in articles, editorials, and other promotional writing leading up to the nationwide television advertisement: "Never place a period where God has placed a comma."[12]

While it is unfair to compare a thirty-second commercial to a feature-length movie, a sketch of the UCC's Christ does emerge in this brief ad. Specifically, allusion is made to a Jesus who traverses the boundaries and the labels society places upon its members. In opposition, perhaps, to the construction of dichotomies that divide the world into categories of good and evil—the apparent function of the bouncers in the ad—the UCC insists upon a quality of inclusion derived from the life of Christ. Instead of the passion (that is, the suffering) of Christ, the ad emphasizes Christ's compassion, his openness to the needs of other and often different people.

This is a promising beginning. Sloganeering, though, does have its limitations. For example, I recently read these words posted on the sign board of a local church (and perhaps composed in response to the UCC's ad campaign): "Don't put a question mark where God put a period." Of the making of bumper stickers, I fear, there will be no end. Content needs to fill the form.

The Faith of the Historic Church

Recognizing the limitations of both slogans, on the one hand, and the popular Christology of Mel Gibson on the other, where does the church turn to construct a Christology for the twenty-first century? As the Preamble to the UCC's Constitution affirms, members of the UCC look to the scriptures and the Reformation faith as it has been appropriated from generation to generation in the church as resources for contemporary witness to the world; as resources, that is to say, for discipleship. Perhaps then, in relation to the Preamble, we can dig a little deeper into the current slogan and ask what it has to do with, and say to, this historical people who make up the United Church of Christ. If, as the church has always believed, "God Is Still Speaking," then the question arises: What further meaning might be derived from the comma that the advertisers have been so insistent about including?

Grammatically at least, the comma offers a resting place before proceeding further. In a sentence it suggests that the reader or speaker should stop for a moment and reflect upon what has already been said or accomplished before moving on. By extension, then, the comma in the UCC's slogan could serve as a reminder to take into account what has gone before. It presents an opportunity to consult the tradition with the question in mind "How has God spoken in the past?" as prelude to an encounter with the new. One of the many resources available to the UCC today is the witness of the saints in its predecessor denominations.

The Mercersburg Movement

The Mercersburg movement arose in the middle of the nineteenth century in the German Reformed Church in the United States, a small denomination located primarily in Pennsylvania but with a significant membership in Ohio and Wisconsin as well. The movement takes its name from the denomination's seminary, originally located in Mercersburg, Pennsylvania, and later moved to Lancaster, where it now resides. The movement's principal leaders were teachers at the seminary: John Nevin, professor of theology, and Philip Schaff, professor of church history. Both Schaff and Nevin were boundary crossers. Schaff had been ordained in the Prussian Union Church in Germany, a union of Lutheran and Reformed groups. He brought this combined perspective to bear on his work in the United States after his arrival in 1844. Nevin had been raised a Presbyterian, and after training at Princeton Theological Seminary and teaching for a decade at the Presbyterian seminary in Pittsburgh, he undertook a thorough study of the German Reformed Church's confessional symbol, the Heidelberg Catechism, in preparation for his duties in his new denomination. His study of the catechism resulted in a series of articles that were published in the *Weekly Messenger*, the newspaper of the German Reformed Church, and served to "rediscover" the lost spirit of the Catechism in the German Reformed Church generally.[13]

Two points of this story are especially significant. First, the German Reformed Church was never narrowly confessional; in particular, they had close ties to German Lutheranism. The Heidelberg Catechism (1563), for instance, though written from a Calvinist perspective, was an irenic document. It was created to engage Lutheran theology (particularly as it developed through Luther's student, Melancthon) and to reconcile Lutheran and Reformed perspectives in the Palatinate, the region of Germany from which the early German Reformed members emigrated.[14] Then, too, as the German Reformed Church developed in Pennsylvania, many church buildings were shared by German Lutherans and German Reformed people who met as separate congregations at different times on Sunday or on alternating Sundays. These German-Americans shared the same iconography in stained glass and the same hymn books, one of which Philip Schaff edited and compiled during his tenure at Mercersburg.[15]

Second, the German Reformed Church was rediscovering its particular confessional heritage at a time when many American churches were abandoning distinction in light of the process historian Nathan Hatch has called "the democratization of American Protestantism."[16] Revivalists such as the famous preacher Charles Finney had introduced "new measures" into worship services in an effort to excite old members and to attract new ones. This method caught on in the German Reformed Church and was even attempted in Nevin's own parish in Chambersburg, Pennsylvania.

The "Anxious Bench"

The methods endorsed by Finney included encouraging extemporaneous prayer in mixed public meetings, often instigated by women; prayer in colloquial, sometimes "vulgar," language; the singing of stirring hymns at strategic moments in the service; and the "protracted meeting"—services that extended for unspecified amounts of time, often late into the night. In an era before radio and television, new measures promised entertainment in addition to salvation. The key element in the new measures catalogue was the "anxious bench," or the "mourner's bench": a special seat or pew reserved for sinners who were anxious about—or mournful over—the condition of their souls. At a particularly charged moment in the service, usually at the end of the sermon, the preacher would call people forward, often by name, to sit on the anxious bench to be preached to and otherwise cajoled toward Christ.

In *The Anxious Bench* (1843), John Nevin focused on the anxious bench as the most visible element in a religious system he deemed riddled with "quackery," that is, "the pretension to an inward virtue or power, which is not possessed in fact on the ground of the mere show of the strength which such power or virtue is supposed to include."[17] For Nevin, the end (converts) did not justify the means (the theatrical practice of the bench). And if "the bench" could not withstand scrutiny, Nevin argued, the whole system that supported it would fall. According to Nevin, the "system of the bench" manufactured a moment of extreme emotional intensity that was misconstrued as a moment of divine intervention. Under the pressure of a badgering preacher and the groans and pleadings of an aroused congregation, the agitated sinner finally rose up from the anxious bench to surrender to Christ. The technique was dangerous, according to Nevin, because it claimed as an end (the moment of coming forward) what was at best a beginning in the development of religious sensibility. For Nevin, religion was a process of growing into and being nurtured in the community of faith, namely the church. Furthermore, the theology informing the new measures assumed that salvation came on account of human initiative rather than through grace freely offered by God. The relationship with Christ was much more than a moment of personal decision, according to Nevin; it was a lifetime of growing "in the bosom of the Church."[18]

Nevin always had in mind the historical church; it would not be entirely anachronistic to call it the "ecumenical Church." In constructing the Mercersburg position, therefore, he made constant reference to what the UCC's Constitution honors as "the basic insights of the Protestant reformers." "The system of the new measures," Nevin argued,

> has no affinity with the life of the Reformation as embodied in the *Augsburg Confession* and the *Heidelberg Catechism*. It could not have found favor in the eyes of Zwingli or Calvin. Luther would have denounced it in most unmerciful terms. His soul was too large, too deep, too free to hold communion with a style of religion so mechanical and shallow.[19]

Nevin pursued this point most sharply in the last chapter of the second edition of *The Anxious Bench* (1844) in his discussion concerning the "system of the catechism," which he elevated in opposition to the "system of the bench." "Where the 'system of the catechism' prevails," Nevin noted, "great account is made of the Church and all reliance placed upon the means of grace, comprehended in its constitution as all-sufficient under God for the accomplishment of its own purposes." As the "mother of all her children," the church provides its members with a variety of gifts including baptism, the family altar, worship, catechetical training, the sacraments, and ministerial visitation in the home.[20]

For the German Reformed Church, and for the Lutherans with whom they occasionally shared church buildings and hymnals, the "system of the catechism" was tangibly enacted in song. Probably the best-known hymn writer among German-speaking people was the Reformer Martin Luther. Luther's purpose in writing hymns—unlike some of Charles Finney's nineteenth-century associates—was not to frame the stress-filled moment in which a potentially "born again" Christian might make a decision for Christ, but rather to educate new generations in the doctrines of the Reformation faith—a foundational tenet of which was that God's crucial decision for humanity had already been made in Christ. This emphasis on the Christian life—both as the life of Christ and as the life of the Christian—is completely congruent with Nevin's concerns. It may be said to have motivated Schaff to compile his own *Gesangbuch* for America's growing German-speaking population. In this regard, it is helpful to consider one hymn written by Martin Luther and used "catechetically," that is, to inculcate children and adults into the mysteries of the faith, particularly an understanding of the nature of Christ. This comes not from a protracted contemplation of Christ's death—as in *The Passion of the Christ*—but rather from an extended meditation upon Christ's birth.

"From Heaven Above"

Vom Himmel Hoch, or "From Heaven Above," written by Martin Luther in 1534, would have been familiar to members of the German Reformed Church from the colonial era onward.[21] Indeed, the key moment in the hymn presents a Christology that the Mercersburg movement would advance in its own hymnody several centuries later. Versions of "From Heaven Above" appear in some form in many contemporary hymnals, including the Lutheran *Book of Worship* and the Presbyterian *Hymnal*. It is also included in the UCC's *New Century Hymnal*—albeit in a form significantly altered from Catherine Winkworth's 1855 translation. *Vom Himmel Hoch*, with all fifteen verses, also appears in the *Evangelisches Kirchengesangbuch* of the Evangelical Church of the Union: the mother church of the UCC's predecessor denomination, the Evangelical Synod of North America; the church into which Philip Schaff was ordained; and the church with which the UCC has maintained particularly close ecumenical ties (*Kirchengemeinschaft*) since 1982.

The hymn begins "from heaven above" with an angelic announcement reminiscent of the one directed to the shepherds in

Luke's Gospel. A lone angel begins to relate "a good new story" that she must sing about and tell, presumably to the whole word. In the first five verses, various affirmations are made about the identity of the child born on Christmas day. He is a "fragile and delicate child"; at the same time, he will make the addressee "clean from all sins." He is the one who supports and carries (*erhält und trägt*) the whole world; yet he is also the one lying in a feedbox wearing dirty diapers. Luther does not hesitate to suggest, in other words, that this child is absolutely—even, humbly—human and his birth is a common one; at the same time, this is an extraordinary birth: one that changes the world forever.[22]

Verses six through thirteen affirm how the world is forever changed, as the angel guides us inside the barn to bear witness alongside the shepherds and to continue to contemplate the mystery of God's presence in human community. At the heart of the mystery is the nature of this child's majesty. Luther asks in verse nine:

> Ah Lord [*Herr*] the maker of us all
> How has thou grown so poor and small
> That there thou liest on withered grass
> The supper of the ox and ass?

Here Luther interrogates the paradoxical nature of Christ's identity and invites Christians into the oldest of the faith's confessions: "Jesus is Lord!" Despite Jesus' status as "the maker of us all," he is not an overlord after the manner of royalty who place themselves above commoners. Rather, Jesus' trajectory, like that of the angel in this song, is from heaven above to earth and, indeed, to the lowliest conceivable place on earth. This is how, in Luke's words, the world is turned upside down (Acts 17:6)—and also the very meaning of words. Jesus exercises lordship in the midst of the downtrodden and, importantly, as one of them. This word "Lord," as Luther places it at the center of this hymn, is an offense. But not because of its inherent hierarchical implications; rather it offends because it becomes the new standard by which all who exercise power must be judged.

There are, of course, social and political implications to the affirmation that this babe in peril of being bitten by beasts, this Jesus, is Lord (or "the one Lord of the one holy, catholic, and apostolic Church," according to the Barmen Declaration).[23] In an engaging article entitled "Martin Luther Between Christmas and Epiphany: The Socioreligious Position of *Vom himmel hoch da kom ich her*," Stephen L.

Wailes argues that "From Heaven Above" was composed in order to redirect religious attention away from the traditional celebration of Epiphany to the far less celebrated Christmas day.[24] For Luther, the manner in which Epiphany, or "Three Kings Day" (*Dreiknigstagö*), was observed served to exemplify everything that was wrong with the Roman Catholic Church of his age: The three kings were associated with papal authority. Wailes demonstrates how paintings of the nativity and the adoration of the Magi during the Middle Ages often featured among the kings the faces of popes, cardinals, and other important members of the church hierarchy. Then, too, Three Kings Day involved pilgrimages to great shrine sites such as Cologne, where a variety of the kings' relics were on display. Luther objected to the whole theory behind pilgrimages because he considered the veneration of relics to be superstitious and pilgrimages to see them another version of the "works righteousness" that opposed the doctrine of salvation by grace. There was also an element of necrophilia in the proceedings: a kind of worship of the dead or a fixation upon death that Luther criticized in both the mass and in the centrality of the crucifixion in the iconography of the church. (One way to understand the logic of Mel Gibson's *Passion* is to allow that only God could endure the violence inflicted upon Jesus in the period leading up to his crucifixion; therefore, Jesus must be God. It is a simplistic truth for an age that detests nuance. Luther's sense of the significance of Christ was far more subtle and complex.)

By focusing on Christmas day, Luther was able to emphasize the significance of incarnation and the key role that grace plays in his understanding of the work of Christ. The point is made particularly poignantly in the thirteenth verse of "From Heaven Above" as translated by Catherine Winkworth (1855) and preserved in the Evangelical and Reformed Church *Hymnal*:

> Ah dearest Jesus, holy child
> Make thee a bed soft undefiled
> Within my heart that it may be
> A quiet chamber kept for thee.[25]

In this verse the intimate relationship between the Lord and his potential disciple is made manifest. Again, the world is turned upside down: the disciple incarnates the Incarnate One; the believer prepares a shrine, a shelter, for the one who, in the words of the Heidelberg Catechism, "protects me so well that without the will of my

Father in heaven not a hair can fall from my head."[26] The intimacy of this relationship is particularly well-established through the use of the second person singular, a conjugation that should be preserved in the hymnody of the church. In opposition to the kind of deferential language one might use in relation to the lords of this world, the conversation with Jesus is personal: as in most renditions of "The Lord's Prayer," it is an "I-Thou" relationship.[27]

"Jesus, I Live to Thee"

Without pressing the case too far, I believe it is safe to say that there is a deep affinity between the piety expressed in Luther's "From Heaven Above" and the theology that emerged from Mercersburg beginning in the middle of the nineteenth century. The overtones from Luther's hymn reverberate throughout the famous Mercersburg hymn "Jesus, I Live to Thee," for example. Written in 1850 by John Nevin's student and eventual successor, Henry Harbaugh, the hymn celebrates both the lordship of Christ and the intimacy of relationship with him. In the final stanza of the hymn, these themes are drawn together in rhyme through a merging of first and second person singular, significantly, in the familiar mode— "my" and "thy"; "thee" and "me"; "thine" and "mine":

> Living or dying, Lord,
> I ask but to be Thine;
> My life in Thee, Thy life in me,
> Makes heaven forever mine.[28]

As in the case of "From Heaven Above," the world is altered: The "kingdom of heaven is at hand" (Matt. 3:2, RSV). Heaven has been made present through the incarnation, and therefore the disciple participates in the life of Christ and Christ participates in the disciple's life.

In other words, we have in this hymn an example of Communion. For the Mercersburg theologian John Nevin, the entire scheme of Christian salvation is anchored in the incarnation and in its representation in the church—as both the body of Christ and, in the Lord's Supper, partakers of the body of Christ. Christ is the principle of a new humanity (a "new Adam"). In his most celebrated book, *The Mystical Presence*, Nevin writes: "He [Christ] took our nature upon him; but in doing so, he raised it into a higher sphere, by uniting it with the nature of God, and became thus the root of a new life for the race."[29] This is not to say that the work of Christ does not include his sacrificial death. But it does means that the death of Christ cannot be understood apart from the life of Christ. And, Nevin insists, this life—or Life—is ongoing.

The church, for Nevin, bears forth the life of Christ into the world. This is what "my life in thee, thy life in me" means. In the Mercersburg tradition, a Christology for the twenty-first century should focus on the life of Christ as he lives out that life in the Gospels and as Emanuel: "God with us." The Christ in whom the United Church of Christ is united is not simply the slaughtered victim and vengeful victor of *The Passion*; he is not the ferocious judge who urges the convicted sinner forward to the anxious bench in a moment of fear-filled decision; and he certainly is not the seemingly-benign "personal savior" of popular movies and the mega-churches.[30] Instead, this Christ Emanuel is the bread-bearer and the healer who welcomes the faithful into *diakone*, that is, service.

The Word of God in the Scriptures (Mark 7:24–31)

At the beginning of Mark's Gospel is Jesus' call to discipleship—a call to enter into, and to participate in, the life of Christ (as Mercersburg would have it). Jesus says to the fishermen Andrew, Peter, James, and John, "Follow me and I will make you fish for people" (Mark 1:17). They drop everything and follow him.

The Missionary Enterprise

In the sixth chapter of Mark's Gospel, the apostles return from their separate missions, having gone out two by two, to cast out demons and call people to repentance. They are anxious to tell Jesus about all they have accomplished, and Jesus invites them to steal away to "a lonely place" where they all might rest a while. The disciples' weariness is understandable, for as Mark notes, "many were coming and going, and they had no leisure even to eat" (6:31). But the crowds follow them all to the "lonely place," and Jesus ends up presiding at a meal for five thousand people. After this meal of thanksgiving, the disciples intend to take the boat to Bethsaida, that is, to a town on the northern shore of the Sea of Galilee. But perhaps on account of their fatigue, and also because of an adverse wind, the boat does not respond to the disciples' efforts. Jesus, meanwhile, is walking on the water with the intention to pass by them, but they call out to him (terrified, because they think he is a ghost). When he gets into the boat, the wind is calm. The disciples, however, are utterly astounded for—referring to the recent miracle of the feeding of the five thousand—"they did not understand about the loaves" (6:52). (What one does and does not understand about bread is a key factor in Mark's Gospel: It functions in much the same way as Christ's blood does in *The Passion*, though the emphasis is on life-giving rather than life-taking.)

After Jesus joins the group and the wind dies down, they arrive not at the comparatively remote village Bethsaida, but on the western shore of Galilee, in the bustling town of Gennesaret, where everyone recognizes Jesus. The lame and the ill are brought to him, and he also engages in debates with the Pharisees and the scribes. After several more days' worth of attempts to find a quiet place to rest, Jesus decides to go somewhere where he is not likely to be recognized. He and his disciples head toward Tyre—to the northwest and beyond Galilee on the Mediterranean coast. Tyre was "largely gentile and despised by Jews."[31] But at least there Jesus and his disciples might finally have some peace and quiet and a chance to talk together.

The Problem of Possession

By this point in his ministry, Jesus is becoming a little overwhelmed by the demands of his work: so many hungry and sick people; no time to get a moment's rest or a bite to eat. And so he pursues the radical strategy of leaving the country, to go into a despised land where, presumably, he will be left alone. But apparently a person with the ability to heal on demand cannot so easily hide from any public. In Jesus' time, as in our own, when it comes to matters of health, religious and political boundaries are often ignored and people just want what works. (Even if, for example, they have to search for it on the Internet and have it shipped down from Canada.)

And so a woman approaches Jesus. She throws herself at his feet and begs him to save her little girl who is possessed by an unclean spirit. There are many ways to understand the role of demon possession in the Marcan text. To begin with, although Jesus heals many different people with all sorts of physical maladies in the Gospel, he is first and foremost an exorcist, a healer. This Jesus, who at the very beginning of the Gospel is possessed by Holy Spirit, is involved in a constant struggle against the evil spirits that invade the lives of innocent people. The paradigmatic figure for this kind of possession in Mark's Gospel is probably the Geresene demoniac in chapter 5, a man who lives in the tombs, the place of the dead, appropriately, for he is truly one of the living dead. He howls in the night and is constantly bruising himself with stones. When Jesus confronts him, the man says, "My name is Legion; for we are many" (5:9). Here Mark ties together the forces that occupy this poor man and the forces that literally occupy the world he lives in, for a Legion is a Roman regiment of approximately six thousand soldiers.

Herman Waetjen, among others, has speculated that the possession that afflicts this poor fellow should be considered in relation to the clash of cultures that was taking place in Palestine at that time. The region had been invaded by the world's only superpower. There was an influx of new consumer goods and a preponderance of foreign gods. The land had been taken over to produce food for the vast numbers of soldiers that made up the occupation army. Some of these foods—like the swine who figure into the story of the Geresene demoniac—were considered unclean by Jews. In short, what might be called culture shock has set in, and many people are completely disoriented; they are lost.[32] Significantly then, once the Geresene demoniac is healed, he goes back home to tell his friends how much the Lord has done for him. In a foreshadowing of the Syrophoenician woman's story, he makes a leap of faith and identifies Jesus as "the Lord" (Kyrie, as the word is sometimes sung in some of our churches).

But it is not just individuals who suffer from the occupation by demonic forces. Institutions, too, are vulnerable. And so Jesus' last exorcism in Mark's Gospel is performed in and upon the temple itself. In the eleventh chapter of Mark, Jesus drives out the merchants and the shoppers from the temple, overturns the tables of the money-changers, and quotes from Isaiah: "Is it not written, 'My house shall be called a house of prayer for all the nations'? But you have made it a den of robbers" (11:17). According to Mark (11:18), these actions become the catalyst for the chief priests and the scribes to look for a way to kill Jesus. He is a threat to the status quo. He subverts the system that keeps certain collaborators with the Romans in power, while all around people are hungry, children are sick, and minds are lost to mental disorder.

The Encounter in Tyre

With the exorcism of the demoniac and of the temple as context, then, we return to the resort town of Tyre where Jesus encounters the poor woman looking for help for her daughter. She does what any parent would do for a child who is in pain, confused, sad, or out of control: She begs Jesus to cast the demon out of her daughter. The Gospel writer is very sparse in detail, but what he does tell us is deeply significant. Mark writes, "Now the woman was a Gentile [the word in the original is *Hellainis*," that is, "Greek"] a Syrophoenician by race" (7:26, author's translation). With the mention of this word "race," Mark invites the attentive listener to consider all sorts of prejudices in the interpretation. First of all, this person is a Greek, not a Jew, so by even addressing Jesus, by coming into contact with him, she is threatening to disrupt longstanding social conventions that enforce the separation of Jews from Greeks in everyday life. (These kinds of social conventions continue to exist today; they are graphically represented in the UCC's television ad, for example, in the persons of the bouncers who regulate admission to the church.)

Not only is she a Greek, but she is a woman. Since she approaches Jesus alone—and not through her husband—it can be assumed that she is a widow. This means that she has absolutely no social status. She is also intervening on behalf of a little girl, and a little orphan girl in this social system is truly the last of all and the least of human beings. She has no dowry because she has no father, and because her mother has no husband she is not likely to survive for very long. And then there's the problem of the demon possession . . .

Even though Jesus is about his father's business (to borrow a phrase from Luke) in his ministry, he remains, after all, a man of his time—at least partially. Some of the prejudices of his age were doubtless difficult to transcend. And so we arrive at what some scholars have called one of "the hard sayings of Jesus." The woman is begging and pleading with Jesus to cast the demon from her daughter, to heal the helpless little girl, and what Jesus says is shocking. Jesus' response, in effect, is something like this: "What do I look like? A universal healthcare provider?" Or, in somewhat more familiar language, "Let the children be fed first, for it is not fair to take the children's bread and throw it to the dogs." (7:27, author's translation)

It appears as if Jesus has not quite abandoned the socially-constructed reality of his day. He uses the epithet "canine" to characterize non-Jews. And he seems perfectly willing to allow a seemingly worthless, orphaned, little Greek girl to meet with her inevitable demise. His healthcare protection, apparently, does not extend beyond a Judeo-centric conception of the cosmos. Granted, Jesus is tired and he has spent the last four or five episodes looking for a place to rest, if only for a moment. So we could attribute this remark in part to fatigue. Still, the rebuke is a harsh one, not fashioned to encourage dialogue or further discussion.

Nevertheless, this remarkable woman is undaunted. She replies, according to the *New Revised Standard Version of the Bible*, "Sir, even the dogs under the table eat the children's crumbs" (7:28). It is important to note that it was a principle of the *NRSV* translators to do away with hierarchical language when it seemed unnecessary. And so the scholars who produced this particular translation chose the word "sir" here to replace the seemingly less-inclusive word that appears in the original. This approach, while commendable in principle, obscures literary and theological nuances in certain key instances. This is one of them. The woman addresses Jesus here as *Kyrie*, that is "Lord." She uses the title associated with the very earliest Christian confession, "Jesus is Lord!"—not Caesar or his heirs to world domination down to the present age. This woman, a resident of Syrophoenicia in the Roman province of Syria recognizes Jesus as Lord, and she is the first person in Mark's Gospel to apply this title directly to Jesus (though, as noted earlier, he was indirectly identified as Lord by the Geresene demoniac, and again on Gentile territory).[33]

She then goes on to say that even the dogs under the table eat the children's crumbs. This retort brings two key aspects of Jesus' ministry together: "bread" as a metaphor for Jesus' ability to heal, and actual bread to feed hungry people. Bread is literally food, as in the feeding of the five thousand and, shortly after this episode in Tyre, the feeding of the four thousand. But bread is also the Word of God that Jesus brings; and on Passover this bread will become his body: the bread of what Christians subsequently call the Eucharist, or Communion.

With all these possibilities activated in that humble reference to crumbs, it is no wonder that Jesus responds to the Syrophoenician woman: "Because of this word [*Logos*] you may go" (7:29, author's translation). But which word? Is it because she has a peculiar insight into the bread that Jesus offers—an insight that even Jesus' closest associates, the twelve disciples, didn't seem to get when the matter of the loaves came up in conversation? Or is it on account of the word she uses to address Jesus, the word "Lord" that acknowledges Jesus' authority above all temporal authority—even in Gentile territory? Or is it because she places herself among the lowest of the low, last of all—as Mark's Gospel, in later chapters, affirms (10:43–44): a dog at the children's table, but nevertheless deserving of the Lord's grace, nevertheless demanding that he attend to her welfare, and the welfare of her single-parent family?

Perhaps all of these factors contributed to Jesus' action. In any case, contrary to his original plan, Jesus repents of his prior intention, he "flip-flops." He turns around and does something entirely unexpected and new. Jesus had originally come to Tyre to avoid contact. Moreover, he had apparently come with the sense that his mission was first of all to the Jews, the people of Israel. In any case, his mission was not meant to extend to the whole world; after all, just preaching and healing in Israel was wearing him out. But because of the Syrophoenician woman, he has a change of heart. In light of new evidence, he alters his plan, he alters his self-understanding, he changes his tactics and his mission.

The New Way

Jesus heals one suffering Gentile child. That is significant enough. But that is only the beginning. Mark offers us another geographic detail to show just how radical Jesus' change of heart is. Mark concludes this episode with these words: "Then he returned from the region of Tyre, and went by way of Sidon to the Sea of Galilee, in the region of the Decapolis" (7:31). This is an oddly circuitous route. From Tyre, Jesus was about a day's journey away from the territory of Galilee to the southeast. But instead of traveling in that direction, he takes a day's journey north to Sidon. He literally turns around, he moves in the opposite direction. This is a physical enactment of *metanoia*, that is, repentance.

And then from Sidon, we are told he travels toward the Sea of Galilee by way of the Decapolis. Perhaps he went as far east as Damascus. In any case, most of the cities of the Decapolis were located on the eastern side of the Sea of Galilee. To give a somewhat inexact parallel, it would be as if a person who lives in Paris went on a visit to Versailles and then decided to return to Paris by way of London and Amsterdam. Jesus takes an extremely indirect route home. But the key to this frivolous itinerary is the fact that the cities of the Decapolis are Gentile cities. Jesus' ministry of healing, therefore, takes him all over Gentile territory until he eventually returns to the shores of Galilee. He does become, as it were, a universal healthcare provider and a provider of food; a healer to Gentile and Jew alike contrary to his own original plan and in response to the Syrophoenician woman's call to conversion.

Conclusion

The Gospels contain stories of many saints, but unlike the named disciples, their likenesses rarely appear on stained-glass windows, and churches are hardly ever named after them. Nevertheless, this obscure saint is responsible for the most amazing turnaround in all of Mark's Gospel: The Syrophoenician woman causes Jesus to reconsider, to re-imagine, the nature and purpose of his ministry. She represents a moment in the life of Christ when "God is still speaking," and it behooves us to take advantage of the comma in that increasingly famous phrase by remembering her in our contemporary context.

As the living Christ in the world, the church would be well-served if it did construct stained-glass windows in honor of the Syrophoenician woman; if churches were somehow named in a way that would recall this worthy saint's story. In any case, her story is a resource for the contemporary church. Her encounter with the living Lord adds substance, flesh and bones, to the slogans we apply to Jesus Christ as we formulate a contemporary Christology. Among other things, it is a good thing for us to be reminded from time to time that the point of faith is not to get ourselves into heaven, but rather to bring that heavenly realm to earth: to heal those who suffer in a world that is deeply divided—a world that still strains for the crumbs that fall from the bountiful tables of those who enjoy health and prosperity. This is what it means to exercise lordship in the twenty-first century in the name of Christ.

CHAPTER NINE

A LIVING CHRISTOLOGY AND THE UNFINISHED BUSINESS OF THE UCC

STEPHEN G. RAY, JR.

Who among us has not heard the quaint, and erroneously trite, quip that the acronym UCC stands for "Unitarians Considering Christ"? This particular jibe represents a profound misunderstanding not only of our identity as a church, but also of the Christological basis for our life in the world. The UCC has historically organized its life and approached its ministry in a tentative and evolving way, which is appropriate to reflecting the life of One who is alive. Life is not static or pristine, so if Christ lives, the people who find themselves joined to him will likewise live in ways that are evolving and unfinished.

CHRISTOLOGY: THE BACKWARD GLANCE

The approach of many who seek to define Christology is to first look at the person and life of Christ and then to draw some contours within which they can articulate a doctrine. What goes unsaid with this approach, and the Christological discussions that emerge from it, is that it proceeds using a language inflected with the past tense. That is, the language of Jesus Christ is the dominant phrase.[1] So, whether it is a statement about the divinity, humanity, or some other aspect of Jesus Christ's person, the dominant glance is a backward one rooted in the belief that the life of Christ has been definitively narrated in scripture and/or tradition. This is different than holding the view that God is definitively made known to us in Jesus Christ and that the contours of life in Christ are made known to us through reflection on scripture, tradition, *and* our contemporary context.

With the first formulation, Christology is the work of recovery; with the second, it is discernment. While as a matter of speculative reflection, the first approach is certainly an important sort of endeavor, when it becomes the basis for the church's reflection on its being and life, the results can be less than helpful. Two specific areas are immediately affected by this backward looking approach: doctrinal purity and effective church membership.

Concern about doctrinal purity is the laudable project of working to ensure that the proclamation and practice of ecclesial life is consonant with what a church holds to be the explicit dogma of the faith. It is the impulse to safeguard the tradition from the ever-present danger of contemporary corruption. This project takes on a particular caste when interpreted by the backward glance. By approaching the question of doctrinal purity with an inordinate attention to an ossified (versus living) tradition and/or a simplistic moralistic reasoning ("What would Jesus do?"), purity often becomes synonymous with custom. Given that custom is the codification of a particular set of social/political relationships, this means that doctrinal purity is often interpreted in such a way that maintenance of a specific definition of normativity becomes the *summum bonum*. The difficulty here, of course, is that the very construction of a specific normativity requires a self-privileging and a marginalizing of the other. This marginalizing process manifests itself in church life when that life is both exclusive and excluding.

A second ramification flows immediately from the first. The issue of effective church membership (as opposed to formal membership) is a significant one that is currently rending the ecclesial life of several communions. Who is truly a member of the church—signified by the opportunity to serve in any office of the church—is a question that bears not just on who may be ordained and who may not, but more significantly on who is claimed as a child of God by the household of God and who is not. Often the answer to this question turns on the normative subject of who stands at the center of the church's sense of itself. More often than not, this subject bears a striking resemblance to those who hold privileged positions in the context within which that church finds itself situated. Those deemed aberrant by dint of race, class, ethnicity, or sexual identity are rarely reflected as the normative child of God.

In bringing attention to these two ecclesial outcomes of a backward-looking Christology I want us to notice not only the untoward effects, but also the connection between church life and talk about the person of Jesus Christ. I believe more than the systematician's sensibility connects the two. This connection is of particular relevance when reflecting on the life of the United Church of Christ because of the hybrid and indeterminate nature of our past, present, and future life. A different approach to Christological reflection—one rooted in a living Christology—is more appropriate to the task of reflecting on Christology in the UCC.

LIVING CHRISTOLOGY

A living Christological discourse begins with three affirmations, which then structure not only the character of the discourse, but also the life of the community engaging in that reflection. The first affirmation is that God definitively discloses Godself to us in Jesus Christ. Here we make the claim that the God who makes Godself known to us in Jesus Christ is truly God. More importantly, we are making the claim that God is disclosing Godself to us today in Jesus Christ. To coin a phrase popular in the church today, "God is still speaking."[2]

This leads to the second affirmation, which answers the question of reception: How do we receive this divine self-disclosure? Here, I draw upon the wisdom of the Reformed tradition: We experience God's disclosure through living in Christ. In a variant of Calvin's assertion that "to share what he [Christ] has received from the Father, he had to become ours to dwell within us,"[3] I believe that it is as we claim a mutually inscriptive existence with Christ that we come to know God in God's fullness.

The third affirmation is that this mutually inscriptive existence is realized as we struggle to exemplify, in the power of the Spirit, the life of Jesus Christ, whose contours are made known to us in scripture and tradition, and given content by our particular context. It is necessary to unpack the implications of this definition, which is seemingly couched in very traditional language.

To say that God is definitively disclosing Godself in Jesus Christ is to make two assertions and an important assumption. The assumption is that, in calling Jesus "Christ," there is more than a nominal connection being made: We are bearing witness to being called by God in Christ.[4] As Paul Tillich helpfully reminds us, when the phrase Jesus Christ is used in a theologically significant way—and not as cultural blather—what is being named is Jesus as the Christ, or Jesus as Immanuel.[5]

This assumption gives rise, then, to the assertion that if, indeed, we name Jesus as the Christ, God has gathered us to Godself in Christ, that Jesus Christ is the definitive disclosure of Godself. This leads to the second assertion that it is the gesture of God that grasps us. The UCC's Statement of Faith makes this recognition: "In Jesus Christ, the man of Nazareth, our crucified and risen savior you [God] have come to us." The import of this is, of course, that when we call Jesus Christ, we are speaking of an active—grammatically present tense—deed on the part of God toward us.

A central affirmation of the Christian tradition is about the mutually inscriptive nature of life in Christ. As Christ lives in us, so also are we a part of Christ living in the world, along with all others who share in that life.[6] When taken in its full theological import, this means more than simply being the "hands and feet" of Christ, more than saying Christ "lives because He lives inside my heart." Each of these popular formulations, while sentimentally meaningful, fails to capture in its fullness the central dogma of the faith that Christ is alive and moving in creation with spiritual and material effect. Whether the effects are seen in spiritual or bodily healing in the face of disease and pestilence, in the resurrection of living souls from the death of demonic degradation and addiction, or in the birth of hope in darkest night of human sinfulness, all are accomplished through the continuing life of Christ in the world. To the extent that we witness and share in these effects, we are sharing in the unfolding life of Christ in the world.

Precisely because Christ's life is still unfolding, so also is our part in that life unfolding. Given that indeterminacy and hybridity are the very stuff of life, it follows that our experience of life in Christ will likewise be ever new and multivalent. This does not, however, mean that this experience of life will be chaotic and meaningless. Rather, it means that we will experience our life as something in which we participate but do not fully control. We can come to know the contours of this life by the witness given to us by scripture and tradition, but we must fully live into our contemporary context to learn what that life in Christ looks like today. A living Christology is therefore a praxio-existential engagement with the person and life of Christ as we struggle to share in that life as a part of our existence.

Before turning to the connection that this view of Christology has for the life of the United Church of Christ, let me highlight some points about this life that we share with Christ.

THE CONTOURS OF LIFE WITH CHRIST

As we seek to give some form to what it is that we mean by life in Christ, an appropriate question is, "What are the sources for reflecting on that life?" The three I believe are most significant are scripture, tradition, and apostolic witness (that is, the witness of the saints). None of these have priority over the others. All are to be taken as inextricably bound to each other and inseparably related to our reflection on Christology. What then do these sources tell us about life in and with Christ?

The narrative of the life of Christ, as given to us by the Gospels and the Epistles, is the story of a life that begins as an overture to the world from God (Matt. 1:18–22; Luke 1:26–56; John 3:16–17). It is a life that is connected to the plan of God to bless all nations and peoples (Gen. 22:17; Matt. 1:2–17) and to heal the ruptured relationship between God and creation (Rom. 8:19–23). The character of this life as it unfolds is that of God's grace penetrating the darkness of brokenness and death (Matt. 4:16), all the while experiencing greater and greater marginalization in the face of the powers of the world as a consequence of bringing the good news and healing to the wounded and brokenhearted (Luke 4:18–21), with the penultimate result being the experience of assault and crucifixion leading to the ultimate reality of resurrection and life in the power and presence of God (Rom. 5). This narrative is given to us by the tradition of the church and its veracity is borne witness to by every generation of saints who have known, and continue to know and experience, the power of God by life in Christ (Matt. 28:16–20).

The importance of paying attention to the contours of this unfolding life is that it gives guidance to the experience of, and participation in it. That is, we may not know immediately what Christ is doing in the world *vis-à-vis* particular events, but we can know what Christ does. The effects of Christ's unfolding life are "the mute speaking, the maimed whole, the lame walking, the blind seeing" (Matt. 15:31). Correlatively, we may not know the specific "geographic" location the

Risen Christ is immediately at work—contrary to the postulations of those spiritual warriors who know with certainty where Christ is not (that is, "third world" unevangelized nations),[7] we do know that Christ is with "the least of these" (Matt. 25:31–45). As well, we may not know the instruments of government or society that God in Christ is using to work out God's providential plan for creation, but we do know that God in Christ is *not* at work in those systems that grind down the poor and leave them bereft (Isa. 3:13–15). Finally, we do know that the unfolding life of Christ is one that takes little notice of itself, but rather pours itself out on behalf of the neighbor in the sure knowledge that such a life cannot be lost (Mark 8:34–36; Luke 10:25–37; John 15:12–17). The contours of this life bear a striking resemblance to the life by which the UCC finds itself grasped. It is appropriate to look at an interpretive account of what this resemblance means for understanding our church and Christology.

UNFINISHED BUSINESS OR AN UNFINISHED LIFE?

In his book *United and Uniting: The Meaning of an Ecclesial Journey*, Louis Gunnemann brings attention to the "ad hoc" nature of life within the UCC—theologically and ecclesially.[8] By *ad hoc*, what I believe he intends is a description of life that is multivalent and in constant process. The source of this unruly quality of life can be traced to the decision by the bodies that formed the UCC to postpone definitive discussions about doctrinal and ecclesiological matters in favor of forming a common life together.[9] These decisions were made with sincere belief that these matters would work themselves out and that, as time passed, more opportunity would arise for substantive engagement with these questions. Put another way, the UCC would come to understand its life better "by and by."

A major consequence of trusting that matters of "theological significance" would be handled in the future was that the church found itself immediately embroiled in the demands of the day. In the 1960s these were, of course, the struggle for civil and human rights. As well, the UCC found itself straightaway dealing with issues of inclusion of "sinners" in the life and ministry of the church.[10] So it was a situation of being pulled this way and that by what Gunnemann identifies in *The Shaping of the United Church of Christ* as "conditions of humanity that touched the Christian conscience."[11] As the church's life unfolded, it seemed to be characterized most profoundly by the invitation to the lost and the least: "Let everyone who is thirsty come. Let anyone who wishes take the water of life as a gift (Rev. 22:16–17). Concomitant with this unfolding character of our life was an increased alienation of the UCC from the reigning paradigm of American Christian life (that is, Evangelicalism), precisely because the church dined too freely with "sinners."

This has led many to believe, erroneously, that the UCC is more concerned with "social action" than with maintenance of the true faith. Quite the contrary. Because of how our life has unfolded, we have come to understand that the Christian life is one in which the "true faith" is most profoundly experienced as life, hope, and well-being that are shared with those on whom the world turns its back (James 2).

The unresolved hybridity that characterizes our ecclesial heritage[12] creates another situation, which profoundly affects how we live. Because there is no single past that we can recover in times of uncertainty, we have had to "make it up" as we go along. This is evidenced in the UCC's propensity to ask not "Who are we?," but rather, to ask "Who, then, shall we be?" In a powerful speech, of the same name, given at General Synod IXX, Paul Sherry asks precisely this question.[13] In this speech, Sherry talks about our journey as a church to the Promised Land. The metaphor of journey is a powerful one in describing the UCC, for it captures not only the verbal character of our existence, but also the character of the faith that enlivens our existence. It is a faith that knows the end of our living but not the paths the journey will take. We, much like the sisters and brothers spoken of in Hebrews 11, are ever looking forward in hope, living forward in Christ.

I contend that interpreting the Christology of the UCC necessitates looking at the life of our church. Put another way, we live our Christology. We live it in a way that presumes Christ is living in the world today—and that we are a part of that life. This is a different way of thinking about Christology than, perhaps, much of the tradition has done so. It is, however, a way of thinking about how Christology not only informs the life of our church, but also how our life together bears witness to the dogma behind all doctrinal formulations of Christology: namely, that Christ Lives!

APPENDIX A

QUESTIONS FOR DISCUSSION

Part One:
Heritage

CHAPTER ONE
The Offices of Christ from Early Church through the Reformers
Max L. Stackhouse

1. How is the idea of an "office" socially significant? What implications does this have for the church? What are some of the difficulties that Stackhouse identifies in applying the categories of the various offices?
2. How might the offices of Christ aid us in interpreting the role of religion and politics in society?
3. Where should the church exercise its prophetic work in modern society? Where does Stackhouse see that work as most necessary?
4. What does it mean to say that Christians must become "deputies, ambassadors, apostles of Christ in every sphere of their lives"? What are some spheres of life that could benefit from this?

CHAPTER TWO
Christology in the Continental and English Reformation
Lee Barrett

1. How does Barrett's use of the "Threefold Office of Christ" differ from Stackhouse's?
2. What are some of the key "plot lines" in the development of UCC Christology?
3. What is the significance for Barrett of what he calls "the priority of the divine agency in Jesus"? Does this have any implications for how we understand Christ's humanity?
4. What changes did the discussion of the divine and the human in Christ undergo in the nineteenth century? Do these developments have anything to say to Christians in the twenty-first century?
5. Does the "forensic" model of the atonement have anything to offer to our understanding of the work of Christ? How is it related to other understandings of Christ as Prophet and King?
6. In what ways is the Christology of the United Church of Christ properly described as a kaleidoscope? What are some of the implications of that description for the unity of the church?

CHAPTER THREE
Jesus Christ in the Texts of the United Church of Christ
Gabriel Fackre

1. What are some of the difficulties in using UCC texts to study Christology? How does Fackre attempt to respond to these difficulties? Does he succeed? Why or why not?
2. What are some of the central texts that Fackre identifies as important in articulating the UCC's understanding of the identity of Jesus Christ? Why these texts? How should we interpret them?
3. What does Fackre mean by the "narrative" framework that characterizes UCC theology? How does "story" as a category help in frame the identity of Jesus Christ?
4. What can UCC texts teach us about the person of Jesus Christ? About the work of Christ?
5. What is the relationship between the narrative and texts of the UCC and the need to restate our faith in light of new insights?

Part Two:
Ecumenical Connections

CHAPTER FOUR
Jesus in God's Plan for Salvation
Lydia Veliko

1. Where does the unity of the "United" Church of Christ lie? How does it exist in light of the UCC's diversity? How is the UCC a "uniting" church?
2. What are some advantages of "pluriformity" in Reformed theology? Can we distinguish between constructive and destructive forms of pluralism? How?
3. What questions are raised by the statement "Jesus Christ is the only way to salvation"? What does the UCC have to say about this?
4. What does it mean today for the UCC to be a "reformed" and "re-forming" denomination?

CHAPTER FIVE
Recognition and the Presence of Christ at the Table
John H. Thomas

1. What is the significance of "recognition" in Thomas's article? What can we learn about the approach to Christology that characterizes the UCC in light of the "recognition stories" that Thomas enumerates?
2. Is sacramental theology important to UCC theology? How does Thomas relate Christology and sacramentology?
3. What is the nature of Christ's "presence" in the Eucharist? How does the approach of Nevin aid us in answering this question? Does the ecumenical reflection on the Eucharist in "Baptism Eucharist, and Ministry" have anything to offer the United Church of Christ's reflection on the issue?
4. What does the Mercersburg theology imply for the ecumenical work of the UCC? How has the work of the United Church of Christ in the Reformed-Lutheran dialogues brought these implications to the surface?
5. What role does worship play in forming our understanding of the identity of Jesus Christ?

Part Three:
Contemporary Issues and Practice

CHAPTER SIX
Pluralism and Mission
Mary Schaller Blaufuss

1. What does it mean to say that "mission is the mother of theology"?
2. What are the "cultures of death" in the modern world? What does Martha's encounter with Jesus in John 11 have to tell us about this?
3. What is the importance of the idea of the "periphery"?
4. What does Christ's encounter with Martha have to say about religious pluralism?

CHAPTER SEVEN
Identity and Ethical Proclamation
Deidre King Hainsworth

1. What is the distinction between understanding Jesus Christ as an "example" and understanding him as an "event"? How are these two dimensions of Christ's identity related to one another? What do they have to say about ethics?
2. What difficulties does the polity of the UCC create in seeking to arrive at a common understanding of the identity of Christ?
3. How is Christ's "prophetic" voice presented in UCC social pronouncements? Is this a helpful way of interpreting scripture?
4. How does Hainsworth argue the prophetic dimension of Christ's identity should be connected to other dimensions of his identity?
5. What does the idea of "transformation" mean in Hainsworth's article? What is the relationship between public pronouncement and personal transformation? Is transformation ethically important?

CHAPTER EIGHT
The Passion and the Compassion of the Christ
Theodore Louis Trost

1. How are *The Passion of the Christ* and the UCC "Still Speaking" campaign examples of "marketplace theology"? Is that good or bad? How are the two similar? How different?
2. What kind of Christ-figure is represented in *The Passion*? How does this compare to the idea of Christ implied by the "Still Speaking" campaign?
3. How does *The Passion* offer an example of "substitutionary atonement"? What is the significance of blood in this understanding of salvation?
4. What characteristics of Christ's identity are implied in the "Still Speaking" campaign's "bouncer" ad? With what view of salvation might this be consistent?
5. How does the tradition of the Mercersburg movement offer another understanding of Christ's identity? How does Lutheran hymnody fit in with this?
6. What does Jesus' encounter with the Syrophoenician woman in the Gospel of Mark say about his identity? Does this have any implications for the contemporary church?

CHAPTER NINE
A Living Christology and the Unfinished Business of the UCC
Stephen G. Ray, Jr.

1. What is the difference between understanding Christology as "recovery" and understanding it as "discernment"?
2. What does Ray mean by a "living Christology"?
3. What implications for Christian life are suggested in Ray's understanding of living Christology?
4. What does it mean to speak of "hybridity" in the United Church of Christ? Is hybridity a good thing?

APPENDIX B

CLASSIC AND CONTEMPORARY CHRISTOLOGICAL CONFESSIONS

The following Christological statements come from a variety of sources. The versions of the Apostles' and Nicene Creeds reproduced here along with the versions of the UCC Statement of Faith come from the *Book of Worship: United Church of Christ* (New York: Office for Church Life and Leadership, 1986). The version of the definition of the Council of Chalcedon is taken from *Christology of the Later Fathers*, edited by Edward R. Hardy (Philadelphia: The Westminster Press, 1954). The statements from the London-Amsterdam Church, the Salem Covenant, and the "Commission" Creed of 1883 are from Williston Walker, *The Creeds and Platforms of Congregationalism* (New York: The Pilgrim Press, 1991). The version of the Barmen declaration is adapted from Robert McAfee Brown, *Kairos: Three Prophetic Challenges to the Church* (Grand Rapids: Eerdmans Publishing Company, 1990), and the selection from the Heidelberg Catechism comes from *The Heidelberg Catechism* (Cleveland: United Church Press, 1962). Many of these resources, as well as others, may also be found at the United Church of Christ's web site (www.ucc.org/faith/index.html). Note that when appropriate, exclusively male language for humanity has been replaced by inclusive language. These substitutions are indicated with braces {}.

APOSTLES' CREED

I believe in God, the Father almighty, Creator of Heaven and Earth.

I believe in Jesus Christ, His only Son, our Lord. He was conceived by the power of the Holy Spirit and born of the Virgin Mary. He suffered under Pontius Pilate, was crucified, died, and was buried. He descended to the dead. On the third day he rose again. He ascended into heaven, and is seated at the right hand of the Father. He will come again to judge the living and the dead.

I believe in the Holy Spirit, the holy catholic church, the communion of saints, the forgiveness of sins, the resurrection of the body, and the life everlasting. Amen.

NICENE CREED

We believe in one God, the Father, the Almighty, Maker of heaven and earth, of all things, seen and unseen.

We believe in one Lord, Jesus Christ, the only Son of God, eternally begotten of the Father, God from God, Light from Light, true God from true God, begotten, not made, of one Being with the Father. Through him all things were made. For us and for our salvation he came down from heaven: by the power of the Holy Spirit he became incarnate from the Virgin Mary, and was made {human}. For our sake he was crucified under Pontius Pilate; he suffered death and was buried. On the third day he rose again in accordance with the scriptures; he ascended into heaven and is seated at the right hand of the Father. He will come again in glory to judge the living and the dead, and his kingdom will have no end.

We believe in the Holy Spirit, the Lord, the giver of life, who proceeds from the Father (and the Son). With the Father and the Son he is worshiped and glorified. He has spoken through the prophets. We believe in one holy catholic and apostolic church. We acknowledge one baptism for the forgiveness of sins. We look for the resurrection of the dead, and the life of the world to come. Amen.

DEFINITION OF THE COUNCIL OF CHALCEDON

Following therefore the holy Fathers, we confess one and the same our Lord Jesus Christ, and we all teach harmoniously [that he is] the same perfect in Godhead, the same perfect in {humanity}, truly God and truly {human}, the same of a reasonable soul and body; consubstantial with the Father in Godhead, and the same consubstantial with us in {humanity}, like us in all things except sin; begotten before ages of the Father in Godhead, the same in the last days for us; and for our salvation [born] of Mary the virgin theotokos in {humanity}, one and the same Christ, Son, Lord, unique; acknowledge in two natures without confusion, without change, without division, without separation—the difference of the natures being by no means taken away because of the union, but rather the distinctive character of each nature being preserved, and [each] combining in one Person and hypostasis—not divided or separated into two Persons, but one and the same Son and only-begotten God, Word, Lord Jesus Christ; as the prophets of old and the Lord Jesus Christ himself taught us about him, and the symbol of the Fathers has handed down to us.

FROM THE HEIDELBERG CATECHISM

Why is the Son of God called JESUS, which means SAVIOR?

Because he saves us from our sins, and because salvation is to be sought or found in no other.

Do those who seek their salvation and well-being in saints, by means of their own efforts, or by any other means really believe in the only Savior Jesus?

No. Rather by such actions they deny Jesus, the only Savior and Redeemer, even though they boast of belonging to him. It therefore follows that either Jesus is not a perfect Savior, or those who receive this Savior with true faith must possess in him all that is necessary for their salvation.

Why is he called CHRIST, that is, the ANOINTED ONE?

Because he is ordained by God the Father and anointed with the Holy Spirit to be our chief Prophet and Teacher, fully revealing to us the secret purpose and will of God concerning our redemption; to be our only High Priest, having redeemed us by the one sacrifice of his body and ever interceding for us with the Father; and to be our eternal King, governing us by his Word and Spirit, and defending and sustaining us in the redemption he has won for us.

But why are you called a Christian?

Because through faith I share in Christ and thus in his anointing, so that I may confess his name, offer myself a living sacrifice of gratitude to him, and fight against sin and the devil with a free and good conscience throughout this life and hereafter rule with him in eternity over all creatures.

Why is he called God's ONLY-BEGOTTEN SON when we also are God's children?

Because Christ alone is God's own eternal Son, whereas we are accepted for his sake as children of God by grace.

Why do you call him OUR LORD?

Because, not with gold or silver but at the cost of his blood, he has redeemed us body and soul from sin and all the dominion of the devil, and has bought us for his very own.

What is the meaning of: "Conceived by the Holy Spirit, born of the Virgin Mary"?

That the eternal Son of God, who is and remains true and eternal God, took upon himself our true {humanity} from the flesh and blood of the Virgin Mary through the action of the Holy Spirit, so that he might also be the true seed of David, like his fellow {human beings}, except for sin.

What benefit do you receive from the holy conception and birth of Christ?

That he is our Mediator, and that, in God's sight, he covers over with his innocence and perfect holiness the sinfulness in which I have been conceived.

From the Second Confession of the London-Amsterdam Church (1596)

8. That in this world Iesus Christ hath reveled watsoever his father thought needful for us to know, beleeue & obey as touching his person & Offices, in whom all the promises of God are yea, & in whom they are Amen to the prayse of God through us.

9. That touching his person, the Lord Iesus, of who Moses & the Prophets wrote, & who the Apostles preached, is the everlasting Sonne of God, by eternall generation, the brightnes of his Fathers glorie, & the engrauen forme of his Person; coessentiall, coequall, & coeternall, god with him & with the holy Gost, by who hee hath made the worlds, by whom hee upholdeth and governeth all the works hee hath made; who also when the fulnes of tyme was come, was made man of a woman, of the Tribe of Iudah, of the seed of Dauid & Abraham, to wyt of Mary that blessed Virgin, by the holy Ghost coming upon hir, & the powre of the most high ouershadowing hir; & was also in all things lyke unto us, sinne only excepted.

10. That touching his Office, hee only is made the Mediator of the new Testament, even of the euerlasting Couenant of grace between God & man, to bee perfectly & fully the Prophet, Priest & King of the Church of God for euermore.

11. That hee was fro euerlasting, by the iust & sufficient authoritie of the father, & in respect of his manhood fro the womb called & separated heerunto, & anointed also most fully & aboundantly with all necessarie gifts, as is written; God hath not measured out the Spirit unto him.

FROM THE SALEM COVENANT DIRECTION OF 1665

I do believe with my heart and confess with my mouth.

Concerning God.
That there is but one only true God in three persons, the Father, the Son and the Holy Ghost, each of them God, and all of them one and the same Infinite, Eternall God, most Wise, Holy, Just, Mercifull and Blessed for ever.

Concerning the Works of God.
That this God is the Maker, Preserver, and Governour of all things according to the counsel of his own Will, and that God made man in his own Image, in Knowledge, Holiness, and Righteousness.

Concerning the fall of Man.
That Adam by transgressing the Command of God, fell from God and brought himself and his posterity into a state of Sin and death, under the Wrath and Curse of God, which I do believe to be my own condition by nature as well as any other.

Concerning Jesus Christ.
That God sent his Son into the World, who for our sakes became man, that he might redeem and save us by his Obedience unto death, and that he arose from the dead, ascended unto Heaven and sitteth at the right hand of God, from whence he shall come to judge the World.

Concerning the Holy Ghost
That God the holy Ghost hath fully revealed the Doctrine of Christ and will of God in the Scriptures of the Old and New Testament, which are the Word of God, the perfect, perpetuall, and only Rule of our Faith and Obedience.

Concerning the Benefits we have by Christ.
That the same Spirit by Working Faith in Gods Elect, applyeth unto them Christ with all his Benefits of Justification, and Sanctification, unto Salvation, in the use of those Ordinances which God hath

appointed in his written word, which therefore ought to be observed by us until the coming of Christ.

Concerning the Church of Christ
That all true Believers being united unto Christ as the Head, make up one Misticall Church which is the Body of Christ, the members whereof having fellowship with the Father Son and Holy-Ghost by Faith, and one with an other in love, doe receive here upon earth forgiveness of Sinnes, with the life of grace, and at the Resurrection of the Body, they shall receive everlasting life. *Amen.*

FROM THE "COMMISSION" CREED OF 1883

VI. We believe that the love of God to sinful men has found its highest expression in the redemptive work of his Son; who became man, uniting his divine nature with our human nature in one person; who was tempted like other men, yet without sin; who by his humiliation, his holy obedience, his sufferings, his death on the cross, and his resurrection, became a perfect Redeemer; whose sacrifice of himself for the sins of the world declares the righteousness of God, and is the sole and sufficient ground of forgiveness and of reconciliation with him.

VII. We believe that Jesus Christ, after he had risen from the dead, ascended into heaven, where, as the one mediator between God and man, he carries forward his work of saving men; that he sends the Holy Spirit to convict them of sin, and to lead them to repentance and faith; and that those who through renewing grace turn to righteousness, and trust in Jesus Christ as their Redeemer, receive for his sake the forgiveness of their sins, and are made the children of God.

VIII. We believe that those who are thus regenerated and justified, grow in sanctified character through fellowship with Christ, the indwelling of the Holy Spirit, and obedience to the truth; that a holy life is the fruit and evidence of saving faith; and that the believer's hope of continuance in such a life is in the persevering grace of God.

IX. We believe that Jesus Christ came to establish among men the kingdom of God, the reign of truth and love, righteousness and peace; that to Jesus Christ, the Head of his kingdom, Christians are directly responsible in faith and conduct; and that to him all have immediate access without mediatorial or priestly intervention.

THE BARMAN DECLARATION

1. "I am the Way and the Truth and the Life; no one comes to the Father except through me." John 14:6
"Very truly, I tell you, anyone who does not enter the sheepfold through the gate but climbs in by another way is a thief and a bandit. I am the gate. Whoever enters by me will be saved." John 10:1, 9
Jesus Christ, as he is attested to us in Holy Scripture, is the one Word of God whom we have to hear, and whom we have to trust and obey in life and in death.
We reject the false doctrine that the Church could and should recognize as a source of its proclamation, beyond and besides this one Word of God, yet other events, powers, historic figures and truths as God's revelation.

2. "Jesus Christ has been made wisdom and righteousness and sanctification and redemption for us by God." 1 Cor. 1:30
As Jesus Christ is God's comforting pronouncement of the forgiveness of all our sins, so, with equal seriousness, he is also God's vigorous announcement of his claim upon our whole life. Through him there comes to us joyful liberation from the godless ties of this world for free, grateful service to his creatures.
We reject the false doctrine that there could be areas of our life in which we would not belong to Jesus Christ but to other lords, areas in which we would not need justification and sanctification through him.

3. "Let us, however, speak the truth in love, and in every respect grow into him who is the head, into Christ, from whom the whole body is joined together." Eph. 4:15–16
The Christian Church is the community of brethren in which, in Word and Sacrament, through the Holy Spirit, Jesus Christ acts in the present as Lord. With both its faith and its obedience, with both its message and its order, it has to testify in the midst of the sinful world, as the Church of pardoned sinners, that it belongs to him alone and

lives and may live by his comfort and under his direction alone, in expectation of his appearing.

We reject the false doctrine that the Church could have permission to hand over the form of its message and of its order to whatever it itself might wish or to the vicissitudes of the prevailing ideological and political convictions of the day.

4. "You know that the rulers of the Gentiles lord it over them, and their great ones are tyrants over them. It will not be so among you; but whoever wishes to have authority over you must be your servant." Matt. 20:25–26

The various offices in the Church do not provide a basis for some to exercise authority over others but for the ministry [lit., "service"] with which the whole community has been entrusted and charged to be carried out.

We reject the false doctrine that, apart from this ministry, the Church could, and could have permission to, give itself or allow itself to be given special leaders [Führer] vested with ruling authority.

5. "Fear God. Honor the Emperor." 1 Pet. 2:17

Scripture tells us that by divine appointment the State, in this still unredeemed world in which also the Church is situated, has the task of maintaining justice and peace, so far as human discernment and human ability make this possible, by means of the threat and use of force. The Church acknowledges with gratitude and reverence toward God the benefit of this, his appointment. It draws attention to God's Dominion [Reich], God's commandment and justice, and with these the responsibility of those who rule and those who are ruled. It trusts and obeys the power of the Word, by which God upholds all things.

We reject the false doctrine that beyond its special commission the State should and could become the sole and total order of human life and so fulfil the vocation of the Church as well.

We reject the false doctrine that beyond its special commission the Church should and could take on the nature, tasks and dignity which belong to the State and thus become itself an organ of the State.

6. "See, I am with you always, to the end of the age." Matt. 28:20
"God's Word is not fettered." 2 Tim. 2:9

The Church's commission, which is the foundation of its freedom, consists in this: in Christ's stead, and so in the service of his own Word and work, to deliver all people, through preaching and sacrament, the message of the free grace of God.

We reject the false doctrine that with human vainglory the Church could place the Word and work of the Lord in the service of self-chosen desires, purposes and plans.

The Confessing Synod of the German Evangelical Church declares that it sees in the acknowledgment of these truths and in the rejection of these errors the indispensable theological basis of the German Evangelical Church as a confederation of Confessing Churches. It calls upon all who can stand in solidarity with its Declaration to be mindful of these theological findings in all their decisions concerning Church and State. It appeals to all concerned to return to unity in faith, hope and love.

Verbum Dei manet in aeternum.
The Word of God will last for ever.

United Church of Christ
Statement of Faith

We believe in God, the Eternal Spirit, Father of our Lord Jesus Christ and our Father, and to his deeds we testify:

He calls the worlds into being, creates man in his own image, and sets before him the ways of life and death.

He seeks in holy love to save all people from aimlessness and sin.

He judges men and nations by his righteous will declared through prophets and apostles.

In Jesus Christ, the man of Nazareth, our crucified and risen Lord, he has come to us and shared our common lot, conquering sin and death and reconciling the world to himself.

He bestows upon us his Holy Spirit, creating and renewing the church of Jesus Christ, binding in covenant faithful people of all ages, tongues, and races.

He calls us into his church to accept the cost and joy of discipleship, to be his servants in the service of men, to proclaim the gospel to all the world and resist the powers of evil, to share in Christ's baptism and eat at his table, to join him in his passion and victory.

He promises to all who trust him forgiveness of sins and fullness of grace, courage in the struggle for justice and peace, his presence in trial and rejoicing, and eternal life in his kingdom which has no end.

Blessing and honor, glory and power be unto him. Amen.

UNITED CHURCH OF CHRIST
STATEMENT OF FAITH
(Inclusive Version, Adapted by Robert V. Moss)

We believe in God, the Eternal Spirit, who is made known to us in Jesus our brother, and to whose deeds we testify:

God calls the worlds into being, creates humankind in the divine image, and sets before us the ways of life and death.

God seeks in holy love to save all people from aimlessness and sin.

God judges all humanity and all nations by that will of righteousness declared through prophets and apostles.

In Jesus Christ, the man of Nazareth, our crucified and risen Lord, God has come to us and shared our common lot, conquering sin and death and reconciling the whole creation to its Creator.

God bestows upon us the Holy Spirit, creating and renewing the church of Jesus Christ, binding in covenant faithful people of all ages, tongues, and races.

God calls us into the church to accept the cost and joy of discipleship, to be servants in the service of the whole human family, to proclaim the gospel to all the world and resist the powers of evil, to share in Christ's baptism and eat at his table, to join him in his passion and victory.

God promises to all who trust in the gospel forgiveness of sins and fullness of grace, courage in the struggle for justice and peace, the presence of the Holy Spirit in trial and rejoicing, and eternal life in that kingdom which has no end.

Blessing and honor, glory and power be unto God. Amen.

Appendix C
For Further Reading

Classic Christological Texts

Anselm, Saint. "Cur Deus Homo." In *Anselm of Canterbury: The Major Works,* edited by Brian Davies and Gill Evans. New York: Oxford University Press, 1998.

Athanasius, Saint. *On the Incarnation.* Crestwood, NY: Saint Vladimir's Seminary Press, 1975.

Athanasius, Saint. "Orations Against the Arians." In *The Christological Controversy,* edited by Richard A. Norris. Minneapolis: Augsburg Fortress Press, 1980.

Calvin, John. *Institutes of the Christian Religion.* 2 vols. Edited by John T. McNeill; translated by Ford Lewis Battles. Philadelphia: Westminster Press, 1960.

Cyril of Alexandria, Saint. *On the Unity of Christ.* Translated by John Anthony McGukin and Anthony McGukin. Crestwood, NY: Saint Vladimir's Seminary Press, 1997.

Gregory of Nazianzus, Saint. *On God and Christ: The Five Theological Orations and Two Letters to Cledonius.* Translated by Frederick Williams and Lionel R. Wickham. Crestwood, NY: Saint Vladimir's Seminary Press, 2002.

The Heidelberg Catechism with Commentary, 400th anniversary ed. Philadelphia: United Church Press, 1963.

Irenaeus of Lyon. "Against Heresies." In *The Christological Controversy,* edited by Richard A. Norris. Minneapolis: Augsburg Fortress Press, 1980.

Leith, John H. *The Creeds of the Churches: A Reader in Christian Doctrine, from the Bible to the Present,* 3rd ed. Louisville, KY: Westminster/John Knox Press, 1983.

Luther, Martin. "Heidelberg Disputation." In *Martin Luther: Selections from His Writings,* edited by John Dillenberger. New York: Anchor Books, 1958.

Tertullian. "On the Flesh of Christ." In *The Christological Controversy,* edited by Richard A. Norris. Minneapolis: Augsburg Fortress Press, 1980.

Important Modern Contributions

Barth, Karl. *The Church Dogmatics.* Vols. IV/1–IV/4. Edinburgh: T&T Clark, 1936–1969.

Bloesch, Donald G. *Jesus Christ: Savior and Lord.* Downers Grove, IL: InterVarsity Press, 1997.

Boff, Leonardo. *Jesus Christ Liberator: A Critical Christology for Our Times.* Maryknoll, NY: Orbis Books, 1978.

Bonhoeffer, Dietrich. *Discipleship.* Minneapolis: Fortress Press, 2001.

———. *Letters and Papers from Prison.* New York: Macmillan, 1972.

Borg, Marcus. *Meeting Jesus Again for the First Time.* San Francisco: HarperSanFrancisco, 1995.

Fackre, Gabriel. *The Christian Story,* vol. 1, *A Narrative Interpretation of Basic Christian Doctrine,* 3rd ed. Grand Rapids, MI: W. B. Eerdmans, 1996.

Grant, Jaquelyn. *White Women's Christ and Black Women's Jesus: Feminist Theology and Womanist Response.* New York: Oxford University Press, 1990.

Hall, Douglas John. *Professing the Faith: Christian Theology in North American Context.* Minneapolis: Fortress Press, 1993.

McFague, Sallie. *Metaphorical Theology: Models of God in Religious Language.* Minneapolis: Fortress Press, 1997.

Moltmann, Jürgen. *The Crucified God: The Cross of Jesus as the Foundation and Criticism of Christian Theology.* Minneapolis: Fortress Press, 1974.

———. *The Way of Jesus Christ: Christology in Messianic Dimensions.* Minneapolis: Fortress Press, 1993.

Niebuhr, H. Richard. *Christ and Culture.* San Francisco: HarperSanFrancisco, 2001.

Niebuhr, Reinhold. *The Nature and Destiny of Man,* vol. 2, *Human Destiny.* New York: Charles Scribner's Sons, 1945.

Pannenberg, Wolfhart. *Jesus: God and Man.* Louisville, KY: Westminster/John Knox Press, 1982.

———. *Systematic Theology.* Vol. 2. Grand Rapids: Eerdmans, 1994.

Ruether, Rosemary Radford. *Sexism and God-Talk: Toward a Feminist Theology.* Boston: Beacon Press, 1993.

Schleiermacher, Freidrich. *The Christian Faith.* Edinburgh: T&T Clark, 1999.

Sobrino, Jon. *Christology at the Crossroads: A Latin American Approach.* Maryknoll, NY: Orbis Books, 1978.

UCC and Ecumenical Texts

Arndt, Elmer J. F. *The Faith We Proclaim: The Doctrinal Viewpoint Generally Prevailing in the Evangelical and Reformed Church.* Philadelphia: The Christian Education Press, 1960.

"Baptism, Eucharist and Ministry" (Faith and Order Paper No. 111). New York: World Council of Churches, 1982.

The COCU Consensus: In Quest of a Church of Christ Uniting, 2nd ed. Princeton: Consultation on Church Union, 1991.

Dunn, David, ed. *A History of the Evangelical and Reformed Church.* New York: The Pilgrim Press, 1990.

Gunnemann, Louis H. *The Shaping of the United Church of Christ: An Essay in the History of American Christianity.* New York: United Church Press, 1977.

Horton, Douglas. *The United Church of Christ.* New York: Thomas Nelson, 1962.

Johnson, Daniel L., and Charles Hambrick-Stowe, eds. *Theology and Identity: Traditions, Movements, and Polity in the United Church of Christ.* Cleveland: United Church Press, 1990.

Nevin, John Williamson. *The Mystical Presence.* Edited by Augustine Thompson, O.P. Eugene, OR: Wipf and Stock, 2000. Previously published by Lippencott, Publishers, 1846.

Nickle, Keith F., and Timothy F. Lull, eds. "A Common Calling: The Witness of Our Reformation Churches in North American Today." Minneapolis: Augsburg Fortress, 1993.

Schaff, Philip. *The Principle of Protestantism.* Edited by Bard Thompson and George H. Bricker; translated by John W. Nevin, 1845. Philadelphia: United Church Press, 1964.

Shinn, Roger Lincoln. *Confessing Our Faith: An Interpretation of the Statement of Faith of the United Church of Christ.* New York: The Pilgrim Press, 1990.

von Rohr, John. *The Shaping of American Congregationalism: 1620–1957.* Cleveland: The Pilgrim Press, 1992.

Walker, Williston. *The Creeds and Platforms of Congregationalism.* Eugene, OR: Wipf and Stock, 2005.

Zikmund, Barbara Brown, ed. *Hidden Histories in the United Church of Christ.* 2 vols. Cleveland: The Pilgrim Press, 1987.

Zikmund, Barbara Brown, general editor. *The Living Theological Heritage of the United Church of Christ.* 7 vols. Cleveland: The Pilgrim Press, 1995–2005.

APPENDIX D

WORSHIP RESOURCES
COMPILED BY FREDERICK R. TROST

EUCHARISTIC CONFESSION:

As we now take and enjoy bread and wine together in accordance with (Christ's) direction, we find comfort and joy in the presence of his body broken for us and his blood shed for us, and therefore in the promise of our life in his coming kingdom. We confess in doing this our thanksgiving for the reconciliation of the world with God that has taken place in him. We also confess herewith that we are bound together as brothers and sisters who must love and assist one another as such. And we affirm herewith our hope in his final manifestation in which he will come and make all things new.

> —Karl Barth, in a letter to Pastor Karl Handrich,
> November 22, 1963, "Confessing Christ Daily Lectionary,"
> Pentecost/Trinity Seasons, 2002/1

A BENEDICTION:

May the grace of the Lord Jesus sanctify us and keep us from all evil;
May he drive far from us all hurtful things,
And purify both our souls and bodies;
May he bind us to himself by the bond of love,
And may his peace abound in our hearts.

> —Gregorian Sacramentary, "Confessing Christ Daily
> Lectionary," Pentecost/Trinity Seasons, 2002/2

FAITH, HOPE, LOVE:

Jesus, the Savior of humankind, who was fastened to the cross with three nails, fasten our hearts to the same cross with the three nails of faith, hope, and love.

—Adrian Parviliers, "Confessing Christ Daily Lectionary,"
Lent, 2003

WE BELIEVE:

In Jesus Christ we believe the God who has become human, crucified and resurrected. In the incarnation, we recognize God's love for his creation; in the crucifixion, God's judgment over all flesh; in the resurrection, God's will for a new world . . .

—Dietrich Bonhoeffer, "Confessing Christ Daily Lectionary,"
Eastertide, 2003

CHRIST IS RISEN, CHRIST IS LIVING:
(CRISTO VIVE, FUERA EL LLANTO)

Christ is risen, Christ is living, dry your tears, be unafraid!
Death and darkness could not hold him,
    nor the tomb in which he laid.
Do not look among the dead for one who lives forever more:
Tell the world that Christ is risen, make it known he goes before.

If the Lord had never risen, we'd have nothing to believe.
But his promise can be trusted: "You will live, because I live."
As we share the death of Adam, so in Christ we live again.
Death has lost its sting and terror, Christ the Lord has come to reign.

Death has lost its old dominion, let the world rejoice and shout!
Christ, the firstborn of the living gives us life and leads us out.
Let us thank our God who causes hope to spring up from the ground.
Christ is risen, Christ is giving life eternal, life profound.

—Easter hymn, from the Church in Argentina,
"Confessing Christ Daily Lectionary," Eastertide, 2003

Eastertide Prayer:

The Day of Resurrection has dawned upon us, the day of true light and life, wherein Christ, the life of believers, arose from the dead. Let us give abundant thanks and praise to God, that while we solemnly celebrate the day of our Lord's resurrection, he may be pleased to bestow on us quiet peace and special gladness; so that being protected from morning to night by his favoring mercy, we may rejoice in the gift of our Redeemer.

—Mozarabic Sacramentary, "Confessing Christ Daily Lectionary," Eastertide, 2003

A Prayer for Others:

O blessed Lord and Savior, who has commanded us to love one another, grant us grace that, having received your undeserved bounty, we may love every one in you and for you.

We implore clemency for all; but especially for the friends whom your love has given to us. Love them, you who are the fountain of love, and make them to love you with all their heart, with all their mind, and with all their soul, that those things only which are pleasing to you they may will, and speak, and do. And though our prayer is cold, because our charity is so little fervent, yet you are rich in mercy. Measure not to them your goodness by the dullness of our devotion; but as your kindness surpasses all human affection, so let your hearing transcend our prayer. Do to them what is expedient for them, according to your will, that they, being always and everywhere ruled and protected by you, may attain in the end to everlasting life; and to you, with the Father and the Holy Spirit, be all honor and praise for ever and ever.

—St. Anselm, "Confessing Christ Daily Lectionary," Pentecost/Trinity Seasons, 2004

Conformity With Christ:

Through suffering with Christ we are conformed to him. Like him we divest ourselves of the "form of God" and put on the "form of a servant." We renounce all pride, all glory and honor before the world and before ourselves, and let ourselves be drawn into Christ's suffering . . . To be conformed to Christ means nothing else but experiencing the fact of the cross also in our lives. When the cross remains not simply a fact of history, but when it is erected in the midst of our life, then we are people who have been conformed to Christ . . . But, of course, it is not in our power to do this. Even with our best-intentioned exertions we cannot compel the "being conformed to Christ;" it is God's gift, not our work. However, we can and should pray for it. For God . . . wants us to be conformed in all things to the image of his Son, and do this altogether voluntarily.

—Walther von Loewenich, reflection on Luther's "Theology of the Cross," "Confessing Christ Daily Lectionary," Pentecost/Trinity Seasons, 2004

Bread of Life:

O Bread of life from heaven, To weary pilgrims given, O manna from above!

The souls that hunger feed thou, the hearts that seek thee lead thou, with thy most sweet and tender love.

—Latin hymn, Tr. Philip Schaff, "Confessing Christ Daily Lectionary," Lent, 2005

O Jesus, My Feet Are Dirty:

O Jesus, my feet are dirty. Come even as a slave to me, pour water into your bowl, come and wash my feet. In asking such a thing I know I am overbold but I dread what was threatened when you said to me, "If I do not wash your feet I have no fellowship with you." Wash my feet then, because I long for your companionship. And yet, what am I asking? It is well for Peter to ask you to wash his feet, for him that was all that was needed for him to be clean in every part. With me it is different, though you wash me now I shall still stand in need of that other washing, the cleansing you promised when you said, "there is a baptism I must needs be baptized with."

—Origen, "Confessing Christ Daily Lectionary," Lent, 2005

God's Will for a New World:

In Jesus Christ we believe the God who has become human, crucified and resurrected. In the incarnation, we recognize God's love for his creation; in the crucifixion, God's judgment over all flesh; in the resurrection, God's will for a new world.

—Dietrich Bonhoeffer, "Confessing Christ Daily Lectionary," Eastertide, 2005

Come To Us: (Epiphany)

Come to us, abide with us, Lord Jesus, Light of the world. Shine in our darkness that the long, bitter night of our doubts might melt away. Redeem the cold stone of our spirits with the strong, warm rays of your truth. Grant that each among us might resonate again to the song the angels sing. Send your Holy Spirit that, humbled and restored to life by the wonder of your love, we might lift up our hearts with great, abounding joy.

—Oratio: A Book of Prayers for the Church Year and for Special Occasions, edited by Frederick R. Trost

A Prayer of Confession: (Epiphany)

Enter, Lord Jesus, the bleak midwinter in which we have, once again, found ourselves. Forgive our cautious ways, our incomplete vision, our hesitant steps, our modest faith, our raw deeds, the often dull and somber approach we bring to life. Do not turn from us, we pray, but in the light of the bright, morning star, set in the heavens for us, hear us as we confess our sin. Grant us grace that we might live in this light and thus in the company of all the saints who praise you and offer you their thanks. Lift us from the depths, accompany us on our way, guide us in the paths of righteousness, that we might rejoice in your truth which abides forever and ever.

—Oratio: A Book of Prayers for the Church Year and for Special Occasions, edited by Frederick R. Trost

EASTER SERMON, 1964:

Dear friends, we were not there when the risen Jesus, in spite of all the folly and mourning of his disciples, in spite of these doors shut from sheer terror, came into their midst. We cannot see him now as directly as they could, nor shall we be able to see him like that until he comes to judge the living and the dead at the end of all time. But in our way, indirectly, that is in the mirror of the narrative and so of the witness, the confession, the proclamation of the first community, we too can and may see him here and now. Many before us . . . have seen him in this and have become glad. For this very reason we celebrate Easter, the festival in memory of that day, to join those people, to see the Lord in that mirror, and so too to become glad. Without seeing the Lord nobody can be glad. Whoever sees him will become glad. Why should this not happen to us as well, to the little Easter congregation of prisoners in Basel's Spitalstrasse with their chaplain and their organist, with all the inmates and warders of this institution and (after all, I suppose I belong here too) with the old professor who occasionally pays a visit here? All of us can see the Lord too. So all of us may become glad too. God grant that this may happen to us.

—Karl Barth, *Call for God*

NOTES

INTRODUCTION
Who Do We Say That He Is?
Scott R. Paeth

1. Roger Lincoln Shinn, *Confessing Our Faith: An Interpretation of the Statement of Faith of the United Church of Christ* (New York: The Pilgrim Press, 1990), 68–69.
2. Dietrich Bonhoeffer, *Letters and Papers from Prison* (New York: Macmillan Publishing Company, 1972), 279.
3. See Louis H. Gunnemann, *The Shaping of the United Church of Christ: An Essay in the History of American Christianity* (New York: United Church Press, 1977).
4. See "The Basis of Union of the Congregational Christian Churches and the Evangelical and Reformed Church with the Interpretations" Article II, n. 3 and Article IV. F in Gunnemann, *The Shaping of the United Church of Christ*, 208 and 211.
5. Gabriel Fackre, "Christian Doctrine in the United Church of Christ," in *Theology and Identity: Traditions, Movements, and Polity in the United Church of Christ*, Daniel L. Johnson and Charles Hambrick-Stowes, eds. (Cleveland: United Church Press, 1990), 140.

Part One:
Heritage

CHAPTER ONE
The Offices of Christ from Early Church through the Reformers
Max L. Stackhouse

1. Robert Sherman, *Priest, Prophet, and King: A Trinitarian Theology of Atonement* (London: T. &. T. Clark, 2004).
2. E. F. Karl Müller, "Jesus Christ: Threefold Offices of," *The New Schaff-Herzog Encyclopedia of Religious Knowledge*, VI, 173ff.
3. John Calvin, *Institutes of the Christian Religion*, vol. 2 (Philadelphia: Westminster Press, 1960), xv.
4. Friedrich Schleiermacher, *The Christian Faith*, 2nd ed. (London: T & T Clark, 1928), Sections 102 to 105.
5. Ibid., Section 103.
6. Ibid., Section 104.
7. Ibid.
8. See A. S. P. Woodhouse, ed., *Puritanism and Liberty*, 2nd ed. (Chicago: University of Chicago Press, 1974).
9. James Luther Adams, *The Prophethood of All Believers*, George K. Beach, ed. (Boston: Beacon Press, 1986).
10. A more accurate portrait of what is going on in globalization can be found in Thomas L. Friedman's *The World is Flat: A Brief History of the Twenty-First Century* (New York: Farrar, Straus & Giroux, 2005), although he does not recognize the influence of religion on these developments. For that, see Lawrence Harrison, et al. *Culture Matters: How Values Shape Human Progress* (New York: Basic Books, 2000).

CHAPTER TWO
Christology in the Continental and English Reformation
Lee Barrett

1. Henry Harbaugh, "Christological Theology," in *The Living Theological Heritage of The United Church of Christ*, vol. 4, *Consolidation and Expansion,* Elizabeth C. Nordbeck and Lowell H. Zuck, eds. (Cleveland: The Pilgrim Press, 1999), 583–90.
2. Lyman Abbott, *The Theology of an Evolutionist* (Boston: Houghton Mifflin Co., 1897).
3. Elmer Arndt, *The Faith We Proclaim* (Philadelphia: The Christian Education Press, 1960), 28–62.

4. Emanuel Gerhart, *Institutes of the Christian Religion*, vol. 2 (New York: Funk & Wagnalls Company, 1894), 223–63.
5. Arndt, *The Faith We Proclaim*, 40.
6. "Creed of 1883" in *The Living Theological Heritage*, vol. 4, 505–07.
7. Roger Lincoln Shinn, *Confessing Our Faith: An Interpretation of the Statement of Faith of the United Church of Christ* (New York: United Church Press, 1990), 64–69.
8. Daniel Irion, *Evangelical Fundamentals, Part Two: Evangelical Belief and Doctrine*, Julius H. Horstmann, trans. (St. Louis: Eden Publishing House, 1916), 63.
9. Zacharius Ursinus, *The Commentary of Dr. Zacharius Ursinus on the Heidelberg Catechism* (Grand Rapids: Wm. B. Eerdmans Publishing Co., 1956), 243–59.
10. Horace Bushnell, *God in Christ* (Hartford: Brown, Parsons, 1849), 135–74.
11. John Williamson Nevin, *The Mystical Presence and Other Writings on the Eucharist*, Bard Thompson and George Bricker, eds. (Philadelphia: United Church Press, 1966).
12. Gerhart, *Institutes of the Christian Religion*, vol. 2, 264–78.
13. Ursinus, *The Commentary of Dr. Zacharius Ursinus*, 169–76.
14. Gabriel Fackre, *The Christian Story*, vol. 1. *A Narrative Interpretation of Basic Christian Doctrine* (Grand Rapids: Wm. B. Eerdmans Publishing Co., 1984) 135–50. See also Gabriel Fackre, "Jesus Christ in the Texts of the United Church of Christ," in this volume.
15. Gerhart, *Institutes of the Christian Religion*, vol. 2, 332–47, 371–76.
16. Nevin, *The Mystical Presence*.
17. Irion, *Evangelical Fundamentals, Part Two*, 66–68.
18. Horace Bushnell in *Horace Bushnell: Selected Writings on Language, Religion, and American Culture*, David L. Smith, ed. (Chico, CA: Scholars Press, 1984).
19. Walter Marshall Horton, *Our Christian Faith* (Boston: The Pilgrim Press, 1945), 21–26.
20. Shinn, *Confessing Our Faith*, 69–72.
21. Fackre, *The Christian Story*, vol. 1, 141–46.
22. "Creed of 1883," in *The Living Theological Heritage of the United Church of Christ*, vol. 4, 507.
23. "Kansas City Statement of Faith" in *The Living Theological Heritage*, vol. 4, 510.
24. H. Richard Niebuhr, *Christ and Culture* (San Francisco: HarperSan Francisco, 2001).
25. Shinn, *Confessing Our Faith*, 40–42.

CHAPTER THREE
Jesus Christ in the Texts of the United Church of Christ
Gabriel Fackre

1. On the latter, see Barbara Brown Zikmund, ed., *Hidden Histories in the United Church of Christ* (New York: United Church Press, 1987).
2. A representative example of such is found in "A Common Calling: The Witness of Our Reformation Churches in North America Today," Keith F. Nickle and Timothy F. Lull, eds. (Minneapolis: Augsburg Fortress, 1993), especially 75–80.
3. A range of formative UCC "texts," going back to the earliest centuries, has been assembled in the seven volume series, *The Living Theological Heritage of the United Church of Christ*, Barbara Brown Zikmund, general editor (Cleveland: The Pilgrim Press, 1995–2005). "Texts" in this remarkable series, however, also include letters, hymns, poems, prayers, essays, and other such documents, all of which are part of the UCC "tradition," though not corporate texts in the sense the term is here used.
4. We have no study of how much these creeds function, pedagogically and liturgically, in the UCC. My own experience is of their widespread use in my ten-year pastoral ministry in the former E&R wing of the church, and as a member in two congregations for thirty years in the heartland of the former Congregational-Christian wing of the church. They were always a standard resource in my required systematic theology courses at both Lancaster Theological Seminary with its E&R roots and Andover Newton Theological School with its Congregational heritage.

   What of the small stream that fed into the UCC called "The Christian Connection," whose slogan was "No creed but Christ"? No creed? Its General Convention in 1874 listed eight of its teachings in the "Belief" section of its Basis of Union, speaking of them as "those fundamental truths, without which Christianity could not exist . . . " See *Living Theological Heritage of the United Church of Christ*, vol. 4, Elizabeth Nordbeck and Lowell Zuck, eds. (Cleveland: The Pilgrim Press, 1999), 128–29.
5. United Church of Christ Constitution, Article V, 13.
6. Interestingly, the Kansas City Statement of Faith appears as a resource in the *Book of Worship: United Church of Christ* (New York: UCC Office of Church Life and Leadership, 1986), 511.
7. See *Churches in Covenant Communion and The COCU Consensus* (Princeton: Consultation on Church Union, rev. ed., 1995), Lutheran-Reformed Joint Coordinating Committee, "A Formula of Agreement" (n.d.) with its foundational study "A Common Calling" and "The Leuenberg Agreement," in *An Invitation to Action: A Study of*

Ministry, Sacraments and Recognition, James E. Andrews and Joseph A. Burgess, eds. (Philadelphia: Fortress Press, 1984), 61–73.

8. See Gabriel Fackre, *The Christian Story*, vol. 2, *Scripture in the Church for the World.* (Grand Rapids: Wm. B. Eerdmans Publishing Co., 1987), passim.

9. Borrowing and altering for our purposes here a phrase coined by UCC theologian Reinhold Niebuhr in describing biblical "myths" to be "taken seriously but not literally."

10. See "Basis of Union of the Congregational Christian Churches and the Evangelical and Reformed Church with the Interpretations," in Louis H. Gunnemann, *The Shaping of the United Church of Christ: An Essay in the History of American Christianity* (New York: United Church Press, 1977), 208.

11. Ibid.

12. Article V, 17 and 19, surrounding V, 18.

13. On the dysfunctional status of not only creed, but also scripture and the historic episcopate, see the indictment of the Episcopal Church in the United States by Episcopal theologian R. R. Reno in *In the Ruins of the Church: Sustaining Faith in a Time of Diminished Christianity* (Grand Rapids: Brazos Press, 2002).

    Pertinent here also is Cardinal Joseph Ratzinger's (now Pope Benedict XVI) public pondering as to whether the doctrinal standards cited by other ecclesial bodies in ecumenical negotiations with the Roman Catholic Church are, in fact, binding, or rather or just "on the books," but no longer adhered to by the people of those bodies. Of course, the same question might be posed to Ratzinger about the degree of loyalty to stated Roman Catholic doctrine by its own constituency, given the notable divisions within that church today.

14. Roger Lincoln Shinn, *Confessing Our Faith: An Interpretation of the Statement of Faith of the United Church of Christ* (New York: The Pilgrim Press, 1990), 3–32.

15. See Williston Walker, compiler, *The Creeds and Platforms of Congregationalism* (Eugene, OR: Wipf and Stock, 2005).

16. See, for example, Bernhard W. Anderson, *The Unfolding Drama of the Bible*, 3rd ed. (Philadelphia: Fortress Press, 1988).

17. The resolution and the clarifying statement by the theological panel in 1990 appear in a full issue on the subject of *New Conversations* 12, no. 3 (Summer 1990).

18. See the detailed study of that usage in scripture and the early church in Larry W. Hurtado, *Lord Jesus Christ: Devotion to Jesus in Early Christianity* (Grand Rapids: Wm. B. Eerdmans Publishing Co., 2003).

19. A move in the rewriting of hymns challenged by a General Synod action.

20. As explored in detail in Richard Christensen, ed., *How Shall We Sing the Lord's Song?* (Allison Park, PA: Pickwick Publications, 1997).

21. For an elaboration of this point and a spectrum of inclusive language proposals, see the writer's "Ways of Inclusivity—the Language Debate," *Prism* 9, no. 1 (Spring 1994): 52–65.

22. See the formulation and exposition in Bjarne Skard, *The Incarnation: A Study of the Christology of the Ecumenical Creeds*, Herman Jorgensen, trans.(Minneapolis: Augsburg Publishing House, 1960), 153–54ff.

23. The authors of this inclusive language version of the Statement realized the importance of asserting the full humanity of Jesus and perhaps, as well, believed that the coming of God into a male Jesus was a statement as to where redemption was most needed in a fallen world. Ironically, those who insist—wrongly in the writer's opinion—on masculine pronouns for God undercut the importance of such usage for the human nature of Christ, that crucial distinction being observed in all the inclusive language renderings of the UCC Statement of Faith. When quoting historic documents in this chapter, the original language is retained. For the writer's views on the theological deployment of inclusive language see the aforementioned *Prism* article.

24. John Murray, *Redemption Accomplished and Applied* (Grand Rapids: Wm. B. Eerdmans Publishing Co., 1955).

25. On the historical importance of Calvin's formulations, see R. S. Franks, *The Work of Christ: A Historical Study of Christian Doctrine* (London: Thomas Nelson and Sons, 1962), 348–51. On its wider use, see the "Decree on the Apostolate of the Laity," in *The Documents of Vatican II*, Walter M. Abbott, S. J., general editor (New York: Guild Press, 1966), 491–92, 501, and passim.

26. Heidelberg Catechism, Question and Answer 31; Westminster Confession, Chapter VIII; Savoy Declaration, Chapter VIII.

27. See The Lutheran World Federation and the Roman Catholic Church, "Joint Declaration on the Doctrine of Justification," English ed. (Grand Rapids: Wm. B. Eerdmans Publishing Co., 2000), and Gabriel Fackre, "The Ecumenical Import of the Joint Declaration," *Reformed World* 52, no. 1 (March 2002): 46–55.

28. Heidelberg Catechism, Question 21.

29. *The COCU Consensus*, "Confessing the Faith," 29.

30. So argued in "Gifts Received: Sovereignty and Sanctification," in Gabriel Fackre and Michael Root, *Affirmations and Admonitions: Lutheran Decisions and Dialogue with Reformed, Episcopal and Roman Catholic Churches* (Grand Rapids: Wm. B. Publishing Co, 1998), 21–43.

31. W. A. Visser 't Hooft, *The Kingship of Christ: An Interpretation of Recent European Theology* (New York: Harper and Bros, 1948).

32. See Barbara Brown Zikmund and Frederick Trost, eds., *The Living Theological Heritage of the United Church of Christ*, vol. 7 (Cleveland: The Pilgrim Press, 2005).

33. See the "God is Still Speaking" segment of the United Church of Christ Internet web site.

34. Karl Barth, *The Word of God and the Word of Man*, Douglas Horton, trans. (Boston: The Pilgrim Press, 1928), 229, 230. Note this first major exposure of Barth to American audiences was published by The Pilgrim Press, and translator Douglas Horton was one of the founders of the United Church of Christ. Barth continued to strike this note, as in the later words cited in footnote 35 below. On Horton, see the excellent biography by Theodore Louis Trost, *Douglas Horton and the Ecumenical Impulse in American Religion* (Cambridge: Harvard University Press, 2002).

35. "But it may well be that the Christian community, assuming that it hears such true words here and now, has still new things to hear and learn which go beyond its dogmas and confessions and which the fathers and brethren could not teach it in the days when these documents were formulated. If these new things . . . are authentic, it may well be expected that their light will somehow be an extension of the line visible in the dogmas and confessions, so that they supplement even though they do not contradict what is stated by them." Karl Barth, *Church Dogmatics*, IV/3/1, G. W. Bromiley, trans. (Edinburgh: T & T. Clark, 1961), 127.

36. Interestingly, while the "God is Still Speaking," project stresses the open-endedness of UCC belief, its web site does list the UCC Statement of Faith II.

Part Two:
Ecumenical Connections

CHAPTER FOUR
Jesus in God's Plan for Salvation
Lydia Veliko

1. "Basis of Union of the Congregational Christian Churches and the Evangelical and Reformed Church with the Interpretations," in Louis H. Gunnemann, *The Shaping of the United Church of Christ: An Essay in the History of American Christianity* (New York: United Church Press, 1977), 208.

2. Louis H. Gunnemann, *United and Uniting: The Meaning of an Ecclesial Journey* (New York: United Church Press, 1987), 82–83.

3. Ibid., 82.
4. For the context of the principle of "mutual affirmation and admonition," see the text of "A Formula of Agreement" (Minneapolis: Augsburg Fortress Press, 1997).
5. Daniel L. Migliore, "The Communion of the Triune God," in *Reformed Theology: Identity and Ecumenicity*, Wallace M. Alston, Jr., and Michael Welker, eds. (Grand Rapids: Wm. B. Eerdmans Publishing Co., 2003), 144.
6. Edmund Za Bik, "The Challenge to Reformed Theology," in *Toward the Future of Reformed Theology: Tasks, Topics, Traditions*, David Willis and Michael Welker, eds. (Grand Rapids: Wm. B. Eerdmans Publishing Co., 1999), 86.
7. Migliore, "The Communion of the Triune God," 142.
8. Ibid.
9. Michael Weinrich, "The Openness and Worldliness of the Church," in *Reformed Theology*, 412.
10. Migliore, "The Communion of the Triune God," 145.
11. See especially Klaas Schilder, "The Main Points of the Doctrine of the Covenant," 1944. Speech translated from an uncorrected stenographic recording of Professor Dr. K. Schilder's speech as it was held at the Waalsche Kerk in Delft, the Netherlands on August 31, 1944. See http://spindleworks.com/library/schilder/ovenant.htm.
12. For a helpful exposition of various perspectives see Gabriel Fackre, "Claiming Jesus as Savior in a Religiously Plural World," published in the *Internet Journal of Christian Theological Research* 8 (2003).
13. Za Bik, "The Challenge to Reformed Theology," 83
14. Philip Schaff, *The Person of Christ: The Miracle of History* (Boston: The American Tract Society, 1865), 104–06, 109.
15. Ibid., 104.
16. Augustine, *Sermons*, 234:2.

CHAPTER FIVE
Recognition and the Presence of Christ at the Table
John H. Thomas

1. See Raymond E. Brown, *The Birth of the Messiah* (Garden City, NY: Doubleday and Company, 1977), 341ff.
2. The phrase "affirmations and admonitions" was coined to describe a way of living together in full communion by the Lutheran Reformed Theological Conversations, 1988–1992, published in Keith F. Nickle and Timothy F. Lull, "A Common Calling: The Witness of Our

Reformation Churches in North America Today" (Minneapolis: Augsburg Fortress, 1993), 66.

3. John Williamson Nevin, "The Mystical Presence, 1846," in *The Mystical Presence and Other Writings on the Eucharist,* Bard Thompson and George H. Bricker, eds. (Philadelphia: United Church Press, 1966), 23.

4. Ibid., 34, 35.

5. Ibid., 256.

6. Ibid., 391.

7. Ibid., 163.

8. Ibid., 109 (emphasis added).

9. Ibid., 38.

10. "Baptism, Eucharist and Ministry," Faith and Order Paper No. 111 (Geneva: World Council of Churches, 1982).

11. Ibid., 11 (Eucharist II.B.6).

12. Ibid., 12 (Eucharist II.B.13).

13. Ibid., 12 (Commentary 13).

14. Ibid., x (Preface).

15. Max Thurian, ed., "Churches Respond to BEM II," Faith and Order Paper 132 (Geneva: World Council of Churches, 1986), 329.

16. *Book of Worship: United Church of Christ* (New York: UCC Office for Church Life and Leadership, 1986), 32.

17. Jaroslav Pelikan, *Credo: Historical and Theological Guide to Creeds and Confessions of Faith in the Christian Tradition* (New Haven, CT: Yale University Press, 2003), 116.

18. "Marburg Revisited," in *An Invitation to Action: The Lutheran-Reformed Dialogue Series III, 1981–1983,* James E. Andrews and Joseph A. Burgess, eds. (Philadelphia: Fortress Press, 1984), 42.

19. Ibid., 42, 43.

20. Ibid., 40, 52.

21. Andrews and Burgess, eds., *An Invitation to Action: The Lutheran-Reformed Dialogue Series II,* 57.

22. Ibid., 56.

23. "The Leuenberg Agreement 18, 19," in *The Leuenberg Agreement and Lutheran Reformed Relationships: Evaluations by North American and European Theologians,* William G. Rusch and Daniel F. Martensen, eds. (Minneapolis: Augsburg Fortress, 1989), 149.

24. "The Leuenberg Agreement 21," in *The Leuenberg Agreement and Lutheran Reformed Relationships,* 149.

25. Marc Leinhard, "The Leuenberg Agreement: Origins and Aims," in *The Leuenberg Agreement and Lutheran Reformed Relationships,* 26.

26. "The Leuenberg Agreement 22," in *The Leuenberg Agreement and Lutheran Reformed Relationships,* 149.

27. "Invitation to Action," in *An Invitation to Action: The Lutheran-Reformed Dialogue Series III*, 16.
28. Minutes of the 17th General Synod of the United Church of Christ, 1989, 112.
29. Ibid., 157.
30. Nickle and Lull, eds., "A Common Calling," 46–47.
31. Ibid., 48–49.
32. At one gathering of Lutherans, a pastor recited the words Luther is said to have spoken to Zwingli at Marburg: "We are of a different spirit," in German! At another gathering, a Lutheran laywoman informed me that "the Reformed don't believe in the real presence" because she had seen "in remembrance of me" carved on a UCC altar. "Lutherans," I was told, "have 'this is my body' on their altars." This was, at the very least, a creative exposition of Luke's version of the words of institution whose "complementarity" may have anticipated that of the authors of "A Common Calling."
33. John H. Thomas and Guy Edmiston, eds., "A Formula of Agreement between the Evangelical Lutheran Church in America, the Presbyterian Church (USA), the Reformed Church in America and the United Church of Christ on entering into full communion on the basis of 'A Common Calling' " (n.d.).
34. *The New Century Hymnal* (Cleveland: The Pilgrim Press, 1995), 1–20, and hymn no. 344.
35. Ibid., no. 348 © Leon Roberts.
36. Ibid., no. 849.
37. Lee C. Barrett, III, "Full Communion or Further Conflict: Can Complementarity Help Lutheran-Reformed Dialogue?" *Prism* (Fall 1996), 76.
38. United Church of Christ Statement of Faith, adapted by Robert V. Moss, 1976, in *Book of Worship*, 512.
39. Barrett, "Full Communion," 73.
40. Gabriel Fackre, "What the Lutherans and the Reformed Can Learn from One Another," *The Christian Century* (June 4–11, 1997): 558.
41. Dietrich Bonhoeffer, *Act and Being* (Minneapolis: Fortress Press, 1996), 90–91.
42. Barrett, "Full Communion," 74, 77.
43. Gabriel Fackre, "Summary Observations," in *The Leuenberg Agreement and Lutheran Reformed Relationships*, 129–30.
44. Barrett, "Full Communion," 76–77.
45. United Church of Christ Statement of Faith.

Part Three:
Contemporary Issues and Practice

CHAPTER SIX
Pluralism and Mission
Mary Schaller Blaufuss

1. Martin Kähler, *Schriften zur Christologie und Mission* (Munich: Chr. Kaiser Verlag, 1971), 190.
2. See David Bosch, *Transforming Mission: Paradigm Shifts in Theology of Mission*, American Society of Missiology Series, no. 16 (Maryknoll, NY: Orbis Books, 1991), 16. See also Walter Russell, "An Alternative Suggestion for the Purpose of Romans," *Bibliotheca Sacra* 145 (1988): 174–184.
3. Bosch, *Transforming Mission*, 9.
4. Ibid., 195.
5. Gail R. O'Day, *The Word Disclosed: Preaching the Gospel of John* (St. Louis: Chalice Press, 2002), 92.
6. Marlene Perera, "Towards the Twenty-First Century: An Asian Woman's Emerging Perceptions on Mission," *International Review of Mission* 81, no. 322 (April 1992): 227.
7. This perspective on globalization is resourced by Roland Robertson and Robert Schreiter. "For present purposes, globalization may be defined simply as the compression of the world. This notion of compression refers both to increasing socio-cultural density and to rapidly expanding consciousness." Robertson, "Globalization and the Future of Traditional Religion," in *God and Globalization: Religion and the Powers of the Common Life*, vol. 1, Max L. Stackhouse, ed. with Peter J. Paris, (Harrisburg, PA: Trinity Press International, 2000), 53. Robert Schreiter contends that globalization, as the context of mission today, is a phenomenon that revolves around the two axes of connectedness and space. Schreiter, "Globalization and Reconciliation: Challenges to Mission," in *Mission in the Third Millennium*, Robert J. Schreiter, ed. (Maryknoll, NY: Orbis Books, 2001), 124–27.
8. Gail O'Day comments that in Jesus' dialogue with Martha we have "echoes of Jesus' conversation with the Samaritan woman" in John 4. In each, Jesus takes the woman seriously without being condescending. There is a give-and-take in the conversations. The encounter with Jesus becomes an occasion for each woman to realize that Jesus is the anticipated one promised to come. Each woman has the meaning of that reinterpreted for her in ways that send her out to share with others the good news of his presence and action of love. See O'Day, *The Word Disclosed*, 103.

9. Mercy Amba Oduyoye, "The Passion Out of Compassion: Women of the EATWOT Third General Assembly," *International Review of Mission* 81, no. 322 (April 1992): 316. Mercy Oduyoye is a former deputy general secretary of the World Council of Churches and coordinated the WCC's Ecumenical Decade of Churches in Solidarity with Women (1988–1998).
10. Bosch, *Transforming Mission*, 23. See also L. Schottroff and W. Stegemann, *Jesus and the Hope of the Poor*, Matthew J. O'Connell, trans. (Maryknoll, NY: Orbis Books, 1986), vii.
11. Bosch, *Transforming Mission*, 31.
12. Ibid., 30.
13. John Dominic Crossan, *The Historical Jesus: The Life of a Mediterranean Jewish Peasant* (New York: HarperSanFrancisco, 1991), 341.
14. Ibid.
15. Ibid.
16. For more on typologies of Christian approaches to religious pluralism see: Paul F. Knitter, *No Other Name? A Critical Survey of Christian Attitudes Toward the World Religions*, American Society of Missiology Series no. 7 (Maryknoll, NY: Orbis Books, 1985); John Hick and Paul F. Knitter, ed., *The Myth of Christian Uniqueness: Toward a Pluralistic Theology of Religions*, Faith Meets Faith Series (Maryknoll, NY: Orbis Books, 1987); Diana Eck, *Encountering God: A Spiritual Journey from Bozeman to Banaras* (Boston: Beacon Press, 1993); Jacques Dupuis, *Toward a Christian Theology of Religious Pluralism* (Maryknoll, NY: Orbis Books, 2001).
17. Many, including those who originally created the typologies, have suggested the limitations and flaws of such categorization. See O. V. Jathanna, " 'Religious Pluralism:' A Theological Critique," *Bangalore Theological Forum* 31, no. 2 (December 1999): 5–6.
18. I first heard the phrase "the new and the now" used by Indian literary critic Susie Tharu in her plenary address at the conference on feminist theologies in India, "Recasting Women," United Theological College, December 2001. She used the phrase to indicate the immediacy of Christ's promises in the midst of many kinds of pluralism and the challenges for the Christian community in India and throughout the world.
19. Stanley J. Samartha, *One Christ—Many Religions: Toward a Revised Christology* (Bangalore: Sathri, 1992), 88.
20. S. Mark Heim, *Salvations: Truth and Difference in Religions*, Faith Meets Faith Series (Maryknoll, NY: Orbis Books, 1995), 219.
21. Jathanna, "Religious Pluralism," 13.
22. Ibid.

23. Ibid. For more background on Jathanna's argument of "critical inclusiveness," see O. V. Jathanna, *The Decisiveness of the Christ-Event and the Universality of Christianity in a World of Religious Plurality* (Berne, Frankfort., Las Vegas: Peter Lang, 1981).

24. Elsa Tamez, "Bible of the Oppressed," *Voices from the Third World* 9, no. 1 (January 1989): 13–18.

25. S. Mark Heim, *The Depth of Riches: A Trinitarian Theology of Religious Ends* (Grand Rapids: Wm. B. Eerdmans Publishing Co., 2001), 56.

26. Constance Tarasar, "Women in the Mission of the Church: Theological and Historical Reflections," *International Review of Mission* 81, no. 322 (April 1992): 190. Tarasar is formerly associate general secretary of the Churches of Christ USA.

27. Heim, *The Depth of Riches*, 52.

CHAPTER SEVEN
Identity and Ethical Proclamation
Deidre King Hainsworth

1. United Church of Christ, *The Constitution and Bylaws of the United Church of Christ* (New York: Executive Council of the United Church of Christ, 1984).

2. These claims echo those of theologian Karl Rahner, whose work on Trinitarian theology was exemplified by his assertion that the imminent Trinity (God's inner relationship) was the economic Trinity (the revealed work of Father, Son, and Holy Spirit in the history of salvation). This is not a claim that our knowledge can encompass the complete mind of God or the scope of God's activity, but rather that God has offered us an understandable and trustworthy account of God's character and intentions.

3. Ellen Leonard details a range of models of Christ that have been proposed as feminist theological alternatives that respond to these challenges of particularity. These include understandings of Christ's incarnation in female form, the incarnation in Jesus as incarnated female divinity, Jesus as prototype or prophet, and Jesus' identity as the founder of egalitarian community. See Ellen Leonard, "Woman and Christ: Toward Inclusive Christologies," in *Constructive Christian Theology in the Worldwide Church*, William R. Barr, ed. (Grand Rapids: Wm. B. Eerdmans Publishing Co., 1997), 326–34.

4. Despite these cultural and social differences, one approach to understanding Jesus' personal and ethical import in recent popular Christian culture jumps over the task of interpretation, simply asking the question "what would Jesus do?" I will argue below that this approach not only omits the task of interpretation, but also mistakes our role and call in relation to God's work.

5. These various "Christological controversies" are well detailed in a recent overview of the topic by Veli-Matti Kärkkäinen, *Christology: A Global Introduction* (Grand Rapids: Baker Academic, 2003).

6. This should be seen in distinction from the Reformed Church, a constituent denomination helping to form the United Church of Christ and one of many denominations with roots in the work of the Protestant Reformation.

7. In the words of the Statement of Faith, "In Jesus Christ, the man of Nazareth, our crucified and risen Lord, he [God] has come to us and shared our common lot, conquering sin and death and reconciling the world to himself." Reprinted in the *Book of Worship: United Church of Christ* (New York: UCC Office of Church Life and Leadership, 1986).

8. Reuben A. Sheares II has described this sometimes difficult balance between denominational unity and diversity in a classic essay in UCC ecclesiology and identity, "A Covenant Polity," in *Theology and Identity: Traditions, Movements and Polity in the United Church of Christ*, Daniel L. Johnson and Charles Hambrick-Stowe, eds. (Cleveland: United Church Press, 1990), 67–78.

9. *Book of Worship*, xi.

10. The discussion of General Synod resolutions and pronouncements is drawn from United Church of Christ, "Minutes of the Twenty-Fourth General Synod" (2003), "Minutes of the Twenty-Third General Synod" (2001), and "Minutes of the Twenty-Fourth General Synod" (1999).

11. Justice and Witness Ministries, United Church of Christ, *2003 Briefing Book*, 5. Located at www.ucc.org/justice.

12. Ibid.

13. Louis H. Gunnemann, *United and Uniting: The Meaning of an Ecclesial Journey* (New York: United Church Press, 1987).

14. Excerpted in *2003 Briefing Book*.

15. Douglas F. Ottati, "The Reformed Tradition in Theological Ethics," in *Christian Ethics: Problems and Prospects*, Lisa Sowle Cahill and James F. Childress, eds. (Cleveland: The Pilgrim Press, 1996), 55.

CHAPTER EIGHT
The Passion and the Compassion of the Christ
Theodore Louis Trost

1. Terry Lawson, "Box Office Bonanza: The Movie Business is Booming," *The Detroit Free Press*, August 22, 2004, http://www.freep.com/ entertainment/movies/lawcol22_20040822.htm.
2. "Priest Who Ministered to Gibson is Disciplined," *Christian Century* 121/19 (September 21, 2004): 16.
3. W. Barnes Tatum, *Jesus at the Movies: A Guide to the First Hundred Years* (Sonoma, CA: Polebridge, 1997), 206.
4. See John Calvin, "The Substitution of Christ," *The Institutes of the Christian Religion*, vol. 2 (Philadelphia: Westminster, 1960), 531–32.
5. See Saint Anselm, "Why God Became Man," in *Anselm of Canterbury: The Major Works*, Brian Davies and G. R. Evans, eds. (New York: Oxford University Press, 1998), 260–356.
6. "Die Passion Christi: Ein Blutbad," *Evangelische Kirche im Rheinland*, March 16, 2004 http://www.ekir.de/ekir/ekir_20840.asp.
7. See for example: Elisha A. Hoffman, "Are You Washed in the Blood?," in *Spiritual Songs for Gospel Meetings and the Sunday School* (Cleveland: Barker & Smellie, 1878) and Lewis E. Jones, "There is Power in the Blood" (1899), which was paraphrased by George W. Bush in his 2003 "State of the Union" address: "There is power—wonder-working power—in the goodness and idealism and faith of the American people" (http://www.whitehouse.gov/news/releases/2003/01/2003012 8–19.htm).
8. Harvey Cox, "Additional Perspectives on *Passion of the Christ*," *Harvard Divinity School Bulletin* 32/3 (Summer 2004): 34.
9. Julie Ingersoll, "Is It Finished? *The Passion of the Christ* and the Fault Lines in American Christianity" in *After the Passion of God*, J. Shawn Landres and Michael Berenbaum, eds. (Walnut Creek, CA: AltaMira, 2005) 84–85.
10. John Calvin, "Catechism of the Church of Geneva," in *John Calvin's Tracts and Treatises, Vol II: On the Doctrine and Worship of the Church*, T. F. Torrance, ed. (Grand Rapids: Wm. B. Eerdmans Publishing Co., 1958), 45. See also "The Geneva Catechism," in *Our Confessional Heritage* (Atlanta: The Presbyterian Church in the United States, 1978), 23.
11. Larry and Andy Wachowski, dirs., *The Matrix Revolutions* (Warner Brothers, 1993); James Cameron, dir., *Terminator 2: Judgment Day* (Carolco, 1991); George Miller and George Ogilve, dirs., *Mad Max Beyond Thunderdome* (Warner Brothers, 1985).

12. The campaign initiative has received continuous coverage in the denomination's major publication The United Church News since its inauguration in spring 2004. See, for example, "Comma Clause: National Ad Campaign Hinges on UCC Members' Financial Support," United Church of Christ News 20, no. 8, (October 2004): 3. See also the web page devoted to the "Stillspeaking Initiative": http://www.stillspeaking. com. I gratefully acknowledge the Louisville Institute whose award of a Religious Institutions Grant for the academic year 2005–2006 made possible my research into the Stillspeaking campaign.

13. The articles, published in the Weekly Messenger during 1840 and 1841 were later published as John Nevin, "The Heidelberg Catechism," Mercersburg Review 4 (1852): 155–86. The qualitative assessment of Nevin's series of articles is made by George W. Richards in his History of the Theological Seminary of the Evangelical and Reformed Church at Lancaster, Pennsylvania (Lancaster, PA: Rudisill, 1961), 267.

14. For a brief history of the Catechism bearing on its irenic nature, see Philip Schaff, The Creeds of Christendom, vol. I, The History of Creeds (Grand Rapids: Baker, 1983; 1877 orig.), 541–50. The creed itself was translated by a committee of the German Reformed Church, including John Nevin. See "The Heidelberg Catechism," in The Creeds of Christendom, vol. III, The Evangelical Protestant Creeds, Philip Schaff, ed. (Grand Rapids: Baker, 1983; 1877 orig.), 306–55.

15. Philip Schaff, ed., Deutsches Gesangbuch: Eine Auswahl geistlicher Lieder aus allen Zeiten der christlichen Kirche (Philadelphia, 1859).

16. Nathan O. Hatch, The Democratization of American Protestantism (New Haven, CT: Yale, 1989).

17. John Nevin, The Anxious Bench, 2nd ed., in Catholic and Reformed: Selected Writings of John Williamson Nevin, Charles Yrigoyen and George H. Bricker, eds. (Pittsburgh: Pickwick, 1978), 19. This discussion of The Anxious Bench is drawn from Theodore Trost, "The Anxious Bench: An Invitation to Lutheran and Reformed Dialogue," The New Mercersburg Review 12 (Fall 1992): 17–19.

18. The Anxious Bench, 111.

19. The Anxious Bench, 12. Nevin's primary detractor among the Lutherans was Benjamin Kurtz, who, in 1843, wrote a series of articles advocating the adoption of new measures in the denominational publication The Lutheran Observer.

20. The Anxious Bench, 110–12.

21. The hymn appeared consistently in the Palatinate German Reformed hymnals from 1567 into the eighteenth century, often alongside Vom Himmel Kam der Engel Schar ("From Heaven Came the Angels' Troops")—a closely related hymn focusing on the role the shepherds play in the nativity scene. The German Reformed people of the colonial

era would have known both hymns from John Philip Boehm's worship book, published at Amsterdam in 1701. See Deborah Rahn Clemens, "Foundations of German Reformed worship in the sixteenth century Palatinate" (PhD diss., Drew University, 1995), 187. Philip Schaff placed *Vom Himmel Kam der Engel Schar* in his *Gesangbuch* to be sung to the tune of *Vom Himmel Hoch*; see Schaff, ed., *Deutsches Gesangbuch*, 84.

22. The German version of the hymn is taken from *Evangeliches Kirchengesangbuch* (Berlin: Evangelische Verlagsanstalt, n.d.), 16. Unless otherwise indicated, the translation is by George MacDonald in *Luther's Works 53: Liturgy and Hymns*, Ulrich S. Leupold, ed. (Philadelphia: Fortress, 1965), 290–92.

23. See "The Theological Declaration of Barmen," in The Office of the General Assembly, Presbyterian Church (U.S.A.), *Book of Confessions* (Louisville, KY: Geneva Press, 1996), 310.

24. See Stephen L. Wailes, "Martin Luther Between Christmas and Epiphany: The Socio-Religious Position of *Vom himmel hoch da kom ich her*," *Internationales Archives für Sozialgeschichte der deutschen Literatur* 15, no. 2 (1990): 13–42.

25. Catherine Winkworth, trans., "From Heaven Above," in *The Hymnal* (Saint Louis: Eden, 1941), 114.

26. "The Heidelberg Catechism," in *Book of Confessions*, 59.

27. This notion of relationship, of course, comes from Martin Buber, *I and Thou* (New York: Scribners, 1958). Although preachers in the mainstream Protestant tradition often point to this work in their sermons, they would have a lot less explaining to do if the churches retained in, rather than expunged from, their contemporary hymnals the word "thou." See, for example, James Crawford et al, trans. (altered) "From Heaven unto Earth I Come" in *The New Century Hymnal* (Cleveland, OH: Pilgrim, 1995), 130.

28. Henry Harbaugh, "Jesus, I Live to Thee," in *The Hymnal*, 254. For contrast, see James Crawford et al (altered), "Jesus, I Live to You [*sic*]" in *The New Century Hymnal*, 457. While the final phrase of the last stanza suggests the immanence of the kingdom of heaven in line with Harbaugh's original ("and heaven on earth be known"), this is undercut (or overshot) in the immediately preceding phrase in which heaven becomes—through the use of the future tense—a symbol of the "great by and by": "My life *will be* your life in me" (emphasis added). This is a complete misunderstanding of Christ's mystical presence here and now.

29. John Nevin, *The Mystical Presence* (Eugene, OR: Wipf and Stock, 2000; 1846 orig.), 197.

30. In *The Matrix*, when Choi receives a much-desired computer program, he says to Neo, "Hallelujah. You're my savior, man. My own personal Jesus Christ."

31. According to the commentators in *The Harper Collins Study Bible* (New York: Harper Collins, 1993), 1931.
32. Herman Waetjen, *A Reordering of Power: A Socio-political Reading of Mark's Gospel* (Minneapolis: Fortress, 1998), 118.
33. The effort to eliminate the word "Lord" from contemporary Christian rhetoric (in the Bible and in the hymnody and liturgy of the church) should be inconceivable. It calls to mind the movie *The Princess Bride*. On numerous occasions the perplexed villain Vizzini (Wallace Shaun) ejaculates the word "Inconceivable!" whenever something unanticipated occurs. His dubious comrade, the swordsman Inigo Montoya (Mandy Patinkin) responds initially with confused looks; eventually, he declares: "I don't think that word means what you think it means." See Rob Reiner, dir., *The Princess Bride* (Castle Rock, 1987).

CHAPTER NINE
A Living Christology and the Unfinished Business of the UCC
Stephen G. Ray, Jr.

1. Examples of this tendency from its earliest manifestation in the Christian theological tradition are found in examples collected by Christopher Norris in *The Christological Controversy* (Philadelphia: Fortress Press, 1980). See especially the introduction.
2. W. Evan Golder, "A Dose of Comma Sense," in *United Church News* December 2003, http://www.ucc.org/ucnews/dec03/dose.htm.
3. John Calvin, *Institutes of the Christian Religion*, vol. 3. John T. McNeill ed., Ford Lewis Battles, trans. (Philadelphia: The Westminster Press, 1960), 537.
4. John 10:26–27.
5. Paul Tillich, *Systematic Theology*, vol. II (Chicago: University of Chicago Press, 1957), 97–99.
6. Romans 12:5.
7. C. P. Wagner, ed., *Territorial Spirits: Insights on Strategic-Level Spiritual Warfare from Nineteen Christian Leaders* (Chichester, England: Sovereign World Ltd., 1991).
8. Louis H. Gunnemann, *United and Uniting: The Meaning of an Ecclesial Journey* (New York: United Church Press, 1987), 28.
9. Ibid., 26–29.
10. For a fuller discussion of the word "sinners" in this context, see the introduction of the author's *Do No Harm: Social Sin and Christian Responsibility* (Minneapolis: Fortress Press, 2002). Here it will suffice to say that this use of the word "sinners" refers to persons and groups whose

social marginalization is speciously attributed to some unique presence of sin in the existence (e.g., gay and lesbian persons).

11. Louis H. Gunnemann, *The Shaping of the United Church of Christ: An Essay in the History of American Christianity* (New York: United Church Press, 1977), 78.
12. Gunnemann, *United and Uniting*, 19–20.
13. Paul Sherry, "Who, Then, Shall We Be?," *Prism* 8, no. 2 (Fall 1993): 4–12.

BELIEVING, CARING, AND DOING
IN THE UNITED CHURCH OF CHRIST
GABRIEL FACKRE
0-8298-1641-0 / paper / 256 pages / $20.00

> Explores the "believing, caring, and doing" dimensions of the United
> Church of Christ and discusses the UCC's inter-relation of its theological
> orientation—as found in key texts, traditions, and movements—its
> ecumenical commitments, and its deeds of justice and peace.

THE EVOLUTION OF A UCC STYLE
Essays in the History, Ecclesiology, and Culture
of the United Church of Christ
RANDI J. WALKER
0-8298-1493-0 / paper / 240 pages / $30.00

> Focuses on the development of the themes that define the UCC:
> inclusiveness, diversity of theological heritage (Reformation, Enlightenment,
> and Pietism), congregational polity (the one and the many), a liberal
> theological approach, and ecumenical spirit.

THE LIVING THEOLOGICAL HERITAGE
OF THE UNITED CHURCH OF CHRIST
BARBARA BROWN ZIKMUND, SERIES EDITOR

> A series of documents, statements, and commentaries that chronicle the
> history, faith, and practices of the United Church of Christ. Hardcover.
>
> Volume 1: Ancient and Medieval Legacies
> 0-8298-1064-1 / $60.00
>
> Volume 2: Reformation Roots
> 0-8298-1143-5 / $60.00
>
> Volume 3: Colonial and National Beginnings
> 0-8298-1109-5 / $60.00
>
> Volume 4: Consolidation and Expansion
> 0-8298-1110-9 / $60.00
>
> Volume 5: Outreach and Diversity
> 0-8298-1111-7 / $60.00
>
> Volume 6: Growing Toward Unity
> 0-8298-1112-5 / $70.00
>
> Volume 7: United and Uniting
> 0-8298-1113-3 / $70.00
>
> Complete 7-Volume Set
> 0-8298-1461-2 / $350.00—Save $90.00